IT Milestones

Englisch für IT-Berufe

von
Dr. Wolfgang Schäfer (Hrsg.)
Jens Eifler
Annely Humphreys
Jason Humphreys
Thomas Roth
Christian Schäfer
Mary Schäfer

Ernst Klett Verlag
Stuttgart · Leipzig

IT Milestones

Englisch für IT-Berufe

Autoren: Dr. Wolfgang Schäfer (Hrsg.), Jens Eifler, Annely Humphreys, Jason Humphreys,
Thomas Roth, Christian Schäfer, Mary Schäfer

Werkübersicht:

Schülerbuch, 978-3-12-808277-6
Milestones Workbook für alle technischen Fachbände mit Prüfungsvorbereitung KMK-Fremdsprachenzertifikat und CD-ROM, Übungsbegleitheft für alle technischen Berufe, 978-3-12-808285-1
Milestones Lehrerhandbuch für technische Berufe inkl. Digitalem Lehrer-Service mit Medien-DVD-ROM + Lehrer-Audio-CDs (6), 978-3-12-808287-5

1. Auflage 1 12 11 10 9 8 | 25 24 23 22 21

Alle Drucke dieser Auflage sind unverändert und können im Unterricht nebeneinander verwendet werden.
Die letzte Zahl bezeichnet das Jahr des Druckes.

Im Lehrwerk befinden sich ausschließlich fiktive Internet-Adressen, die deshalb auch mit ww#. beginnen anstatt wie üblich mit www.
Die im Buch abgedruckten Mediencodes führen zu interaktiven Zusatzübungen und Hörverständnistexten auf www.klett.de. Die Mediencodes leiten ausschließlich zu optionalen Unterrichtsmaterialien, sie unterliegen nicht dem staatlichen Zulassungsverfahren.

Projektleitung: Matthias Rupp
Redaktion: Volker Wendland, Helen Smyth
Herstellung: Angelika Lindner

Satz und Gestaltung: Satzkiste, Stuttgart
Umschlaggestaltung: Projektteam des Verlages
Reproduktion: Meyle + Müller Medien-Management, Pforzheim
Druck: Druckhaus Götz GmbH, Ludwigsburg

Printed in Germany
ISBN 978-3-12-808277-6

9 783128 082776

IT Milestones bietet Ihnen praxisorientiertes Fachenglisch für IT-Berufe an Berufsschulen, Berufsfachschulen, Fachschulen sowie für technisch ausgerichtete Englischkurse in der Erwachsenenbildung.

IT Milestones im Überblick:

- Konsequente Berücksichtigung neuester Lehrpläne (Lernfelder) sowie durchgängiges Sprachkompetenztraining nach dem Gemeinsamen Europäischen Referenzrahmen (Sprachstufen A2 – B2).
- 21 kompakte 4-seitige Module: Fachmodule mit Schwerpunkt auf Fachenglisch wechseln sich mit Modulen (A – H) ab, in denen der Schwerpunkt auf der beruflichen Kommunikation liegt.
- Schnelle Orientierung im Buch durch Übersicht der Lernziele jeweils am Modulanfang.
- Die Kompetenzen auf einen Blick: Viele Aufgaben bereiten bereits gezielt auf die Anforderungen des KMK-Zertifikats hin. Diese Aufgaben sind mit den Kürzeln R (Rezeption), P (Produktion), I (Interaktion) und M (Mediation) gekennzeichnet.
- Typische Sprachhandlungssituationen im Berufsalltag werden multimedial mit Audio- und Videounterstützung (u.a. Originalvideos der BBC) trainiert.
- Zahlreiche Partner-, Gruppen- und Internetaufgaben werden durch Texte und Aufgaben zur Arbeitssicherheit *(Safety first)* abgerundet.
- In den Modulen befinden sich hilfreiche Verweise auf die nach beruflichen Situationen geordneten Redewendungen *(Phrases)*.
- Unter der Überschrift *Understanding technical English* befinden sich Hinweise und Aufgaben zum richtigen Umgang mit englischem Fachvokabular.
- Möglichkeit zur Binnendifferenzierung durch anspruchsvollere Aufgaben sowie Aufgaben zur Vorbereitung auf das KMK-Fremdsprachenzertifikat in verschiedenen Stufen.
- Auf den Fachwortschatz in den jeweiligen Modulen kann über die *Word Bank* (auf jeder Doppelseite) direkt zugegriffen werden.
- Online-Grammatiktraining über die Milestones-Codes 🌐 3u5mw9 in den Modulen A – H.
- Vertieftes Grammatik- und Hörverstehenstraining im Workbook mit Prüfungsvorbereitung auf das KMK-Fremdsprachenzertifikat inklusive CD-ROM mit allen technischen Milestones-Fachbänden- und Workbook-Audios (MP3).

Weiterführendes Material

Milestones Workbook für alle technischen Fachbände mit Prüfungsvorbereitung KMK-Fremdsprachenzertifikat und CD-ROM

Lehrerhandbuch für alle technischen Milestones-Fachbände mit 6 Audio-CDs + Digitaler Lehrer-Service (Lehrer-Software mit multimedialen Schülerbüchern, Audios, Videos, Lösungen, Übungsmaterial, Übungsgenerator, Dokumentenpool mit veränderbaren Materialien)

Videos, Anhang, Symbole ▶

Üben interaktiv: Online Grammatiktraining

Modul A: 3u5mw9	**Modul E:** 5zw8jx
Modul B: gc2x9w	**Modul F:** pf5r3n
Modul C: x3gj95	**Modul G:** 3b9c4h
Modul D: cy8yn5	**Modul H:** 842j42

Die Module A – H legen den Schwerpunkt auf die Skills zu Business Communication, die im Workbook intensiv trainiert werden.

V 1 Company tour

V 2 Telephoning

V 3 Job interview

V 4 Technical support

V 5 Waste – the future's most valuable resource

V 6 Pipe inspection

V 7 High voltage work

V 8 Ras Laffan

V 9 Pipelines

V 10 Robots in the hospital

V 11 Portable power stations

V 12 Car speed control

Appendix

Umschlagseiten

Modulelemente

Nach diesem Modul	Lernziele
WORD BANK	Fachvokabular
UNDERSTANDING TECHNICAL ENGLISH	Hinweise und Aufgaben zu englischem Fachvokabular
SAFETY FIRST ⚠	Aufgaben zur Arbeitssicherheit
Video Lounge	Aufgaben zu authentischen Videos (die Videos und die Videoskripte befinden sich im Lehrerhandbuch)
→ **PHRASES:** Telephoning	Verweis auf Phrases (Telephoning) im Anhang

Symbole

◎ A 1.27	Audioverweis mit Tracknummer (CD1 – Track 27)
P, M, I, R	Produktion, Mediation, Interaktion, Rezeption
(Globus-Symbol)	Aufgabe mit Internetrecherche
(Dreieck-Symbol)	Anspruchsvollere Aufgabe (advanced)
(Personen-Symbole)	Partner- und Gruppenaufgaben
(Globus-Symbol) 3u5mw9	Grammatiktraining online über www.klett.de
KMK II	Aufgabe zur Vorbereitung auf die Prüfung des KMK-Fremdsprachenzertifikats (Niveaustufe II)

01

NACH DIESEM MODUL:

- ✓ kenne ich einige englische Bezeichnungen für Berufe und Qualifikationen im IT-Bereich,
- ✓ kann ich die Organisation innerhalb einer IT-Firma beschreiben,
- ✓ kann ich mich auf eine Stelle auf Englisch bewerben.

1

2

3

4

People and jobs in IT

Today computers are everywhere you turn – not only in office jobs, but also in engineering, production, entertainment, and many more. In fact, it is hard to imagine working in a job that does not use a computer at some point. Despite this, only a small majority of computer users can be called experts, and an even smaller number of people understand what happens behind the screen. It takes IT experts to create and service the machines and applications that so many people depend on. And these experts need to have a wide range of qualifications and skills to provide the quality and support necessary.

P **1** Look at the photos and describe what the people in the pictures are doing. Do you meet people in these positions in your daily work? Report to the class about it.

I **2** Discuss with your partner what the job responsibilities, skills and requirements for each of the jobs above might be. Can you describe other jobs in IT?

P **3** Write a short paragraph in which you describe the necessary qualifications, skills and requirements for your own job.

4 What made you decide to choose your profession? Give reasons.

P **5** Describe some activities during a typical day at work.

6 Imagine becoming self-employed and starting your own IT company. Make a list of the advantages and disadvantages of being self-employed. Discuss your list in class.

A | Job descriptions

R **1** Who says what? Match the texts (1–4) with the jobs (a.–d.).

a. IT Consultant 1	c. Network Administrator 3
b. Computer Programmer 4	d. Web Developer 2

1 "My main task is to look for ways of applying IT to business processes. To do this, I have to keep up to date with new technical developments and trends. I also have to advise my clients on their different options, about the costs, benefits and risks of my suggestions as well as about their impact on other parts of the business. I need a thorough education in Computer Science and Business along with strong analytical and communication skills, both verbal and written. I must be good at presentations, too."

2 "I design and develop websites for companies, and I integrate SQL Server databases into them. My focus lies on design and functionality. I also assist the head of the company in developing the overall company strategy with regard to web performance. I need to know a lot about programming, including several programming languages, and a lot about databases. Of course, it also helps to have skills in graphic design, and an eye for detail."

3 "Mostly, I install, upgrade and troubleshoot networks, both hardware and software. Another aspect of my work is the maintenance of our LAN/WAN, for which I recommend, schedule and execute repairs. I need strong analytical and communication skills. I work alone or in a team, and much of the information or material I handle is confidential. A broad education in IT systems and several internationally recognized certificates have helped me in my career."

4 "What I mostly do is develop new applications, from the first idea right through to their implementation, but I also maintain and update existing programs. Another focus lies on innovating data visualisation and presentation techniques. For my work I must be able to apply technical standards, theories and techniques. Also, I must have some experience in database systems and programming languages, along with problem solving capabilities and both verbal and written communication skills."

M **2** Read the four texts again and make a list in German outlining the responsibilities, skills and qualifications required for each job.

Beruf	Zuständigkeiten	Fertigkeiten	Qualifikationen

3 Search the Internet. Find information about other jobs in IT, e.g. systems analyst. Use the table above and report your findings to the class.

I **4** Choose one of the jobs without telling your partner. Your partner asks (Yes-/No-) questions to find out your job title. Then swap roles.

Example: "Do you normally work in a team?" "Yes, I do."

WORD BANK

database – Datenbank
IT consultant – IT-Berater(in)
LAN – lokales Netzwerk
network – (Computer)netzwerk
network administrator – Netzwerkadministrator(in)
programmer – Programmierer(in)
systems analyst – Systemberater(in)
WAN – Weitverkehrsnetz
Web Developer – Webentwickler(in)
website – Internetseite

B | A new company

Michael Petersen is training to become an IT Technician. In the course of his apprenticeship he is sent to a partner company in Glasgow for three months to get some international experience. On his first day he meets his tutor, Iain MacIntosh, who welcomes him to CompuTech UK.

R **1** The following organigram is wrong. Listen to the dialogue and draw the correct
⊚ A 1.8 organigram on a separate sheet of paper.

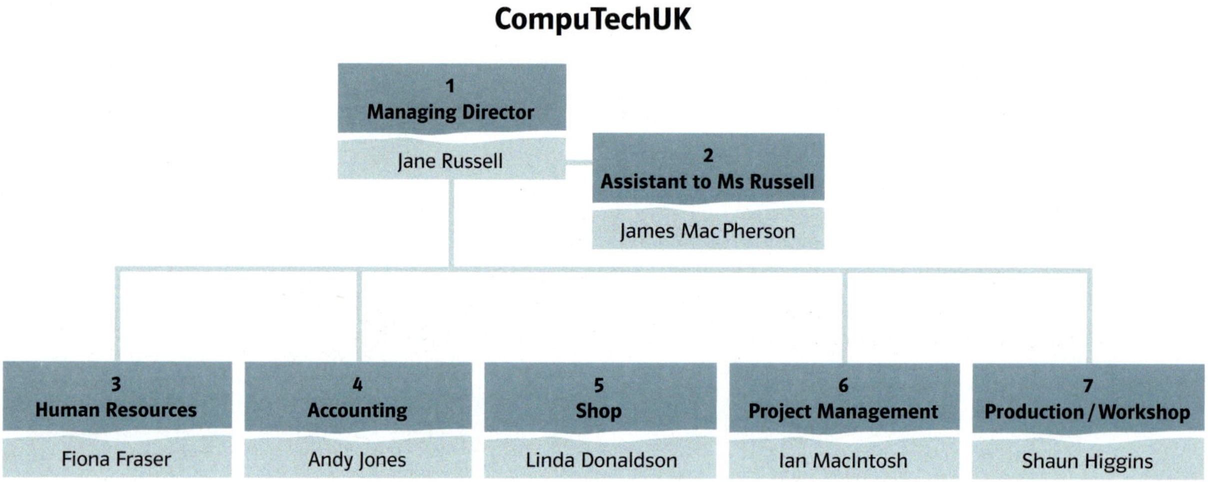

R **2** Listen to the dialogue again and match the following tasks with the departments
⊚ A 1.8 in the organigram.

a. purchases and sales 4
b. taking on repair orders 5
c. planning and designing networks 6
d. talking to customers 5
e. assessing customers' needs and wishes 5
f. repair of faulty devices 7
g. advising customers buying hardware 5
h. customer field service 7
i. enquiries, orders and offers 4

M **3** Give a brief description of CompuTechUK in German.

4 What do you think Michael will be doing during his stay at CompuTechUK?

P **5** Prepare and hold a presentation of your company, e.g. using an organisation chart. → **PHRASES:** Presentations

C | Applying for a position

Gegen Ende seiner Ausbildung sucht Michael Petersen eine Anstellung. Da ihm sein Aufenthalt in Schottland sehr gut gefallen hat, zieht er auch in Betracht, im Ausland zu arbeiten und sucht nach entsprechenden Angeboten. Dabei stößt er auch auf die unten stehende Anzeige.

R **1** KMK II **Geben Sie die wesentlichen Punkte der Anzeige stichwortartig auf Deutsch wieder.**

Network Administrator / Network Support

London, West End
Basic salary up to £48,000

Network Administrator / Network Support required on a permanent basis by a leading blue chip company in London.

The ideal candidate will have a broad range of network support skills including VOIP network support. Experience in Cisco switches is essential.
Your responsibilities will include all forms of support, administration and implementation of servers and networks as well as budgets.

You will also be expected to document network functions and occasionally travel to other sites. People skills and the ability to communicate well are essential for the position.

Required knowledge and skills:
CISCO Switches, Routers, Firewalls (ASA), Wireless Access Points, WAAS, IPS, ACS, Solarwinds, TCP/IP, Qos and TMS.
In return our client is offering a basic salary up to £48,000 plus benefits and bonus.

For more information please apply online to personnel@IT-Company.co...uk

P **2** KMK II **Schreiben Sie auf Englisch eine Mail, in der Sie sich auf obige Stelle bewerben. Hängen Sie Ihren eigenen oder einen fiktiven Lebenslauf an.**

→ **PHRASES:** Applications

3 **Find equivalents for the following German terms and phrases in the job advertisement above.**

1. Zusatzleistungen
2. Sozialkompetenz
3. ein erstrangiges Unternehmen
4. ein breites Spektrum an Fähigkeiten
5. als Gegenleistung
6. unerlässlich, unentbehrlich

WORD BANK

network support – Netzwerkunterstützung

A

NACH DIESEM MODUL:

- ✓ weiß ich, wie man sich auf Englisch begrüßt,
- ✓ weiß ich, wie ich mich selbst und andere einander auf Englisch vorstelle.

Meeting people

In the world of work you will often meet new people and it will be necessary to introduce yourself. In all industries developing relationships with colleagues and customers is the key to success. Not only is it important that you are polite, confident and friendly, but also that you know what to say, what information to include, and what the differences between formal and informal situations are.

1 **Match the parts of the dialogues to form short conversations. Start with Speaker A.**

Speaker A	Speaker B
1. Morning, Tom. That was a great game last night, wasn't it?	a. Nice to meet you, too, Hannah.
2. Hi guys, my name's Natalie.	b. Goodbye Mr Horvath. It was nice meeting you.
3. Goodbye, Mr Bauer. See you next week.	c. Morning Chris. Yeah, it was amazing!
4. It's nice to meet you, Simon.	d. Hi Natalie, I'm Mark. Welcome to the team.

2 **Now match the conversations above with the appropriate picture (1–4) and decide which are formal and which are informal.**

P **3** **Which other phrases do you know for greeting somebody and saying goodbye? Make a list.**

A | Saying "hello" and "goodbye" and giving your name

A trainee from Denmark has just arrived at Neureuther und Söhne in Kiel for a three-month internship.

R **1** ◎ A 1.1 **Listen to the two dialogues and write down the names of the people and their positions in the company.**

R **2** ◎ A 1.1 **Listen again and write down the phrases the people use for greeting and introducing one another.**

R **3** **Match the replies to the greetings and goodbyes in the two boxes.**

Formal greetings / goodbyes	Formal replies
1. Good morning. How are you today?	a. Good morning. I'm fine, thanks. And you?
2. Good night. Have a nice evening, Mr Dachs.	b. Goodbye, Mr Schäfer, and thanks for everything.
3. Goodbye, Mr Horvath. Have a nice journey home.	c. Good night, Ms Kistner, you too.
4. Good night, Silke.	d. Good night, Ms Hornbach.

Informal greetings / goodbyes	Informal replies
1. Hello, Mike. Haven't seen you for a long time.	a. Bye, Thomas. Give me a call, will you?
2. Lena, how are you this morning?	b. You, too, Florian. Thank you.
3. Morning. How was your weekend?	c. Fine, thanks. How about yours?
4. Bye-bye, Sevda.	d. I'm good, thanks. Yourself?
5. Have a nice weekend, Joe.	e. Yes, I was away on a trip last week.

P **4** **Make dialogues from the following prompts and present them to the class. Look at your lists of phrases from exercise 2 and check the info box on the next page.**

Example:

A: Hello, my name is Marina Kohler. I represent Toolcell in Leipzig.
B: Hello, Ms Kohler. I'm Amy Strong from Easytools in Bern. Nice to meet you.
A: Nice to meet you, too, Ms Strong.

Names: Denise Hofmann • Marina Kohler • Alice Campbell • Abel Kazich • Tanja Neuhäuser • Rudolfo Orvieto • Ursula Braun • Stefan Helm • Gerard Mathieu • your name

Job descriptions: I'm a trainee / intern • I work for … • I come from … • I represent … • I'm training to be a … • your job

Companies: Toolcell GmbH in Leipzig, Germany • Easytools in Bern, Switzerland • Tools Expert Pontypridd, Wales • DWT Electronics, Stuttgart • Smart EDV, Kiel • Xiang Piong Ltd, Hong Kong • Naturholz GmbH • your company

Situations: a first meeting with a new customer • a meeting with an existing customer / colleague • a party • a company open day • a trade fair • a job fair for trainees • the first day in a new company

WORD BANK ◎

intern – Praktikant(in)

5 **Introduce the people to each other according to the following structure. Use the prompts on the previous page.**

→ **PHRASES:** Meeting people

A: Fragen Sie **B** und **C**, ob sie sich schon kennen. B und C antworten mit Nein.
A: Stellen Sie **B** und **C** einander vor.

B: Begrüßen Sie **C** freundlich.

C: Sie grüßen **B** zurück und stellen eine Frage zu **Bs** Firma

B: Sie geben eine Auskunft über Ihre Firma. Sie fragen **C** nach seiner Tätigkeit.

C: Sie beantworten **Bs** Frage.

INFO BOX: Meeting people

First meeting / Formal introduction

A: Hello, my name is Ines Sacher.
B: Nice to meet you, Ms Sacher. My name is Joshua Hamsung.
A: Nice to meet you, too, Mr Hamsung.
Women – married or not – are addressed as Ms, not Miss.

A: Mr Jacobs, this is Mr Sykes.
B: How do you do?
C: How do you do?
"How do you do?" is rarely used for first introductions.

A: I'm Frank Warren of Wood Tools in Manchester.
Please call me Frank.
B: Pleased to meet you, Frank. My name is Joanne McNeill.
Do call me Joanne.
In English-speaking countries first names are often used from the start of a business realtionship. In South America or Asia, however, you don't usually use first names right away.

I hope you had a good trip. /
I hope you had no trouble finding us. /
Welcome to our stand.
Phrases like these are used to break the ice after an introduction.

Second meeting

A: Good morning, Ms Sacher. Do you remember me?
I'm Joshua Hamsung from Bell & Co in Chicago.
B: Good morning, Mr Hamsung. Nice to see you again.

Informal meetings

A: Hello Ines. Great to see you again. How are you?
B: Hi Joshua. Lovely to see you, too. I'm fine. And you?

B | Intercultural awareness

M **1** KMK II **Ihr Betrieb wird in Zukunft für einen amerikanischen Auftraggeber arbeiten. Ihre Vorgesetzte interessiert sich daher für folgenden Artikel aus einer englischen Fachzeitschrift. Sie bittet Sie, die wesentlichen Aussagen des Artikels stichpunktartig in übersichtlicher Form für sie auf Deutsch herauszuarbeiten.**

Intercultural awareness

Politeness, pleasantries and profitability

Americans are known to be direct, but they do like to take a few minutes to chat before getting down to work. They may ask after your health, or if your trip was pleasant, or about where you are from. This gives both parties a chance to form an impression of the other and establishes a basis on which to do business.

Americans, including the president, like to be called by their given name. This is not an invitation to be personal, as you would expect in Germany if someone suggested using the familiar "Du". It is a way to set a framework for working together. While it is usual in business, it would not be expected in dealing with a doctor, a teacher or a professor, and in any case, you should wait until it is offered: "Hello, I'm James Smith, vice-president in charge of sales. Call me Jim." "Pleased to meet you! I'm Walter König; please call me Walter." (Note that in the United States you state your *given* name and then your *family* name, and not the other way around, except perhaps on a form that you have to fill out.)

Americans don't like to waste time. They get to the point, in conversations as well as in conferences. Although Milton Berle, a comedian from the 1950s and 1960s, is quoted as saying: "A committee is a group of people that keeps minutes and wastes hours."

Americans are generally very polite, and they tend to smile much more than we are used to. An American tourist was quite upset that perfect strangers didn't smile back at her when she walked through the streets of a small town in Germany. On the other hand, a German woman in New York became quite tired of being asked, again by perfect strangers, the person at the cash register, the bus driver: "How are you doing?" and commanded to "Have a nice day!" These pleasantries are intended to show that you are noticed and respected. More than "Thanks!" is not expected.

P **2** **Check the Internet to see what advice people from other countries get to prepare for meetings in Germany. Make a list of ten useful tips.**

02

NACH DIESEM MODUL:

- √ kann ich die wesentlichen Bauteile von Computern und ihre Funktionen auf Englisch benennen und beschreiben,
- √ kann ich wichtige externe Geräte auf Englisch beschreiben,
- √ kann ich eine englische Montageanleitung für PCs erstellen.

1

2

3

4

Computer hardware

It is almost impossible to imagine a home or a company without a computer. Computer hardware refers to the devices and components which form the building blocks of personal computers. Some hardware components are necessary for the computer to function, and others are more like accessories which can optimise performance and user-friendliness.

1 Look at the photos and ask your partner to describe them, to name the components and to say what they are needed for.

2 What other internal computer components do you know? Use your dictionary and tell the class about their functions.

3 List the devices in the box below in two groups: input and output devices. One device is used for both input and output. Which device is it? Complete your lists with other devices you know.

> projector • keyboard • plotter • mouse • scanner • gamepad • microphone • touch screen • joystick • printer • webcam • graphics tablet • monitor • optical bar code reader • touch pen • graphic digitizer • light pen • track ball • speaker

UNDERSTANDING TECHNICAL ENGLISH

Beamer = ~~beamer~~ projector

A | Internal components

Computers come in all different shapes and forms, but the main components that make up a computer are generally the same. Each component plays a very important part – and if just one of them fails, the whole PC may no longer work. First, there is the chassis, also known as system unit. This is the outer encasement which houses all the internal components, e.g. the power supply unit (PSU) which transforms incoming power to the voltage needed by the computer and connects to the other components. Then, there is the mainboard, a big printed circuit board (PCB) to which most components are fitted, such as the central processing unit (CPU) which handles all requests and calculates all processes. Also on the mainboard you will find the random access memory (RAM), also called primary or volatile memory, that hosts all proccesses currently running on the computer. Sometimes you find expansion cards, devices for additional features such as audio, graphics or internet access. Most modern mainboards, however, have these integrated (onboard). Next, there is the hard disk drive (HDD), the main storage device (also called secondary or permanent storage) that holds all stored data including the operating system (OS) or other applications installed on your machine. Finally, there is the optical disk drive. This is used to read from or write onto external storage media such as CDs, DVDs or Blu-ray Discs.

R **1** **Read the text above and match these components with their descriptions.**

Component	Description
1. chassis / system unit	a. primary storage medium in all desktop computers
2. power supply	b. necessary for optical storage devices
3. CD drive	c. can handle optical storage media with larger capacity
4. DVD drive	d. the 'brain' of your system
5. hard drive	e. the size of this determines which and how many parts fit in
6. RAM	f. needs to be installed unless a device is installed on the motherboard
7. motherboard	g. often associated with types of memory
8. CPU	h. only needed these days to deal with PC gaming
9. heat sink / fan	i. determines the type of components that can be used with the machine
10. VCD	j. used to cool the computer
11. graphics card	k. your computer won't work without it

2 **Search the Internet for up-to-date examples of the components above and find their best prices. Use a table like the one below. Report your findings to the class.**

component	specifications	price
case	Mid Tower design	$29.99

P **3** **Write an email to an online-supplier and enquire about all the necessary components for assembling your own PC. Then swap enquiries with your partner and answer the email. Thank him / her for his enquiry and submit a corresponding offer.**

WORD BANK

access – Zugriff
application – Anwendung
capacity – Fassungsvermögen
chassis – Gehäuse
component – Bauteil
CPU – Prozessor
device – Gerät
drive – Laufwerk
expansion – Erweiterung
external – extern, außen
fail (v) – ausfallen
feature – Eigenschaft
graphic digitizer – Grafikdigitalisierer
hard disk – Festplatte
input – Eingabe
install (v) – einbauen, einsetzen
internal – intern, innen
keyboard – Tastatur
light pen – Lichtgriffel
mainboard- Hauptplatine
memory – Speicher
operating system – Betriebssystem
optical bar code reader – Strichcodeleser
output – Ausgabe
PCB – Platine
plotter – Zeichengerät, Plotter
power supply – Stromversorgung
projector – Projektionsgerät, Beamer
shape – (äußere) Form
speaker – Lautsprecher
storage – Speicherung
system unit – Gehäuse
track ball – Rollkugel
volatile – flüchtig
voltage – Spannung

→ **PHRASES:**
Written communication

B | External components

The Internet has become a location where an increasing amount of private, public and commercial data can be stored and processed.

R **1** ◎ A 1.9 **An IT expert is talking about peripheral devices for a computer. Listen to him and make a list of the devices mentioned in the text.**

M **2** **Give a short summary in German of the important information in the text.**

R **3** **Find synonyms from the audio text for the following words or expressions.**

1. commands
2. to join/link
3. usual
4. to enter
5. to favour
6. something with many different functions
7. to combine
8. in current times
9. audio
10. nevertheless

P **4** **Explain the colour code on the right. Which device should be connected to which port?**

5 **Match the devices (1.–10.) with the appropriate descriptions (a.–j.).**

1. web cam
2. trackball
3. image scanner
4. head set
5. game pad
6. monitor
7. microphone
8. mouse
9. interface
10. keyboard

a. connects external to internal devices
b. modern forms are of the TFT-version
c. helps you navigate on the screen
d. controller that needs fingers and thumbs to provide input
e. used for inputting commands or data and for navigating on the screen
f. analyses images, text, or objects
g. a combined input/output device
h. converts sound into electric signals
i. pointing device consisting of exposed ball housed in a socket
j. used to provide visual input that can be easily transferred online

6 **Ask your partner to describe the function of the devices above to you. Use structures like:**

Example: What is a … used for? It is used to …

C | Assembling a computer

In Ihrer Klasse haben Sie zur Zeit einen Austauschschüler aus England, der ein Praktikum in Ihrem Betrieb absolviert. Der Austauschschüler bittet Sie, ihm im Rahmen des Projekts „Aufbau eines PCs" zu helfen.

P/M
KMK III

Übertragen Sie folgende Montageanleitung mit Hilfe Ihres Wörterbuches stichwortartig ins Englische.

Arbeitsauftrag:
Benutze die Anweisung und die verfügbare Hardware und baue den Computer schrittweise zusammen.

1. Das Gehäuse
Entferne die Schrauben auf der Rückseite des Gehäuses. Öffne dann die seitlichen Gehäusewände. Jetzt kannst du die Seitenwände vom Gehäuse abnehmen. Lege das Gehäuse auf seine rechte Seite (von vorne gesehen).

2. Das Netzteil
Setze das Netzteil im oberen Bereich des Gehäuses ein. Achte darauf, dass das Netzteil so eingebaut ist, dass die Lüfter frei liegen und nicht von der Gehäusewand verdeckt sind.

3. Das Mainboard
Montiere das Mainboard in das Gehäuse. Achte darauf, die richtigen Schrauben zu verwenden. Die Schrauben dürfen nicht zu stark angezogen werden! Anschließend muss das Mainboard an das Netzteil angeschlossen werden. Benutze dazu die Bedienungsanleitung für das Mainboard.

4. Der Prozessor
Die CPU ist bereits samt Lüfter auf dem Mainboard montiert.
Schließe den Lüfter an das Mainboard gemäß der Bedienungsanleitung des Mainboards an.

5. Der Arbeitsspeicher
Auf dem Mainboard findest du den DIMM-Sockel für den Arbeitsspeicher. Öffne vorsichtig die Klammern am Sockel und drücke den RAM-Riegel gleichmäßig und kräftig runter, bis die Klammern einrasten. Achte darauf, dass du den Riegel richtig herum einsetzt. Eine Kerbe am Riegel lässt nur eine Möglichkeit zu.

6. Die Grafikkarte
Montiere die Grafikkarte auf der entsprechenden Schnittstelle des Mainboards. Achte darauf, dass die Sicherungsklammer einrastet. Fixiere anschließend die Grafikkarte mit einer Schraube am Gehäuse.

7. Die Festplatte
Setze die Festplatte in den im Gehäuse dafür vorgesehenen Einschub ein und positioniere sie so, dass an beiden Seiten jeweils eine Schraube zur Fixierung angebracht werden kann. Verbinde dann die Festplatte mit dem Mainboard und dem Netzteil.

8. Das DVD-Laufwerk:
Führe das DVD-Laufwerk von vorne in das Gehäuse ein. Fixiere es auf beiden Seiten mit den dazugehörigen Schrauben. Schließe das DVD-Laufwerk an Netzteil und Mainboard an.

9. Inbetriebnahme
Kontrolliere, ob alle Kabel angeschlossen sind.
Schließe jetzt das Gehäuse.
Schließe Maus, Tastatur, und Bildschirm an den Rechner an und überprüfe seine Funktion.

WORD BANK

interface – Schnittstelle
peripheral device – Peripheriegerät

gc2x9w

B

NACH DIESEM MODUL:

- ✓ kann ich verschiedene Firmenabteilungen auf Englisch erklären,
- ✓ kann ich Arbeitsplätze und Tätigkeiten auf Englisch beschreiben,
- ✓ kann ich eine Firmenstruktur auf Englisch beschreiben.

Your company

Regardless of whether your company builds houses, repairs cars, or makes furniture, there is likely to come a time where you will be required to talk about yourself, your job and your company in English. Whether you are greeting an English-speaking visitor, giving a tour of the factory, or talking to suppliers from another country, it is important you have the skills and vocabulary to express yourself clearly.

1 **Work on your own. Look at the photos and brainstorm words that describe what is shown in each of them.**

I/P **2** **Compare your list of words with your partner and work together to describe the pictures. Use these words to help you:**

building site • cable • construction worker • grease • hard hat • car mechanic • overalls • ratchet • server • timber • tools • wires • work gloves

WATCH OUT!

She ~~wears~~ a hard hat. She is wearing a hard hat.

P **3** **With your partner, think of three questions you would like to ask each of the four young workers shown in the photos.**

A | The company and its departments

P **1** **Use the words and phrases in the table to explain what the departments of Krone Elektronik GmbH do.**

Example: Sales and Marketing advertises and sells the products.

Department		
Sales and Marketing	distribute	the products are not damaged.
Production Planning	*advertise and sell*	new employees.
Accounts	check	raw materials.
HR (Human Resources)	buy	*the products.*
Production	deal with	the computer network.
Logistics	recruit and train	the finished products.
Purchasing	maintain	customer problems.
Customer Service	handle	the company's finances.
R&D (Research and Development)	make	new products.
IT (Information Technology)	organize	production schedules.
Quality Control	develop	the products to the customers.

P **2** **Use the information in the table to form sentences using *responsible for / in charge of*.**

Example:
The Production department is responsible for making the products.
The Production Planning department is in charge of …

P **3** **Look at the departments again and write down three questions. Then close your book and ask your partner.**

Example:
A: What is the Quality Control department responsible for?
B: It is responsible for …
A: Which department is in charge of …?
B: The … department is in charge of …

R **4** KMK I ⊙ A 1.2 **Der Ausbildungsleiter von Krone Elektronik, Herr Kirchner, zeigt Sean, einem Elektrotechnikstudenten aus Belfast, das Firmengelände und die einzelnen Abteilungen. Hören Sie sich das Gespräch an und beantworten Sie die folgenden Fragen auf Deutsch.**

1. Wann wurde Krone Elektronik GmbH gegründet, und von wem?
2. Wo hat die Firma ihren Hauptsitz?
3. Wie viele Produktionsanlagen hat Krone Elektronik insgesamt?
4. Wo wird nächstes Jahr eine neue Produktionsanlage eröffnet?
5. Wie viele Leute beschäftigt die Firma?
6. Woran arbeitet die Forschungs- und Entwicklungsabteilung gerade?
7. Welche drei Abteilungen befinden sich in dem Hauptgebäude?
8. Wo wird Sean zuerst arbeiten?
9. Wie viele Zylinderköpfe werden jährlich bei Krone Elektronik hergestellt?
10. Was passiert momentan in der IT-Abteilung?

WORD BANK

grease – Fett, Schmierfett
ratchet – Knarre
raw materials – Rohmaterialien
recruit (v) – anwerben
tool – Werkzeug

B | Tasks and responsibilities

Industrial companies are made up of many different people, who all have a variety of tasks and responsibilities. DWG Tech GmbH in Stuttgart manufactures machine parts for the automotive and aviation industry. Below, Tim Schieber, a DWG Tech GmbH employee, talks about his job and daily activities on DWG Tech GmbH's English website.

R **1** **Read the text and answer the following questions in your own words.**

1. What do CNC machines do?
2. What problems can occur with CNC machines?

Hi, my name is Tim Schieber and I work as a CNC machine operator here at the DWG Tech headquarters in Stuttgart. I've been with the company since completing my apprenticeship three years ago and next summer I am going to work at the DWG Tech branch in Detroit.

In my opinion, what we do here is very important. CNC is all about precision, and it is therefore essential that I concentrate at all times. These machines drill, shape, cut and polish the parts for automobiles and aeroplanes. As a CNC machine operator I am responsible for one machine. As I said, this job is all about precision, and the machines are programmed specifically for each job. I do not do the programming myself, but I learnt programming during my apprenticeship and I sometimes have to intervene when something goes wrong – such as a vibrating workpiece or broken cutting tools.

The CNC process is almost entirely automatic. It is my job to set up the machine for the production process, which means loading the machine with the correct tools and workpieces. Once the programming for an operation is done, I enter the commands into the machine. To do this we use a computer network. The next step is to let the machine work its magic.

The main part of my job is to monitor the machine and spot problems. This means checking that the machine is running smoothly, measuring finished workpieces to check that the dimensions are correct, and sometimes replacing tools. It is also important that the machine is kept cool and lubricated with a special lubricating oil – but this is also done automatically. Of course, another of my tasks is to make sure the machine is kept clean, and that the working area is safe.

My working day depends on what shift I am on. We generally work either early shift or late shift. Early shift is from 6am until 2pm, and the guys on late shift begin at 2pm and clock out at 10pm. Sometimes, if we have a lot of work to do, there is also a night shift – but that doesn't happen too often. I actually prefer early shift. Even though I don't enjoy waking up at 4:45am, it is great to have the afternoon to do whatever I like – especially in the summer.

I really enjoy my job and I am proud to be working for an international company like DWG. My colleagues and I are always very busy and it can be fairly stressful. But I love working with the machines and it is interesting to see the many technological developments in the industry.

2 **Find the synonyms in the text for the following words:**

1. to finish
2. very important
3. cars
4. accuracy
5. to observe
6. usually
7. to like
8. workmates
9. quite

R **3** **Decide whether the statements are true or false. Give reasons for your decisions in German.**

1. Tim is currently doing an apprenticeship as a CNC machine operator.
2. Once the machine starts running, Tim's work is over.
3. One of Tim's tasks is making sure that the cutting tools are not broken.
4. Tim rarely works in shifts.
5. Accuracy is very important for CNC work.
6. The technology used in CNC machining has hardly changed over the years.

P **4** **Your boss has asked you to write a short text for your company's English website. Make sure you include some basic facts about your company and details about your daily tasks and responsibilities. Use some of the phrases in Tim's text, e.g. *I work as, I've been with the company since,* etc.**

→ **PHRASES:** Your company

P/I **5** **Check the Internet for a job in your industry that interests you. Make notes on the daily tasks and responsibilities.**

I **6** **Explain the job you researched to your partner, but don't mention the job title. Your partner must guess what the job is from the description you give. Then swap roles.**

C | Organisational structure

P/M KMK II **Sie sind Auszubildende(r) in der DWG Tech GmbH. Ihr Vorgesetzter benötigt eine Übersicht über die Ingenieursabteilung der DWG Tech GmbH Niederlassung in Detroit. Auf deren Firmen-Homepage finden Sie die folgenden Informationen zu den Mitarbeitern. Zeichnen Sie ein Organigramm nach der vorliegenden Beschreibung.**

Who's who in DWG Tech GmbH Detroit's engineering department?

DWG Tech GmbH Inc. employs around 60 people in its engineering department. The department is led by Chief Engineer Dr. Adam Foster, who is supported by his Personal Assistant Helen Green and DWG Tech's Assistant Chief Engineer Dr. Tim Bayliss. The engineering department is split into two core areas: automotive and aviation. Shift leaders Chris Falsone and Sandra Borowski report to Michael Kellermann, the foreman. They all belong to automotive which is run by experienced Chief Automotive Engineer, Dr. Torben Brinkema. DWG Tech's aviation department is in the capable hands of Dr. Judith Sommer, Chief Aviation Engineer, who has been with the company for over 15 years. Dr. Sommer is supported by foreman Frank Kapowski. Barry Richardson and Jens Schmelzer are the two shift leaders and work closely with Mr Kapowski.

WORD BANK

aviation – Luftfahrt
CNC (computerized numerical control) – CNC (computerisierte numerische Steuerung)
dimensions – Maße
drill (v) – bohren
lubricated – geölt
lubricating oil – Schmieröl
measure (v) – messen
polish (v) – schleifen, polieren
precision – Genauigkeit
shape (v) – fräsen, formen
vibrate (v) – vibrieren
workpiece – Werkstück

WORD BANK ⊙

braking system – Bremsanlage
cylinder head – Zylinderkopf
interface – Schnittstelle
manufacturing plant – Produktionsbetrieb
operating system – Betriebssystem

03

NACH DIESEM MODUL:

- ✓ kann ich Speicherarten und Speichermedien auf Englisch benennen und ihre unterschiedlichen Funktionsweisen beschreiben,
- ✓ bin ich über einige neue Entwicklungen informiert und kann mich auf Englisch zu ihnen äußern.

1

2

3

4

Storing data

1 Look at the illustrations: What do they all have in common, what are the differences between them? Say a few words about each.

2 Which storage devices do you use every day? Do you have any favourites? What do you use them for? Discuss with a partner, then report to the class.

3 The units in the box are all used to describe storage capacity. Put them in ascending order and present your result to the class.

> Kilobyte (KB) • Petabyte (PB) • Yottabyte (YB) • Megabyte (MB) • Zettabyte (ZB) • Terabyte (TB) • Gigabyte (GB) • Exabyte (EB)

Example:

Kilobyte (KB) 10^3 Byte = 1.000 Byte

P **4** Search the Internet for information about cloud-computing. What is it? Who will probably be the providers and customers? Have you used it yourself? If not, would you try it? Why/why not? Prepare a short report.

A | Storage devices

M **1** You have come across the following text on computer memory. Summarize the main points in German.

Storage devices

Storage devices are used in computers to store data. These devices come in many shapes and sizes, and the technologies used to store the data are also very different. There are two kinds of memory: the primary memory, which is volatile, and the secondary memory, which is non-volatile. Volatile memory is erasable whereas the contents of non-volatile memory cannot be erased. Basically, when we talk about data storage devices we refer to the secondary memory, which is used to store data permanently in the computer.
Memory devices vary according to their architecture and design. Some, for example, are optical data storage memory devices, others are magnetic or mechanical storage media, or flash memory devices. The most common secondary storage device is the hard disk drive, which is used in almost all computer systems. Other secondary storage devices and techniques include floppy disk drives, CD ROM and DVD ROM, flash memory, USB data cards and Blu-ray.
CDs and DVDs can have two types of storage. In the first type the data cannot be erased, but is stored permanently. The second type of CD or DVD is called rewritable: here the data that has been written can be erased completely and the same storage device can be re-used for storing different data.
The data in a storage device can be in the form of files, databases, digital video and audio, etc. Non-volatile memory devices can store data permanently until the user decides to erase it. This is the case with hard disk drives or floppy disk drives. However, most of the drives that are used for the purpose of data storage are fragile and the data in them can be easily corrupted.
Data storage devices used to be expensive but are becoming cheaper day by day. The technology is constantly improving, and memory storage capacity has now risen to terabyte (TB).

P **2** Describe the types of storage media and give examples for each.

I **3** One of you is an IT expert, the other is a journalist. Prepare questions and answers using the information in the text. Practise an interview, then act it out for the class.

R **4** Find words or expressions from the text that match the following definitions:

1. can be deleted
2. permanently mounted device
3. not retaining stored information
4. can be written on many times
5. damaged
6. disk space

WORD BANK

corrupt (v) (data) – (Daten) beschädigen
erasable – löschbar
flash memory – Flash-Speicher
floppy disk drive – Disketten-laufwerk
fragile – hier: anfällig
hard disk drive – Festplatte(nlaufwerk)
rewritable – überschreibbar
storage device – Speichergerät, Datenspeicher
volatile (memory) – flüchtiger (Speicher)

B | Past and current developments in data storage

R **1** Put the following paragraphs into the correct order.

A short history of data storage

By contrast, a holographic memory could store several thousand holograms on an area similar to that of a DVD. You would still have a laser beam reading the information but it would be able to "see" and access the different holograms on that area, and you would be able to store up to 25 times more data and access it 25 times faster than you could with a DVD. **1**

However, information technology is developing so quickly that we may see holographic storage devices enter the consumer market in the near future. According to rumours in the industry, one big manufacturer is already thinking about using holographic storage for its next generation of game consoles. So what is different about it? **3**

The key difference between today's standard optical storage systems (DVDs, Blu-ray discs, etc.) and holographic storage is that standard optical discs store the data using only two dimensions. A laser beam scans the surface of the disc for lows and highs, which reflect the beam back to its source. The software of the disc drive then translates this information into zeros and ones and so on. **5**

No one knows for certain what new high capacity storage devices the future will bring. The first hard disc drive (HDD) was invented in 1956 by Rey Johnson. Back then, of course, the massive amounts of data we are able to store on an HDD now would have seemed like science fiction. However, in 1988 an effect called Giant Magneto Resistance (GMR) was discovered, which made a much denser storage of data on magnetic hard disc drives possible. GMR increased the storage capacity enormously. **2**

Today scientists and engineers are working on several exciting new technologies that may change the way we store data and the amounts we can store. One of those technologies is holographic memory. The idea has been around since the 1960s. But at that time the underlying technology was so expensive that it seemed unlikely holographic memory would ever become an everyday reality in office or household computers. **4**

R/P **2** Decide whether the following statements are true or false according to the above text. Give reasons for your answers.

1. HDDs first appeared in the 1960s.
2. The GMR was discovered soon afterwards.
3. The idea of holographic storage is brand-new.
4. Holographic storage was made available to the mass market in the beginning of the 21st century.
5. The main difference between optical and holographic storage is in the number of dimensions both work with.
6. The software transforms the information it gets from the laser into binary code.
7. The number of holograms to be stored on the same area is limited to several hundred.
8. The speed of the different storage technologies would be roughly the same.

C | The next storage revolution

R **1** Complete the following text with words from the box:

9 brains 6 · bacteria 2 · quantum mechanics 11 · data 8 · incredible 14 · mirror 6 · experiments 15 · 90 GB 5 · process 13 · quantum computing 17 · mass · petabytes 10 · molecule chains 7 · seconds 16 · market ready 4 · revolution 1 · information 3

Quantum computing – Science Fiction?

Holographic data storage, however, is just the beginning of the next data storage **1**. Researchers are already looking into storing data in things such as **2**. In 2010 a Chinese team from the University of Hong Kong successfully managed to encode **3** in a colony of E.coli. Their method is far from **4** and will require many more years of research to perfect, but, in theory, using just one gram of bacteria one could store up to **5**.

However, to get new ideas for data storage you don't have to look into a microscope. Simply look into the **6**. Our brain stores memories, which are really also just bits and bytes of data, by forming new **7** and storing them. Yes, we may sometimes forget where we put our car keys, but the amount of **8** we can store in the memory centres of our **9** is estimated to be somewhere around 2.5 **10**. So researchers are also looking into storing data using similar molecule chains.

But all of the above seems laughable when you start looking at **11**. Today we cannot begin to imagine the amounts of **12** we will be able to store and **13** at truly **14** speeds. None of us alive today may live to see the day when mankind starts using quantum computers to store data. At present, in scientific **15**, quantum computers and storage only function for a few **16**, but one day, and that day may still be a century or more away, **17** will become a reality.

WORD BANK

holographic – holographisch
Magneto Resistance – Magnetwiderstand
molecule chains – Molekülketten

WORD BANK ◎

CERN – ein internationales Forschungslabor
cluster – Anhäufung, Gruppe
framework – Rahmenwerk, Rahmenbedingungen
relational databases – relationale Datenbank
search engine – Suchmaschine
source code – Quellcode
toolbox – Werkzeugkasten

P **2** Search the Internet for information on the developments above, or for other, perhaps even newer approaches. Prepare a short presentation and give it to the class.

→ **PHRASES:** Presentations

I **3** Should one push research to boundaries yet unimaginable, or should one accept limits, e.g. the capacity of the human brain? Discuss the pros and cons.

M **4** KMK III ◎ A 1.10 Ihre Vorgesetzte hat Sie gebeten, ihr für eine betriebsinterne Fortbildung zu neuen Entwicklungen in der Informationstechnologie Informationen zusammenzustellen. Im Rahmen Ihrer Recherche sind Sie auf folgenden Podcast gestoßen. Hören Sie sich den Podcast an und geben Sie seine wesentlichen Inhalte sinngemäß auf Deutsch wieder.

P **5** Verfassen Sie auf Englisch eine kurze, stichwortartige Beschreibung der Anwendung.

C

NACH DIESEM MODUL:

- ✓ kenne ich die wichtigsten Redewendungen um ein Telefongespräch zu führen,
- ✓ kann ich Maße, Namen und Adressen am Telefon auf Englisch weitergeben.

Telephoning

When you are on the job, chances are you will have your mobile phone with you – it does not matter what line of work you are in. Whether you are repairing a server, fixing a leak, or installing a telephone line, your phone can ring at any time. It could be a customer with a complaint, you may have to ring a supplier or check the status of an order. And if you have to talk in English, you need to have the necessary skills to understand and be understood, no matter what the situation.

P **1** **Look at the photos. What might the people be talking about on the telephone? Compare your answers with a partner. Use these words to help you:**

materials • problem • delay • support • help • breakdown • repair • solution • angry • confused • crash • computer network room

2 **Match the German words below with the English equivalents.**

1. Handy	a. message
2. Anrufbeantworter	b. hands-free device
3. Festnetz	c. extension number
4. Nachricht	d. mobile / cell phone
5. Durchwahl	e. answering machine
6. Freisprechanlage	f. area code
7. Vorwahl	g. country code
8. Ländervorwahl	h. landline

A | Making and receiving a phone call

R **1** **Which of the following phrases are used for making calls and which ones for receiving calls? Make a list.**

1. Could you put me through to Mr Warren, please?
2. I'm sorry, but Mr/Ms ... is in a meeting at the moment.
3. How can I help you?
4. Thank you. I'll ring back later.
5. Can I ask what your call is about?
6. Would you like to leave a message?
7. Thank you very much for your help.
8. My name is Barry Potter and I'm calling from ...
9. May I take your name, please?
10. I'd like to speak to somebody in the production department, please?
11. Hold the line, please. I'll put you through.
12. Could you tell him/her that ...?

M **2** **Read the telephone conversation below and find the English equivalents for the following German expressions.**

→ **PHRASES:** Telephoning

1. Haben Sie etwas zum Schreiben?
2. Soll ich Ihnen seine Handynummer geben?
3. Er ist leider zurzeit nicht im Büro.
4. Ich hätte gerne mit ... gesprochen.
5. Einen Moment, bitte.
6. Wie kann ich Ihnen helfen?

Christoph:	Smart EDV, Christoph Fink.
Caller:	Er, yes, hello. Do you speak English?
Christoph:	Certainly. How can I help you?
Caller:	This is the Smart IT company in Kiel, isn't it?
Christoph:	Yes, that's correct.
Caller:	Great. My name is Erik Pedersen and I'm calling from Danske Onlinebank Copenhagen. I'd like to speak to Mr Gebhardt, please.
Christoph:	Sorry, but Mr Gebhardt is not in the office at the moment. Can I take a message, or would you like his mobile number?
Caller:	Can you give me his mobile number, please?
Christoph:	Ok, do you have a pen?
Caller:	Just a second, please ... ok, go ahead.
Christoph:	The number is 0049-170 557624.
Caller:	Sorry, I didn't catch that. Could you speak up a bit?
Christoph:	Yes, of course. The number is 0049-170 557624.
Caller:	Thank you very much.
Christoph:	You're welcome. Maybe you can give me your phone number.
Caller:	Certainly. It's 0045, that's the country code for Denmark, 32, the area code for Copenhagen, and then 54 58 11. Oh, and my extension number is 944.
Christoph:	0045-32 54 58 11, extension 944. Thank you very much. Goodbye.
Caller:	Goodbye.

WORD BANK

breakdown – Störung, Ausfall
crash – Absturz
leak – Leck

INTERCULTURAL BOX

Intercultural awareness – Telephoning in English-speaking countries

When talking on the phone in English it is important that you use suitable and polite phrases. For example, if you know the person you are calling, it is common to make a little small talk before getting down to business. One thing to remember: Although it is common for English people to quickly switch to first names, it is still important to remain polite and remember that you are talking to a customer or a colleague, and not your best friend.
Example: *How are you? I haven't spoken to you for a while.*
If you have to give bad news or talk about a problem, then you should begin with *I'm afraid …* or *Unfortunately … .*
Example: *I'm afraid we cannot install your wireless internet connection this week.*
A request often begins with *Could you possibly …* or *I would be grateful if you would / could … .*
Example: *I would be grateful if you would call me back later.*
When someone thanks you for your help, or for a job well done, you can simply say *You're welcome.* And be careful! Whereas in German, just saying *yes* or *no* may be fine, this is considered to be quite impolite in England. Instead, just say *Yes, I think so,* or *No, I'm afraid not.* If you call somebody, you should give your name, where you are calling from, and say who you would like to speak to.
Example: *Hello, my name is Felix Hirschbach, calling from Crown Electronics. Could I speak to Ms Cameron, please?*

P **3** **How would you say the following things more politely?**

→ **PHRASES:** Telephoning

1. Eh? Say it again!
2. Give me your number!
3. What do you want?
4. What's your name?
5. I can't hear you!
6. What?
7. He's not here!
8. Give me Ms Bauer!

I **4** KMK I **Sie arbeiten im International Calls Service Center von Smart EDV in Kiel und erhalten einen Anruf. Führen Sie das folgende Telefongespräch mit einem Partner auf Englisch.**

Smart EDV GmbH, Kiel.	Stefanie Berg, dänische Kundin
Nehmen Sie den Anruf entgegen. →	Nennen Sie Ihren Namen. Sie möchten mit Herrn Gebhardt sprechen.
Sagen Sie, dass Sie die Anruferin schlecht verstehen und bitten Sie sie, etwas lauter zu sprechen. →	Sprechen Sie etwas lauter und fragen Sie, ob Sie jetzt besser zu verstehen sind.
Bejahen Sie und fragen Sie, worum es geht. →	Erklären Sie, dass die Firma Smart EDV gestern in Ihrer Firma neue Hardware und Software installiert hat, und dass heute Morgen der Server abgestürzt ist. Es ist dringend!
Sagen Sie höflich, dass Herr Gebhardt in einer Sitzung ist und sich später melden wird. Fragen Sie, ob Herr Gebhardt die Nummer der Anruferin hat. →	Bejahen Sie. Bedanken Sie sich und beenden Sie das Gespräch.
Bedanken Sie sich auch und verabschieden Sie sich.	

B | Giving information over the phone

Making a quick call is often the fastest and easiest way of passing on valuable information, such as measurements or figures. However, misunderstandings can happen very quickly, so it is important to make sure any information is delivered clearly and correctly.

1 Match the English word to the German translation.

1. height	a. Breite
2. length	b. Gewicht
3. width	c. Höhe
4. weight	d. Tiefe
5. depth	e. Länge

INFO BOX: Saying weights and measurements

nine **point** five milimetres (9.5 mm)	100 **by** 30 **by** 15 (100 x 30 x 15)
thirty one **square** metres (31 m²)	twenty **cubic** metres (20 m³)
one **point** two five litre engine (1.25 l)	6000 revolutions **per** minute (6000 rpm)
170 kilometers **per** hour (170 kph)	two hundred **and** twenty volts (220 V)

2 What are the adjectives for the nouns in exercise 1?

I **3** Sit back to back with a partner. Take turns in giving each other different information over the phone. Partner A uses role card A, Partner B uses role card B (see Appendix).

I **4** Sit back to back and spell your name, the name and address of your company, and your email address. Use the table below to help you.

Symbol	Name	Example
@	at	info@
B / b	capital letter / lower case	NYC / asap
-	hyphen / dash	t-online
ö	o-umlaut / oe / o with two dots	Schönberg
:	colon	http:
/	slash / stroke / forward slash	org/news
\	backslash	\docs
.	dot	.de
_	underscore	customer_info

R **5** KMK I ◎ A 1.3 Alex Bauder works for Fertighaus Henke in Magdeburg and is called by Mr. Reid, an English customer who lives in Germany and who is currently building a house near Magdeburg. Listen to the conversation and answer the following questions in German.

1. Who is Mr Deschler?
2. Why can't Mr Reid speak to him personally?
3. Why does Mr Reid want to speak to Mr Deschler?
4. When will Fertighaus Henke begin building Mr Reid's cellar?
5. Why does the extractor fan need to be moved to the left?
6. Which changes is Mr Deschler not responsible for?
7. What should Mr Deschler do next?

R **6** ◎ A 1.3 Now listen to the conversation again and make notes of the changes Mr Reid wants, where he wants them, and details about the measurements, where given.

WORD BANK

cubic metre – Kubikmeter
revolutions per minute – Drehzahl
socket – Steckdose
square metre – Quadratmeter

WORD BANK ◎

construction manager – Bauleiter
diameter – Durchmesser
extractor fan – Dunstabzugshaube
foundation pit – Baugrube
hob – Kochfeld

04

NACH DIESEM MODUL:

√ kann ich mit den englischen Fachbegriffen in Bezug auf BIOS und Betriebssysteme umgehen,

√ kann ich Vorgänge im BIOS auf Englisch beschreiben.

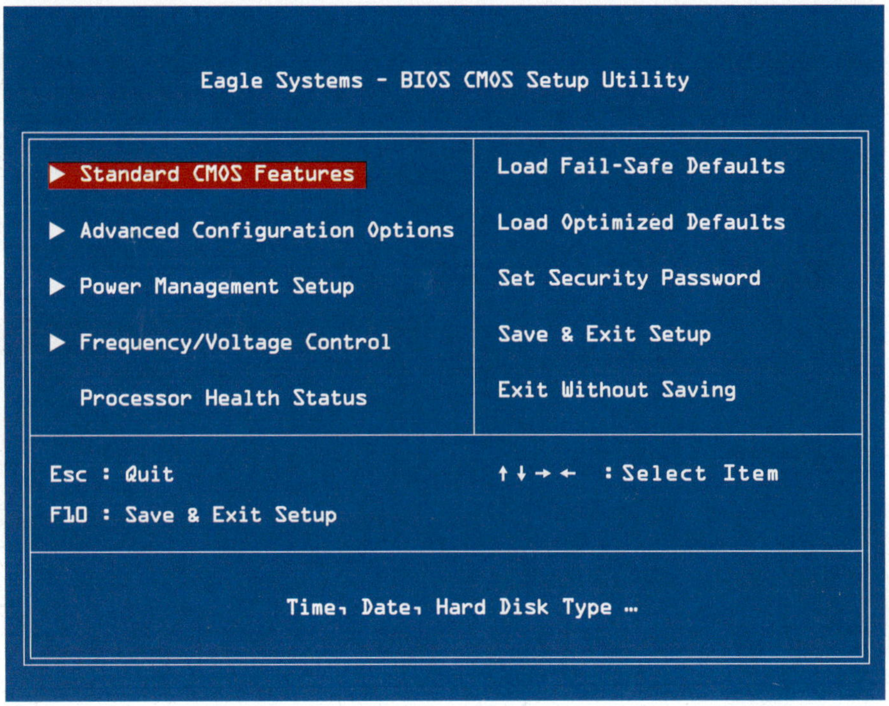

BIOS and operating systems

The **B**asic **I**nput / **O**utput **S**ystem (BIOS) is firmware that gives the software access to the hardware in a PC. This firmware is already included on the motherboard. If you build your own computer, you have to install and configure the operating system and sometimes even the BIOS yourself. The BIOS only accepts keyboard input. Depending on the BIOS, you enter the setup by pressing a special button. Then you usually navigate the setup using the arrow keys.

1 Match the sentences with the corresponding BIOS entries in the screenshot.

1. This allows you to regulate the energy consumption of your computer.
2. Here you can set the time and date.
3. Select this option when you need to load a fail-safe configuration.
4. This menu entry protects the BIOS setup from unauthorised access.

P **2** Explain how you would enter the BIOS setup on your computer and then check the temperature of the CPU.

P **3** SAFETY FIRST ⚠

1. Find out the average temperature of your processor.
2. Which device ensures that the temperature does not get too high?

A | BIOS or solving the chicken-or-the-egg dilemma

R **1** **Read the text and do the tasks.**

1. Define the dilemma the BIOS aims to resolve in your own words.
2. Describe how the BIOS resolves this dilemma.
3. Give examples of other information stored in the BIOS.

Every PC needs an operating system (OS). It is stored on a hard disk drive or a solid state disk. The OS handles which commands are loaded into and executed by the central processing unit (CPU). The CPU is nothing more than an integrated circuit designed for logic and arithmetic functions. It cannot 'remember' anything unless it is already executing a program. Since the first instruction of the OS has not already been loaded into memory, it is not ready to be executed by the CPU. Consequently, it cannot do anything with the OS's machine code. The OS in turn cannot load its instructions into the CPU unless it is already running. This is what constitutes a so-called "chicken-or-egg dilemma", i. e. which step must come first? Fortunately, this dilemma is resolved by the BIOS, a basic system on a chip. The BIOS is tailor-made to 'know' the layout of the motherboard, the location of the disk containing the OS, the circuits leading to and from the CPU, and how the main memory can be accessed. In other words, the BIOS knows where the bootloader is located. This is a software that loads the components of the OS in the startup process. The BIOS also knows what needs to be done, and what needs to be loaded from where into the processor and the main memory to boot the computer. The BIOS never forgets this information, because

it comes with a small battery that constantly supplies the BIOS's memory with power. In this way, the BIOS can keep track of the date and time, even when the computer is turned off. The BIOS can also store the settings for the boot process and other things such as the correct processor frequency and power management settings.

2 **Put the steps for booting a computer into the correct order.**

1. BIOS initializes the PC's other components and devices.
2. BIOS turns over control to the bootloader.
3. BIOS loads its instructions into its memory.
4. BIOS looks for the boot disc containing the operating system.
5. BIOS loads the bootloader from the master boot record of the boot disc.
6. The bootloader loads the operating system.

M **3** **Describe the process of booting a computer in German.**

P **4** **UNDERSTANDING TECHNICAL ENGLISH**

Find the German meanings for the technical terms. Use an online dictionary.

1. to execute
2. main memory
3. to access
4. integrated circuit

WORD BANK

BIOS – Basis-Eingabe-Ausgabe-System
central processing unit (CPU) – Hauptprozessor
firmware – Software in einem persistenten Speicherbaustein
initialize (v) – initialisieren
machine code – Programm-Code in einer Maschinensprache
motherboard – Hauptplatine
operating system – Betriebssystem
setup – Programm zur Festlegung von Konfigurationsvariablen

B | Network booting

Booting is not limited to using local discs. It is also possible, and not uncommon, to boot a computer via a concept referred to as network booting.

Complete the text about network booting using the words in the box.

complex · network · capacity · operating system · computer users · server · efficiency · network connection · central · location · discs

In the case of network booting the **1** is not stored locally. Instead it is kept at a different **2** where it is accessible via a network. **3** will not even notice the difference. However, a fast and stable **4** is required. The operating system is loaded from a network **5**. The operating systems for all users are managed from a **6** point. In a **7** booting environment the computers can be so-called thin clients. Sometimes these computers do not have local **8**. However if they do, they do not have a high **9**. Thin clients are less **10** computers. This means lower costs and higher **11**.

C | Troubleshooting

Robert Leiske is doing an IT course at a college in Cologne. Robert gets a phone call from Victor, an American exchange student of online marketing from CalTech. Victor has got a computer problem and he needs Robert's help.

R **1** ⓐ A 1.11 **Listen to the dialogue. Decide whether the statements are true or false. Correct the false statements.**

1. Robert thinks that the hard disc drive in Victor's computer must be broken.
2. Victor accidentally overwrote the bootloader of the mOS.
3. Robert tells Victor to edit a configuration file.
4. Robert suggests that Victor reinstall the operating system.

R **2** ⓐ A 1.11 **Listen to the dialogue again. Explain Victor's problem and write down the steps Robert suggests to solve it.**

P **3** **What bootloader do you use in your computer? Explain how you can change its configuration.**

4 **Find out detailed information about GRUB on the Internet. You can focus on the operating systems it supports and also on the filesystems it can handle. Report your results to the class.**

D | Selecting an operating system

M **1** KMK III

Sie arbeiten in der IT-Abteilung einer international tätigen Firma. Die Geschäftsleitung will die IT-Infrastruktur modernisieren und hat folgende Vorgaben in einer E-Mail an alle Mitarbeiter geschickt. Ein englischer Kollege, der gerade bei Ihnen arbeitet, bittet Sie, die anstehenden Änderungen für ihn kurz auf Englisch zusammen zu fassen. Geben Sie folgende Vorgaben sinngemäß im Englischen wieder.

An: Alle
Von: Dietmar_Herrmann@herrmanns...de
Betreff: Modernisierung der IT-Struktur

Unser Unternehmen hat in der Vergangenheit zu viel Geld für IT ausgegeben. Die zukünftige Infrastruktur muss vor allem kosteneffektiv sein.

1. IT Sicherheit
Wir glauben, dass die Bedrohung durch digitale Angriffe stark übertrieben ist; folglich muss das Budget für solch leichtsinnige Verschwendungen drastisch reduziert werden.

2. Energieverbrauch
Die zukünftige Infrastruktur muss Energie effizienter sein. Dadurch sollen einerseits Kosten eingespart werden, andererseits soll unser Bild in der Öffentlichkeit grüner werden.

3. Benutzerfreundlichkeit
Die Systeme müssen einfacher in der Bedienung sein.

4. Wartung
Um effizienter Arbeiten zu können, soll es möglich sein, kommerziellen Support in Anspruch zu nehmen.

P **2** KMK III

Ihrer Firma sind mehrere Vertriebsgesellschaften angeschlossen, u. a. in London, die ebenfalls von der Modernisierung der IT-Infrastruktur betroffen sind. Ihr Vorgesetzer bittet Sie, eine Präsentation für die Vertriebsgesellschaft in London zu erarbeiten. Sie sollen die Unterschiede zwischen drei Betriebssystemen herausarbeiten, die in der engeren Auswahl stehen. Fassen Sie die wichtigsten Unterschiede in der Tabelle auf Englisch zusammen.

	mOS²	Centrix Linux	Pear OS
price per client	300 €	free	100 €
price per server	3200 €	800 €	not available
support available	yes	no	yes
open source	no	yes	no
incl. firewall	yes	yes	no
incl. virus scanner	no	yes	no
can function as server	yes	yes	no
can function as client	yes	yes	yes
network boot	no	yes	yes

WORD BANK

configuration file – Konfigurationsdatei

WORD BANK ◎

boot menu list – Liste von Betriebssystemen
cfg – häufig verwendete Endung für Konfigurationsdateien
default bootloader – Standard-Bootloader
design application – Software zum Gestalten von z. B. Webseiten oder Druckerzeugnissen
text editor – Textaufbereitungsprogramm

D

NACH DIESEM MODUL:

- ✓ kann ich auf Englisch kurze Anfragen, Angebote und Bestellungen als Brief, E-Mail oder Fax erstellen,
- ✓ kann ich englische Briefe, E-Mails und Faxe beantworten.

1

2

3

4

Written communication

Written communication such as emails, faxes and business letters play an essential role in business, both in the office and the workshop. For any company to run efficiently, it is necessary to have an effective communication system – making sure that enquiries are answered promptly, offers are made on time, and orders are placed and processed correctly. The standard business letter has been replaced in recent years by the faster email, and to a lesser extent, the fax. In all areas of business today it is common to have dealings with countries across the globe, meaning you need to be able to understand written communication in English.

P **1** Look at the pictures above and describe them in your own words.

P **2** What are the advantages and disadvantages of the forms of written communication shown in the pictures? Create a list. Use these words to help you:

> confidential • instant • easy • time-consuming • reliable • signal • misunderstanding • slow • personal • formal • informal

3 Compare your lists with a partner and come up with a final list for each form of communication. Share your final list with the class.

A | Enquiries

Business transactions generally begin with an enquiry. In the example below, a car garage is looking for a new supplier of tools.

M **1** **Stephen Bains from City Garage in Wolverhampton, England is interested in buying some tools from Hauch Werkzeuge KG in Gelsenkirchen, a toolmaking company specializing in tools for car mechanics. Read Stephen's enquiry and summarise the main points of the enquiry in German.**

Dear Sir/Madam,	a. appropriate salutation
Automotive mechanic tool supplier	b. subject line
We saw your advertisement in this month's edition of *Under the Bonnet* magazine regarding your selection of tools for car mechanics.	c. source of address
We are a family-run car mechanic company in Wolverhampton, England, with over 20 employees.	d. introduction of your firm
We have recently expanded and are looking for a new supplier of quality tools for our new workshops. Therefore we would ask you to send us a copy of your latest catalogue and price list.	e. reason for enquiry f. request to send catalogue and price list
Please also inform us about your export prices and possible discounts as well as terms of payment and delivery and delivery times.	g. request for information on prices and discounts and terms of payment and delivery
As we would like to test your tools, we would appreciate it if you could send us some samples.	h. further requests
Thank you for your attention to this enquiry and we look forward to hearing from you.	i. closing phrase
Yours sincerely,	j. complimentary close

R **2** **Match these parts of an enquiry with the descriptions (a.–j.) above.**

1. Best wishes.
2. Your company was recommended to me by a colleague.
3. We are a large production company, specialising in machine components.
4. Please let us have a detailed cost estimate for configuring our IT network.
5. We hope to hear from you soon.
6. What are your terms of payment for regular customers?
7. As we are convinced that your products will sell well on the American market …
8. A visit by your representative would be greatly appreciated.
9. Please let us know whether you can supply from stock.
10. Machine component supplier

WORD BANK

bonnet – Motorhaube
car mechanic – KFZ-Mechaniker(in)
toolmaking company – Werkzeugmacher
workshop – Werkstatt

B | Offers

P **1** **Read the offer email below and complete it using the words from the box.**

bank transfer • discount • interest • business • working days • sample • attachment • delivery period • stock • orders

From: mailto:t.wolf@hauch...de **Sent:** 201_-05-30 14:52
To: mailto:info@citygarage.co...uk
Cc: mailto:k.mueller@hauch...de
Subject: Your enquiry

Attachments Hauptkatalog_2012.pdf

Dear Mr Bains

Thank you for your enquiry and your **1** in our products.

We are sending you our latest brochure and price list as an **2**.
For **3** of 200 units or more we are able to grant a quantity **4** of five per cent.
For large orders (over 250 units) we require a **5** of 10–14 **6**.
Smaller orders can be delivered from **7** and within 3–5 working days.

Our usual terms of payment are by **8** to our account with the GDB Bank in Gelsenkirchen.

One **9** case of ratchets, sockets, wrenches and screwdrivers has been dispatched to you this morning and should reach you in the next few days.

Thank you again for your enquiry. We look forward to establishing regular **10** with you.

Yours sincerely

Tim Wolf

P **2** **Use the following notes to write an enquiry and an offer in English.**

→ **PHRASES:** Written communication

Enquiry
(You work at Construct World.)

- large DIY store in Poland (Construct World), looking to buy quality German-made tools
- saw your company (Hauch Werkzeuge KG) at a trade show in Hannover
- would like information about delivery times, discounts, copy of catalogue
- would like some samples to inspect
- polite ending

Angebot
(Sie arbeiten bei Hauch Werkzeuge.)

- Bedanken Sie sich für die Anfrage.
- Gerne schicken Sie Ihren aktuellen Prospekt inklusive Preisliste zu.
- Lieferzeit (nach Polen):
  große Bestellungen (über 500 Stück): 5–10 Werktage,
  kleine Bestellungen: 2–4 Werktage
- Preisnachlass ab Bestellwert von 2.500 € möglich (5 %)
- Sie würden sich freuen, mit Construct World zusammenarbeiten zu dürfen.
- höflicher Schluss

C | Orders

1 **Read the order fax below and complete it using the prepositions in the box below.**

for (2 x) • by • of • to (3 x) • with

TELEFAX Message

City Garage
17 Gorsebrook Rd.
Wolverhampton WV6 5PI
Tel.: 0044 (0)1902 554997… • Fax: 0044 (0)1902 554998…

To: Hauch Werkzeuge KG
Schmiedstrasse 44
45879 Gelsenkirchen
Germany

Attention: Mr Tim Wolf

Fax: 0049 209 721965…

From: Stephen Bains

Subject: Order

Dear Mr Wolf

Thank you very much **1** your email **2** 30 May.

Thank you also for sending us your catalogue and price list.
We were very impressed **3** your range of tools for car mechanics and would like to place a trial order **4** 16 socket sets, 16 screwdriver sets, 30 adjustable wrenches and 16 torque wrenches.

Please confirm this order indicating the bank account **5** which you wish to have the sum in question transferred.

Please deliver the tools **6** our workshop at 17 Gorsebrook Rd., Wolverhampton, WV6 5PI.

We look forward **7** receiving the consignment soon and to placing further orders **8** you.

Best regards

S.Bains

Stephen Bains

M **2** KMK II **Sie arbeiten bei Hauch Werkzeuge KG in Gelsenkirchen. Ihr Chef bittet Sie, das obige Fax für ihn auf Deutsch zusammenzufassen, damit er über den Auftrag informiert ist.**

WORD BANK

ratchet – Knarre
screwdriver – Schraubenzieher / -dreher
socket – Steckdose, Stecknuss
torque wrench – Drehmomentschlüssel
(adjustable) wrench – (verstellbarer) Schraubenschlüssel

05

NACH DIESEM MODUL:

- ✓ kann ich gängige Computerarten auf Englisch beschreiben,
- ✓ kann ich einige ihrer typischen Nutzer und Einsatzgebiete auf Englisch erläutern,
- ✓ kann ich einfache Beratungssituationen auf Englisch bewältigen.

1

2

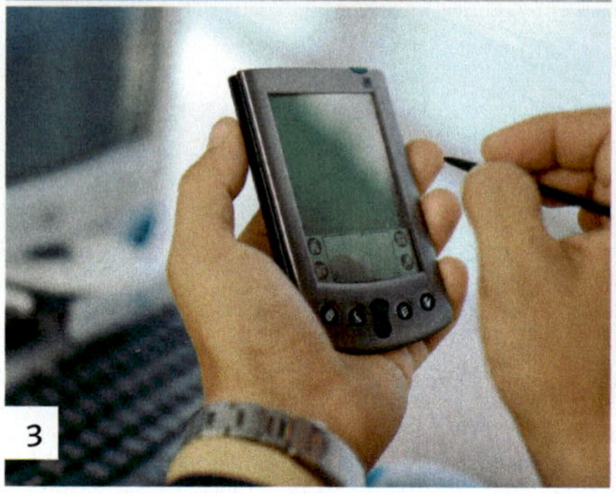

3

4

Types of computer

Almost all of us use computers every day, and depending on personal preferences and lifestyle we may own a number of devices. In the office we might have a stationary tower computer and a monitor. When we are on the move, a notebook, netbook or tablet are more useful. Smartphones come with most of the functions that PDAs had in the past as well as a lot of other functions.

1 **Interview a partner about his/her use of computers. Find out the following information and report your results to the class.**

1. Which of the devices in the photos does your partner know?
2. Does he or she use one or more of these devices at home or at work?

2 **Compare notebooks to tablet PCs. Make a list of the advantages and disadvantages of both devices. Use the words below and any other aspects you can think of.**

keyboard · memory · external devices · display size · portable · powerful · lightweight · functional

3 **Answer the following questions using your ideas from exercise 2.**

1. Which type of work is a notebook more suitable for?
2. Which type of work is a tablet PC more suitable for?

A | Mainframes, minicomputers and microcomputers

R **1** **Read the text below and do the following tasks.**

1. Outline the basic characteristics of a modern computer.
2. Name some input and output devices.
3. Describe the type of computer engineers use to design a new car.
4. Define the term 'server' in your own words.

Modern computers are made up of a lot of electronic components such as integrated circuits and transistors. The main characteristic of computers is that they contain microprocessors and can be programmed, i.e. software programs tell the computer what to do. The software can be adapted to suit the needs of groups of users, or even an individual user. Computers also have one or more processors, memory, and different input and output devices, e.g. a mouse or a screen. Different types of computers vary greatly as regards price, size, speed and what we can use them for, although the distinctions are not sharp, and there is some overlap.

Mainframes and supercomputers are the largest, most powerful machines. The term 'mainframe' refers to the cabinet that contains the central processing unit (CPU) of such a machine. Mainframes are used by companies, for example, to process huge numbers of transactions. In cases where huge processing power is needed – weather forecasting is a good example – you will normally find a supercomputer.

A minicomputer is a midsized machine with less processing capacity than a mainframe but more processing power than a microcomputer. This last category of computer includes workstations, which are used for engineering or design applications (CAD/CAM), desktop publishing and other programmes requiring a moderate amount of processing power as well as high graphics capabilities. Most workstations are single-user computers like PCs, yet another type of microcomputer. In a home or small company network, a workstation can be used as a mid-range server for multiple users. The term 'server' describes not so much a type of computer as a usage: it is a machine dedicated to server applications such as web servers, e-mail servers, file servers or database servers. In networking, any computer connected to a LAN is referred to as a workstation, even if it is a personal computer.

2 **Search the Internet for information about mainframes and workstations. Find out who uses them and what for. Present your findings to the class in a table like the one below.**

Type of computer	Who uses the computer	What they use it for
Mainframe		
Workstation		

3 **UNDERSTANDING TECHNICAL ENGLISH**
Find the general and technical meanings of the words.

1. processor   2. server   3. file

WORD BANK

application – Anwendung
capacity – Leistungsfähigkeit
central processing unit (CPU) – Prozessor, Zentraleinheit
component – (Bau)teil
database – Datenbank
input – Eingabe
integrated circuit – Schaltkreis
keyboard – Tastatur
mainframe – Großrechner
memory – Speicher
microprocessor – Mikroprozessor
output – Ausgabe
transistor – Transistor

B | Microcomputers of today

Sven has just started an apprenticeship with a company in Stuttgart and he is now planning to buy a new PC. As he is not really an expert, Sven asks Naomi, an IT specialist from the company's UK branch, for advice.

R **1** Listen to the dialogue and write down Sven's plans for the new computer.
A 1.12

R/P **2** Listen to the dialogue again. Describe the computers Naomi and Sven talk about.
A 1.12

3 Complete the text with the words in the box.

voice • palmtop • web browsers • devices (2) • keyboard • Internet • input • disc drives • costs • screen • functions • features • network • provider • needs • apps

For people on the move – which is most of us nowadays – mobile computers open up lots of possibilities. The first hand-held **1** were PDAs (Personal Digital Assistants) or **2** computers which were small enough to fit into the palm of your hand. You use a stylus to write on the touch-sensitive **3** or to touch icons or characters on a virtual **4**. Some PDAs also have **5** recognition technology. Due to their size, most handheld computers do not include **6**, instead they have slots, so users can connect them to external **7** or their computers. Originally devised for PIM (Personal Information Manager) **8** such as an address book or a diary, modern PDAs can be used as portable media players, **9** and smartphones. Most can access the **10** via Bluetooth or WiFi connection.

Nowadays PDAs have largely been replaced by smartphones, which combine the **11** of a PDA and a cellphone. Although smartphones may seem to be cheaper than PDAs, one also has to consider **12**, such as fees for data services when you are connected to a cellular **13** to surf the Internet. Also, smartphone users usually have a contract with one **14**, whereas PDAs are carrier-independent. Tablet PCs are portable PCs which can mainly be used to read or view data. Their principal **15** device is a rotatable touchscreen and a virtual keyboard. In addition to their system software, both tablet PCs and smartphones support application software or **16** which allow users to personalise devices or do specific tasks. At the end of the day it is up to the users to decide which device best suits their **17**.

4 Match the definitions to the types of computers.

a. tower PC	1. a form factor for stationary computers
b. notebook	2. a lightweight, mobile computer with integrated LED screen
c. tablet PC	3. a computer of medium capacity with high graphics performance
d. mainframe	4. The name describes the cabinet that housed the huge CPU of the early models.
e. multimedia computer	5. a portable machine into which you input data via the screen
f. CAD-workstation	6. a midsized computer with lower performance than a mainframe
g. minicomputer	7. a computer used for office work, to play music, watch films and access the Internet

C | Advising customers

M 1
KMK II

Sie arbeiten als Aushilfe in einem großen Computerladen. Ihr Vorgesetzter, der folgende englischsprachigen Kunden bedient, bittet Sie, deren Wünsche ins Deutsche zu übertragen.

"I'm into gaming and I also like going to LAN parties. However, recently my computer has been having problems with the newer computer games."

"I need a computer mainly for work. It has to have all of the main office applications. I travel a lot and need to stay in contact with head-office, and with my customers, too."

"I need a computer for college: Writing papers, doing research in the Internet, preparing and holding presentations and doing my emails. I also want to stay in touch with my friends on social networks."

Customer A

Customer B

Customer C

M 2
KMK II

Ihr Vorgesetzter *(Speaker A)* führt ein Beratungsgespräch mit einem englischsprachigen Kunden *(Speaker B)* und bittet Sie dazu, ihm behilflich zu sein. Übertragen Sie sinngemäß die Kundenwünsche ins Deutsche und die Antworten Ihres Vorgesetzten ins Englische.

Speaker A		Dolmetscher(in)		Speaker B
old laptop/six years old; battery/recharge every two days; new laptop/graphics card	→	?	→ ←	Laptop mit HD-Grafik/Hochleistungsgrafik und Medienverarbeitung
phone/girlfriend/boyfriend/in Australia	→	?	→ ←	Modell mit integrierter Webcam/Mikrophon/Headset dazu kaufen
student/tight budget/limit €449	→	?	→ ←	haben einige Modelle/zeigen welche, die passen

WORD BANK

app – Anwendung
battery – Akku
icon – Icon, Bildschirmsymbol
processing power – Rechenleistung
recharge (v) – wiederaufladen
rotatable – drehbar
slot – Einbaustelle
stylus – Stift

WORD BANK ◎

battery pack – Akku
chassis – Gehäuse
handwriting recognition – Handschrifterkennung
LCD, liquid crystal display – Flüssigkristallanzeige
optical disc drive – optisches Laufwerk
power supply – Stromversorgung
processing power – Rechenleistung
storage – Speicherung
store (v) – speichern
touchpad – Tastfeld
wireless – kabellos

E

NACH DIESEM MODUL:

- ✓ kann ich eine Stellenanzeige auf Englisch verstehen,
- ✓ kann ich meine Fähigkeiten und Qualifikationen auf Englisch beschreiben,
- ✓ kann ich eine Bewerbung auf Englisch schreiben.

1

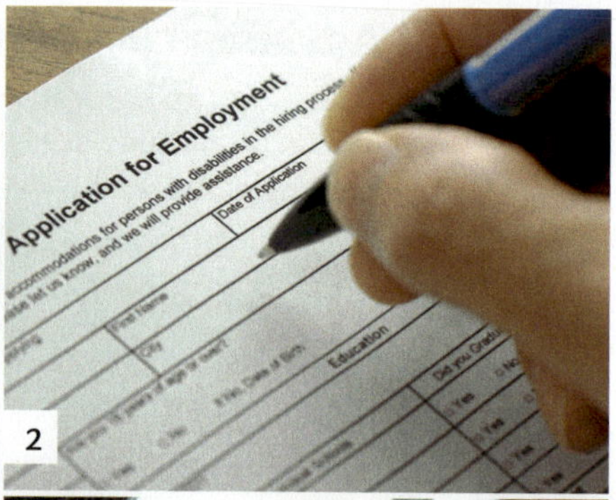

2

3

4

Applications

The world today is full of opportunities. You might decide to work in your hometown, a big city, or even another country. Maybe you want to work for a small family-run company or a major corporation with branches across the globe. Whatever you decide, the opportunities are out there, but it is up to you to take them.

1 **Look at the pictures above and describe them using the words below.**

> to apply • job advertisement • letter of application • CV • to search • job interview • employment contract • to invite • newspaper • to write

2 **Put the steps of the application process shown in the pictures above into the correct order.**

P **3** **Work on your own. What skills and qualifications do you need for a job in your industry? Make a list. Use these words to help you:**

> hard-working • motivated • logical • good with numbers • good with your hands • communicative • good team player • technical skills • able to understand plans and diagrams • attention to detail • computer skills

4 **Work with a partner and decide upon a final list. Share it with the class.**

A | Job advertisements

M/R **1** **Read the three online job advertisements below and find the English translations for the following German words and expressions.**

1. verantwortungsbewusst
2. aktiv, praktisch
3. Bewerber
4. Störungssuche
5. pünktlich
6. lernbereit
7. begeistert
8. gültige Fahrerlaubnis
9. Erfahrung
10. abgeschlossene Ausbildung
11. gute Bezahlung
12. fließendes Englisch
13. teamfähig
14. Montage
15. Grundkenntnisse in CAD
16. freie Stelle

http://www.totaljobs...com

1	City Garage – Car mechanic (full-time)	City Garage in Wolverhampton is looking for a recently-qualified car mechanic to join our busy team. Are you enthusiastic, willing to learn, responsible and punctual? If so, then contact us. We offer good rates of pay and a pleasant working atmosphere. Applicants must have a clean and valid driver's license. Please send a written application and a CV to Michael McCarthy at the following address: City Garage 17 Gorsebrook Rd. Wolverhampton WV6 5PI Tel.: 0044 (0)1902 554997...
2	Harper Shipping Client Support Technician	We are looking for a client support technician for our IT team to provide support and troubleshooting for hardware and software installation. You will also be responsible for new system configuration and maintaining the desktop client software. You should have two years experience, good English skills and be able to work as part of a team. Salary: negotiable Email application to: careers@HS...com
3	Trafford Tools Mechatronic Technician	Trafford Tools is a leading supplier of high-quality tools. We have a vacancy for a hands-on person to work as a mechatronic technician. Tasks: fault finding, maintenance, assembly, assist with installation. Skills: completed apprenticeship, basic CAD skills, good knowledge of tools, fluent English. Contact: James Truman J.truman@TT...co.uk Tel: 0044 (0)161 929496...

I/M **2** **One of your colleagues does not speak English and asks you to tell him about one of the job ads. Choose one of the ads and give him a brief summary in German. Swap roles.**

WORD BANK

branch – Filiale
family-run company – Familien-unternehmen
job application – Bewerbung
maintain (v) – warten
opportunities – Möglichkeiten
qualifications – Qualifikationen
skills – Fähigkeiten
troubleshooting – Fehlerbehebung

B | Letter of application

R **1** **Read the letter of application and decide whether the following statements are true or false. Give reasons for your decisions.**

1. Erkan is in the final year of his apprenticeship as a car mechanic.
2. He has always wanted to be a car mechanic.
3. Erkan had a holiday job at *Werkstatt Kuhn*.
4. He is looking forward to working abroad.
5. Erkan has included his CV in the application.

Erkan Celik • Waldstrasse 48 • 50679 Köln • Germany

Michael McCarthy
City Garage
17 Gorsebrook Rd.
Wolverhampton
WV6 5PI
England

12 June 20_

Dear Mr McCarthy,

Application for job as car mechanic

I am writing to apply for the advertised position of a car mechanic at City Garage. I completed my apprenticeship as a car mechanic at a technical college here in Germany six months ago. I have been interested in cars since I was a child and being a car mechanic is my dream job.
As you will see from my CV, I recently completed a six-month internship at Werskstatt Kuhn. This not only gave me the opportunity to put my theoretical skills into practice, but I also had the chance to gain more experience with customers.
I am a very enthusiastic person. I am also reliable, responsible and willing to learn. Furthermore, I have good English skills and I would welcome the opportunity to gain some experience working in another country.
Thank you in advance for considering my application. If you require any further information, please contact me.

Yours sincerely,
Erkan Celik

Encl.: CV

WATCH OUT!
I am interested ~~for~~ cars. I am interested <u>in</u> cars.

M **2** KMK I **Fassen Sie mit Hilfe der unten stehenden Stichworte die wichtigsten Inhalte des Bewerbungsschreibens auf Deutsch zusammen.**

1. Beruf, für den sich Erkan bewirbt **2.** Berufserfahrung **3.** Motivation
4. Persönliche Qualifikationen/Fähigkeiten **5.** Kontaktperson

C | The CV

R **1** KMK II ⓞ A 1.4

Andrea Wagner ist Auszubildende bei einer IT-Firma in Nürnberg. Sie möchte sich für eine Praktikumsstelle in der englischen Niederlassung ihrer Firma bewerben und fragt David, einen Praktikanten aus England, ob er ihr ein paar Tipps geben kann. Hören Sie das Gespräch an und vervollständigen Sie die folgenden Sätze auf Deutsch.

1. Andrea möchte sich für eine Praktikumsstelle in ? bewerben.
2. Sie bringt am Montag ? mit ins Büro.
3. Der Lebenslauf sollte nicht länger sein als ? .
4. Man sollte niemals einen Lebenslauf ohne ? senden.
5. Man sollte den Lebenslauf dazu benutzen, seine ? und ? hervorzuheben.
6. Wenn man seine Arbeitserfahrung auflistet, sollte man mit ? anfangen.
7. In England muss ein Lebenslauf kein ? enthalten.
8 Man sollte sicherstellen, dass man zwei ? nennt.
9. Man sollte niemals ? .
10. Wenn der Lebenslauf fertig ist, sollte man ihn auf ? und ? überprüfen.
11. Es ist eine gute Idee, den Lebenslauf ? zu geben.
12. Wenn man den Lebenslauf abschickt, sollte man ? behalten.

P **2** KMK II

Verfassen Sie ein Anschreiben für eine der in Modulteil A ausgeschriebenen Stellen auf Englisch. Arbeiten Sie dabei die unten aufgeführten Inhalte ein.

→ **PHRASES:** Applications

- Wählen Sie einen geeigneten Betreff.
- Nehmen Sie Bezug auf die Stellenanzeige und bekunden Sie Ihr Interesse an der ausgeschriebenen Stelle.
- Sie werden bald Ihre Ausbildung als … abschließen.
- Bringen Sie zum Ausdruck, dass Sie ein geeigneter Bewerber sind: organisiert, erfahren, hoch motiviert, teamfähig, flexibel, lernbereit, zuverlässig. Sie haben gute Englischkenntnisse.
- Beenden Sie den Brief angemessen und unterschreiben Sie.
- Weisen Sie auf Ihren Lebenslauf hin.

WORD BANK

consider (v) – betrachten
gain (v) – sammeln
internship – Praktikum
letter of application – Bewerbungsschreiben
reliable – zuverlässig
require (v) – benötigen

INFO BOX: Translating German school types and qualifications

It is not always possible to find the equivalent of your school type or qualification in English. However, the following table gives some useful translations.

Schools			
Grundschule	Elementary school / Primary school	Berufsschule (Duales System)	Part-time vocational school (dual system)
Hauptschule	General secondary school	Berufsfachschule	Full-time vocational school
Realschule	Intermediate secondary school	Fachschule für technische Berufe	Technical college
Gymnasium	Upper secondary school	Fachoberschule	Upper secondary vocational school
Gesamtschule	Comprehensive school	Fachgymnasium	Specialized upper secondary school

Qualifications			
Hauptschulabschluss	secondary modern school qualification	Fachabitur	advanced vocational certificate of education
Mittlere Reife	secondary school leaving certificate	Zusatzqualifikation	additional qualification
Abitur	A level/high school diploma		

06

NACH DIESEM MODUL:

- ✓ kenne ich die englischen Begriffe für gängige Netzwerkgeräte,
- ✓ kann ich mit den englischen Fachbegriffen im Bereich Netzwerktechnik umgehen,
- ✓ kann ich auf Englisch beschreiben, wie man ein Netzwerkkabel crimpt.

1

2

3

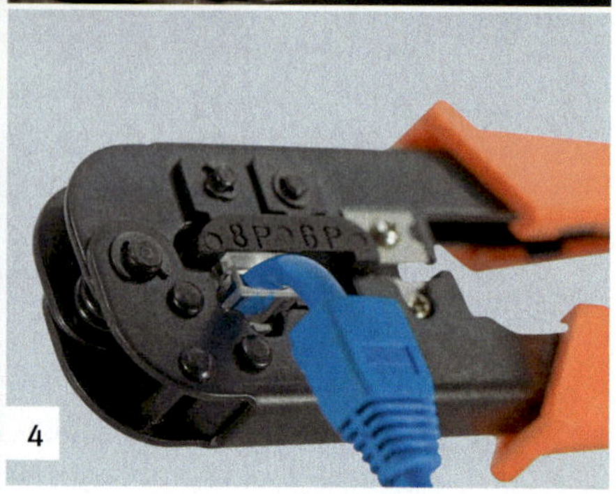
4

Networks

The term 'network' is not only used in computer technology, but it has also become a synonym for a 'computer network'. A network can interconnect a number of computers or even devices like smartphones. The purpose of a network is to share resources, e.g. data storage, Internet access, printers or services.

1 Match the words in the box with the photos.

crimping tool • network interface card (NIC) • server room • network switch

2 Put the jumbled descriptions into the correct order. Then match the descriptions with the words in exercise 1.

1. room • a server • multiple servers • houses. The • protection system • is • air conditioned • room • has • and often • a fire
2. device • this • interconnects • other network devices • various. 256 cables • it • ports • can easily have • for up to
3. this • your • computer's or server's • is • if • broken • built-in • connection • network • can • you • install
4. tool • this is • a • for • network • crimping • your own • cable

A | Introduction to networks and associated protocols

1 Complete the text using the words in the box.

physical connection • UDP • concept • TCP • lowest • Local Area Network • voice communication • medium • traffic • protocols

In order to make a network possible first of all you need a transport **1**. This can be a **2**, such as a copper wire or optic fibre, or it could be the air (WLAN). In order to get **3** flowing, you need protocols ruling how data is sent, received and interpreted by the networked devices.
The **4** are stacked in several layers and together they make up the Internet Protocol Suite. On the **5** layer (the Link Layer) there is a protocol dealing with digital electronics. In a LAN or **6**, this is the Ethernet Protocol. On top of this comes the Internet layer (yes, it is called that even in a LAN). Here we have – among others – the Internet Protocol. From this point on a **7**, referred to as IP addressing, becomes available. Next, in the Transport Layer, we find the Transmission Control Protocol or **8** for short, and User Datagram Protocol (**9**). Again, there may be other protocols in this layer. One more layer up is the Application Layer, which has protocols we know from everyday use, such as HTTP, SMTP and also protocols for P2P (peer to peer) **10**.

R **2** Describe in your own words how the Internet Protocol suite is organized.

3 List the layers of the Internet Protocol Suite in a table like the one below, starting with the highest layer. Then match the protocols in the box with the corresponding layer.

HTTP • UDP • SMTP • FTPIP • TCP • Ethernet • ATM

Protocols	Layers

P **4** **UNDERSTANDING TECHNICAL ENGLISH**

1. Give the technical and general German translations of the terms.

1. port
2. client
3. network
4. traffic
5. virus
6. switch
7. packet
8. service

2. Translate the sentences into German.

1. A virus is a software which can infect whole networks and all the clients on it.
2. A switch makes sure that the traffic on a network (i.e. all the network packets) is handled correctly.
3. Each service is assigned to one or more ports specifically reserved for that service.

WORD BANK

copper wire – Kupferkabel
data storage – Datenspeicher
device – Gerät
IP addressing – IP-Adressierung
optic fibre – Glasfaser
protocol – Protokoll

B | Network topologies

The network topology refers to how a network is arranged. The topology includes the nodes and connections.

P ▲ **Read the text and do the tasks.**

1. Say which protocols your network at home or at work uses.
2. Explain how the devices are connected to each other, i.e. what topology does the network follow?

Once a network reaches a certain size, you need to pay attention to its topology. Line and ring networks are not very efficient. To reduce the time the data needs to travel from one point to another, you can add more connections. When you do this, you get a mesh topology. If you connect all of the devices with one another, you have a fully connected mesh network. While this improves data delivery speed, it also makes the network more expensive. Alternatively, you can connect all of the devices at a single point (star topology). However, if the central node goes down, the whole network is down (single point of failure), too. Today you are most likely to find hybrid topologies which combine the features of at least two topologies. This allows cost effective and resilient topologies.

Types of network topologies

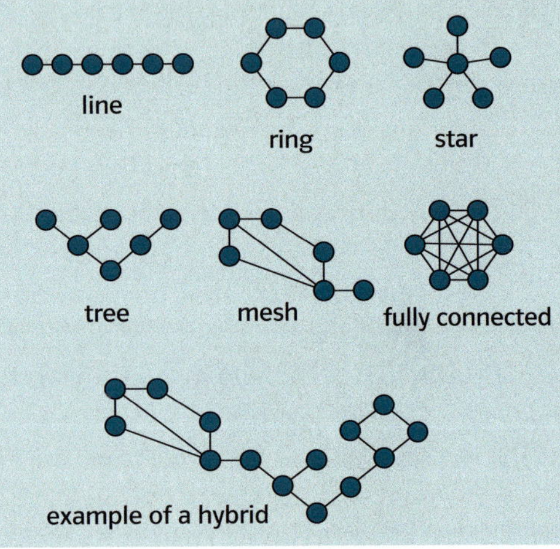

C | Troubleshooting: Network access

Linda Stratton works as a network administrator at Westham Drilling Ltd. in London. It is her job to make sure that staff have access to the network resources they need. Part of her job is to handle the IT helpdesk.

R **1** **Listen to the call to the helpdesk and answer the questions.**
A 1.13

1. Why is Michael calling the helpdesk?
2. What questions does Linda ask first? Why does she ask these things?
3. What does Michael need in order to access the company's network?

R **2** **Listen again and put the instructions into the correct order.** •
A 1.13

1. Install the VPN client software.
2. Check if the ethernet cable is plugged in.
3. Enter the correct username and password.
4. Download installer at ww#.westhamdrilling.co.uk/support/vpn.

3 **Find out more about the security aspects of VPNs and present your results to the class.** → **PHRASES:** Presentations

1. What software solutions are there?
2. How expensive is it to set up a VPN?

R

KMK III

D | Crimping your own cable

Sie arbeiten als Netzwerk Adminstrator in einem deutschen Unternehmen. Ein Kollege muss ein neues Netzwerkkabel krimpen und hat folgende Anweisung aus dem Internet heruntergeladen. Da er nur wenig Englisch kann, bittet er Sie um Hilfe. Lesen Sie den Text durch und führen Sie folgende Schritte aus:

1. Erstellen Sie eine Liste der Werkzeuge und Materialien, die er brauchen wird. Geben Sie auch die deutschen Bezeichnungen an.
2. Erstellen Sie eine stichwortartige Liste der einzelnen Arbeitsschritte auf Deutsch.

http://ww#.10minutetutorials.net

Tutorial number 3 | **Crimping your own CAT5 ethernet cable**

- Cut off the desired length plus a few extra centimetres from the cable roll.
- Strip the outer insulation of both ends using the insulation stripping pliers.
- Strip away about 20mm of the outer insulation. It will make it easier to work with the inner wires.

  ! Safety notice: Do this with great care so as not to damage the insulation of the inner wires.
- Examine the inner wires. If you have damaged the insulation, you will have to cut away the exposed wire and start again. Damaged insulation and subsequently bridging the wires may cause crosstalk.
- There are 8 wires with different colours. Two of them are twisted together at a time to form four twisted pairs.
- Untwist those pairs. Next align them from left to right as follows:

  white orange | orange | white green | blue | white blue | green | white brown | brown
- Once the wires are correctly arranged, shorten the inner wires by about 12 mm.
- This is done to ensure that the wires will fit neatly into the RJ-45 plug later.
- Recheck the alignment and insert the wires into the plug. Make sure that you push the wires all the way to the front end of the plug.
- Insert the wired plug into the crimping tool and firmly but evenly squeeze the handles. You should hear a ratcheting sound.
- Release the pressure on the handles and let them return to the starting position.
- Better safe than sorry so crimp it once more.
- Repeat the steps for the other end of the wire.
- When you are done, test the new wire with the circuit indicator.

WORD BANK

central node – zentraler Knotenpunkt
data delivery – Datenauslieferung
go down (v) – ausfallen
helpdesk – Hotline
insulation – Isolierung
mesh – Gitter
node – Knotenpunkt
plug in (v) – einstecken

WORD BANK ◎

engineering department – Konstruktionsabteilung
IP address field – IP-Adressfeld
mail server tab – Mail-Server-Karteireiterkarte
menu bar – Menüleiste
operating system – Betriebssystem
secure connection – sichere Verbindung
VPN client installer – Installationsprogramm für den VPN Client

F

NACH DIESEM MODUL:

- ✓ kann ich *Small Talk* auf Englisch machen,
- ✓ kenne ich die Regeln des *Small Talk*,
- ✓ kann ich auf Englisch Essen erklären und bestellen.

1

2

3

4

Socialising

Socialising is very important. It can strengthen relationships with your colleagues and improve the working atmosphere in a company. It can also be a good way of getting to know your customers or potential customers a little better. And in today's global world, English has become the world's language. So although the people you meet and work with are likely to come from a wide range of cultural backgrounds, you will often be required to communicate in English. That means that it is important to not only have the necessary language skills, but also the intercultural knowledge so that you can make a good first impression and develop professional and personal relationships.

I **1** **Look at the pictures above. What relationship do you think these people might have to each other? Discuss with your partner.**

2 **Brainstorm a list of topics these people might be talking about.**

P **3** **Choose one of the pictures and create a small dialogue.**

4 **Look at photo 1. Brainstorm what cultural misunderstandings could take place when a German employee meets a person from another country.**

P **5** **Make a list of situations when a German technician might have contact with foreign colleagues – for example, customers, suppliers, manufacturers, etc.**

A | Small talk

Your company has visitors from a subsidiary in Poland. Fabian, a German trainee, has been asked to show Jan, a Polish trainee, around the company.

R **1** Listen to the dialogue between Jan and Fabian. Take notes of the topics the two are talking about. Then listen again and make a list of the phrases they use.
A 1.5

2 Name other topics that Jan and Fabian could also talk about.

3 Which of the following topics would / wouldn't you talk about? Why? Discuss in class.

> free-time activities • films you have recently seen • sex • your job or school course • politics • money • personal problems • fashion • sports • food • the boss's wife • the weather • your favourite music • religion

P **4** Small talk is not that difficult. All that is needed is an 'ice breaker' to get things going. Look at the following examples and come up with appropriate answers.

→ **PHRASES:** Socialising

In the workshop:

a. Did you see the game last night?
b. How was your weekend?
c. It's warm today, isn't it?

At a trade fair:

a. Did you have any problems finding our stand?
b. Would you like a brochure?
c. If you like, I could give you a demonstration.

In the car:

a. How was your trip / flight?
b. Is this your first time in Germany?
c. How's the weather in Sao Paolo?

In the canteen:

a. Have you tried the tiramisu? It's amazing!
b. Is anybody sitting here?
c. Ah! I see you like spicy food.

P **5** Now it's your turn to break the ice! Think of at least three ice breakers for each of the following situations:

→ **PHRASES:** Socialising

1. You are at a bar with colleagues on Friday evening.
2. You work with a new colleague one afternoon.
3. You are at the "Green Technology" conference. It's time for a coffee break.
4. You've just arrived at work and you're in the lift. A person you don't know enters.

I **6** Choose one of the four situations above. Start a conversation and try to keep it going for as long as possible. Then end the conversation politely and act it out in front of the class.

→ **PHRASES:** Socialising

P **7** Check the Internet and create your own 'Dos & Don'ts' guide to making small talk and present it to your class. Also include some intercultural aspects.

Dos	Don'ts
Make eye contact.	Ask personal questions.

WORD BANK

subsidiary – Tochtergesellschaft
trainee – Auszubildende(r)

B | Small talk in business

R **1** KMK II

Ihr Arbeitgeber hat im Internet folgenden Artikel gefunden. Da er nur wenig Englisch kann, bittet er Sie, die folgenden Fragen auf Deutsch zu beantworten.

1. Was wird oft in abwertender Weise über Small Talk gesagt?
2. Was passiert, wenn man sich nicht am Small Talk beteiligt?
3. Was sind die positiven Auswirkungen von Small Talk?

Small talk in business

Small talk is often dismissed as a waste of time, or as the art of saying nothing with a lot of words. Some people say it has no place in the business world, since the subjects discussed are often 'unimportant' – i.e. the weather, sports, fashion or other trivial matters. However, if you don't take part in small talk, your business partners might feel that you are being unfriendly or antisocial. When people just stand next to one another, without any signs of communication between them, it can lead to a feeling of uneasiness, and even tension. And this is certainly not good for future business or private relations. Small talk is in fact a very important and effective tool for avoiding an awkward silence between people who don't know each other, especially business partners who may want to form a relationship. Making small talk with strangers helps to break the ice; you discover what they like or dislike, so you can find a common ground of some sort. It helps, for example, if you support the same football team, like the same kind of car, or read the same kinds of books. However, it is also important to know who you are making small talk with. The rules of small talk are not international and different cultures have their own dos and don'ts. For example, you may have been told to always make eye contact when talking to your counterpart – but this may offend a material supplier in China. If you are going to have contact with someone from a different cultural background, it is a good idea to do a little research to avoid any embarassing mistakes.

M **2** KMK II

Ihr Arbeitgeber bittet Sie, für die Mitarbeiter stichwortartig ein kurzes Merkblatt anhand dieses Textes auf Deutsch zu erstellen.

R **3**

Sind Sie ein guter Smalltalker? Bewerten Sie die Aussagen zum Small Talk in einem Online-Test mit „Yes“ oder „No“. Notieren Sie die entsprechenden Buchstaben.

Statements	Yes	No
1. Small talk deals with rather unimportant topics. Another word for it is chitchat.	a	c
2. Religion always makes a good topic, because it is controversial.	d	e
3. Answering questions with 'yes' or 'no' during small talk is appropriate.	i	e
4. A good answer when asked if you'd like something to drink is: "I'd love a cup of coffee, thank you."	g	h
5. "That's great" is an acceptable answer to the statement: "I got the job!"	b	i
6. The noun "talk" can also mean speech.	a	c
7. Small talk is an icebreaker.	b	f

Addieren Sie die Buchstabenwerte a = 3, b = 3, c = 1, d = 0, e = 3, f = 1, g = 3, h = 1, i = 1.
Wer hat die höchste Zahl? (Maximum 21)

C | Eating out

1 Look at the German words (1. – 16.) below and match them with the English equivalent (a. – p.).

1. Speisekarte	a. well-done
2. Rechnung	b. pork
3. Rind	c. side order
4. Vorspeise	d. bill
5. Schweinefleisch	e. game
6. Wild	f. dessert
7. durchgebraten	g. savoury
8. Hauptgericht	h. fork
9. Geflügel	i. menu
10. Kellner(in)	j. main dish
11. Nachtisch	k. beef
12. Trinkgeld	l. poultry
13. Beilage	m. starter
14. vegetarisch	n. waiter / waitress
15. herzhaft	o. vegetarian
16. Gabel	p. tip

I/M **2** Partner 1: You are taking a foreign colleague out to dinner in a traditional German restaurant. Study the menu below and explain the dishes to him / her.
Partner 2: Take the role of the foreign colleague and ask questions about the menu.

Gasthaus Sonne

Tagesmenu (10,95 €)

Vorspeisen
Lauchcremesuppe **oder** *kleiner gemischter Salat*

***

Hauptgerichte
Rinderrouladen mit Kartoffelklößen & Sauerkraut
oder
Putenschnitzel mit Pommes Frites
oder
Forelle Müllerin mit Salzkartoffeln

***

Nachtisch
Rote Grütze mit Sahne **oder** *Gemischtes Eis*
(Vanille / Erdbeere / Schoko)

Inklusive ein alkoholfreies Getränk (0,3 l)

WORD BANK

avoid (v) – vermeiden
awkward – unangenehm
common ground – gemeinsame Basis
dismiss (v) sth. as – etwas abtun als
tension – Spannung
trivial – unbedeutend
uneasiness – Unbehagen

I **3** Now the two of you are ready to order. The young German waitress / waiter doesn't mind taking the order in English. Study the eating out phrases at the end of the book and create a role play. Practise, and perform it in front of the class.

→ **PHRASES:** Socialising

07

NACH DIESEM MODUL:

- ✓ kann ich mich auf Englisch über vergangene, gegenwärtige und zukünftige Telekommunikationstechnologien unterhalten,
- ✓ kann ich Technologien auf Englisch vergleichen und deren Vor- und Nachteile abwägen.

1

2

3

4

Telecommunications

The goal of communication is to deliver messages from one person to another. The goal of telecommunications is to do the same thing over long distances and in a short time frame. Over the last century, the time frame that we accept for delivery has been shortened to an instant or even real time.

1 Match the descriptions with the above photos.

1. These towers form wireless cells, within which one can use a cell phone (*BE* mobile phone). The towers and phones operate using microwaves. The range depends on the power of the transmitter and factors like the weather.
2. High bandwidth fibre optics networks are the backbones of modern telecommunications. Signals travel at the speed of light (approximately 300,000 km per second) as opposed to the slower electrons in metal fibres.
3. Samuel Morse invented the telegraph in 1836. He sent the first telegram over a distance of 3 km.
4. Was the telephone invented by a German, an American, an Englishman or a Canadian? Maybe we'll never know. What is certain is that this invention changed the world forever.

2 Decide whether the types of technology described in exercise 1 are digital or analogue.

P **3** **UNDERSTANDING TECHNICAL ENGLISH**

Use a dictionary to find out the general and technical meanings of the words.

1. backbone 2. cell 3. range

A | Telecommunication in the past and the present

The telegraph was one of the first forms of electrical telecommunication. It allowed people to encode and transmit messages around the world. Nowadays most of our communications infrastructure is still based on wired technologies.

R **1** **Read the text and decide whether the statements are true or false. Correct the false statements.**

If two people want to exchange information, they first need to decide on a transport medium. With the telegraph, this medium is an electrical connection from one place to another. Next, they need to figure out a way to send the message over the transport medium. Since you cannot transmit the full message, you have to break it down into smaller parts. Then, you convert the individual characters into electrical signals. This conversion is called 'encoding'. You use a code – also referred to as an encoding scheme such as Morse code, – to convert a message.
Morse code uses two characters: the letters of the alphabet and the numbers from 0 to 9 are encoded using dots and dashes, or rather electrically 'short on' and 'long on', which is three times a 'short on'. A short pause, which is one dot long, separates the ONs. The individual characters are separated by a medium pause (three dots long). Words are separated by a long pause (seven dots long).
So you have a total of five kinds of signals. This makes Morse code an analogue communication as opposed to digital communication, which uses ones and zeros.
The recipient puts the message together again or 'decodes' it. The process chain, 'break apart – encode – send – decode – reassemble', and the definition of how it is done is called a protocol.
The principal behind protocols is still vitally important for the way we communicate. So, even though the telegraph was not digital, and it took decades for everybody to agree to use the same protocol, all it took to send us on our way into the telecommunications age were a dot and a dash.

1. Morse code is based on three different characters.
2. You need five types of signals to encode a message into Morse code.
3. In Morse code it is not necessary to separate the characters or words.
4. Morse code uses pauses which vary in length.

M **2** **Define the word 'protocol' in German as it is described in the text.**

3 **Complete the text about modern telecommunication using the words in the box.**

copper • telecommunication • dirty interface • good • connection • wires • UMTS and LTE • reliable • technologies

Wireless **1** make network access simpler. However, **2** are not obsolete. The backbones of **3** rely on wires for one main reason: Wireless devices interface with each other through the air. In physics, air is referred to as a **4** because it is unreliable. The difference between **5** and bad connections can simply be weather conditions. In general, the **6** quality in the air is much lower than with fibre optics. Underground fibre optic wires provide fast and **7** long-distance lines for telecommunication. Most broadband Internet users connect using **8** wire-based digital subscriber lines (DSL) yet more and more people are using **9**.

WORD BANK

bandwidth – Bandbreite
broadband – Breitband
digital subscriber line (DSL) – eine Art von Breitband-Internetverbindung
dirty interface – fehleranfällige Schnittstelle
fibre optics – Glasfaser
high bandwidth network – Netzwerk mit hoher Bandbreite
interface – Schnittstelle
long-distance line – Langstreckenverbindung
long on – langes An
LTE (long term evolution) – Mobilfunkstandard mit Bandbreite bis zu 300 Mbits
process chain – Ablauf-Kette
short on – kurzes An
transmit (v) – übertragen
transmitter – Sendeeinrichtung
transport medium – Übertragungsmedium
UMTS (universal mobile telecommunications system) – UMTS-Mobilfunkstandard

B | Telecommunications networks: future problems

A telecommunications network is made up of nodes, links and terminals. Messages are sent from terminals along links, passing a number of nodes before they reach the recipient's terminal. The nodes send messages in the correct direction.

R **1** ⓞ A 1.14 **Listen to the discussion between two computer science students, Jo Engel from Würzburg and Andrew Taylor from London. Then answer the questions.**

1. What does Andrew think of the concept of wired communication?
2. How does Andrew connect to the Internet?
3. What is the bandwidth of Andrew's connection?

R **2** ⓞ A 1.14 **Listen to the discussion again and say what the numbers 1–4 refer to.**

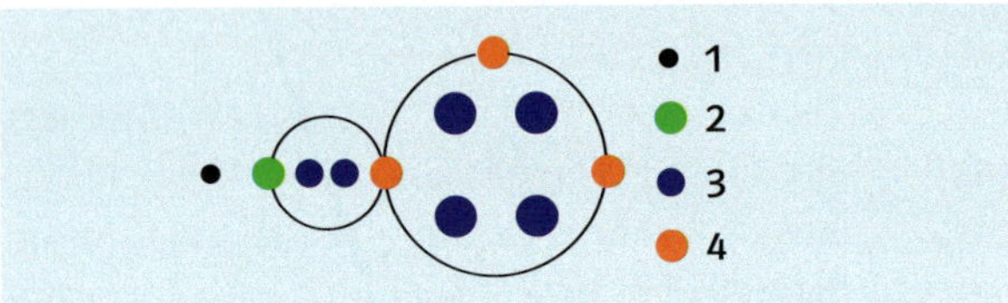

I **3** **Act out the rest of the discussion in English.**

Jo	Andrew
1. Sagen Sie, dass die Reichweite heutiger Drahtlos-Technologien noch sehr begrenzt ist.	2. Antworten Sie, dass diese Technologien im Durchschnitt doch eine 45 km Reichweite haben.
3. Sagen Sie, dass das zwar stimmt, aber dies immer noch nicht ausreicht.	4. Bitten Sie ihn, es Ihnen anhand eines Beispiels zu erklären.
5. Erklären Sie, dass der nächste Backbone für die Internet-Anbindung sich in München (ca. 280 km Entfernung) befindet.	6. Antworten Sie, dass 280 km Glasfaserkabel *(fibre optics wire)* doch sehr teuer sind.
7. Geben Sie ihm recht, aber erklären Sie weiterhin, dass man beim Kabel nur den Anfangs- und Endpunkt braucht. Bei einer drahtlosen Verbindung bräuchte man mindestens sechs Knotenpunkte, um die Distanz zu überwinden.	8. Fragen Sie, was das Problem dabei ist.
9. Antworten Sie, dass das teure an Kommunikationsverbindungen nicht die Strecke ist, sondern die Anzahl der Knotenpunkte.	10. Fragen Sie, ob das der einzige Grund dafür ist, dass man noch immer Glasfaser-Verbindungen benutzt.
11. Antworten Sie, dass Kabelverbindungen unter der Erde nicht anfällig für schlechtes Wetter sind.	12. Bedanken Sie sich für die Erklärung.

4 **Search the Internet for one of these technologies. Find out when it was introduced, what bandwidth it provides and where it is in use. Present your results in class.**

→ **PHRASES:** Presentations

1. LTE
2. WiMax
3. ATM
4. Carrier Grade Ethernet

C | Finding the right telecommunications provider

M **1**
KMK II

Sie arbeiten in der IT-Abteilung einer international tätigen Firma, für die einige hundert Außendienstmitarbeiter(innen) weltweit unterwegs sind. Ihr Unternehmen möchte die Verwaltung der Internetanschluss-Verträge vereinfachen, um Kosten zu senken. Daher soll für alle mobilen Internetanschlüsse in Zukunft nur noch ein Anbieter zuständig sein. Sie sollen auf Englisch einen Fragebogen erstellen, um die Anforderungen der Außendienstmitarbeiter(innen) zu erfassen. Fertigen Sie den Fragenbogen mit folgenden Punkten an.

Questionnaire

1. Welche Geräte	❍ notebook ❍ tablet ❍ smartphone
2. Welcher Provider momentan	❍ Komtel ❍ 03 ❍ Voxphone
3. Minuten pro Tag am Telefon	______
4. Tage pro Woche außer Haus	______
5. Hauptsächlich wo unterwegs:	❍ Stadt ❍ Land
6. Hauptnutzen:	❍ Telefongespräche ❍ Internetverbindungen
7. Benötigtes Datenverkehrsvolumen pro Monat	______

R **2**
KMK II

Anhand der Ergebnisse der Fragebogenaktion haben Sie nun einen Überblick über den Bedarf der Außendiensmitarbeiter(innen) bekommen. Der Anbieter Komtel hat ein Komplettangebot gemacht. Vergleichen Sie die Anforderungen der Mitarbeiter(innen) mit dem Angebot. Ermitteln Sie die wesentlichen Daten aus dem Ergebnis der Studie und ordnen Sie sie den Zahlen in der Tabelle unten zu.

Results of the questionnaire

Most of the sales representatives take netbooks with them when they travel.
All of our employees use smartphones. The most common providers are Komtel and O3, very few people use Voxphone. Employees use their phones for calls for an average of 180 minutes per month.
On 16 out of 20 working days employees are out of office. So their main means of telecommunication is their smartphone. Most of our sales representatives travel around cities and rural areas, where there is usually good mobile phone reception.
Phone calls from smartphones are currently more important than Internet connections, but trends show that within the next two years the importance will shift towards Internet connections.
Users currently use a data traffic volume of ca. 1 GB a month. On average they do not require a bandwidth that is greater than 1.8 Mbits.

	Komtel's offer	employees' requirements
supported devices	all devices	1
free minutes per month	unlimited	2
main focus of network coverage	cities	3
best suited for	Internet users	4
data traffic per month	unlimited	5

M **3**
KMK II

Ihr Vorgesetzer möchte wissen, welches Ergebnis die Umfrage geliefert hat. Fassen Sie die Ergebnisse der Fragebogenaktion auf Deutsch zusammen.

WORD BANK

data traffic – Datenverkehr
link – Verbindung
network coverage – Netzabdeckung
node – Verbindungsknoten
reception – Empfang
terminal – Endpunkt einer Verbindung

WORD BANK ◎

access node – Zugangsknotenpunkt
core network – Verbindungsnetzwerk, das mehrere MAN miteinander verbindet
HSDPA (high-speed downlink packet access) – Erweiterung des UMTS-Standards
MAN (metro area network) – regionales Netzwerk, z. B. für eine größere Stadt
service node – Serviceknotenpunkt, der Daten von einem Netzwerkformat in ein anderes übersetzt
Tier 1 provider – Stufe 1 (Internet-) Anbieter
transport node – Transportknotenpunkt, der entscheidet wohin Daten weitergeleitet werden
WAN (wide area network) – Weitverkehrsnetz

G

NACH DIESEM MODUL:

- ✓ kann ich eine englische Präsentation vorbereiten,
- ✓ kann ich auf Englisch präsentieren.

1

2

3

4

Presentations

At some point in your career you may be required to present your company, or their products or services, either informally or on a more formal level. This could mean presenting a new product to a potential customer, or presenting the company as a whole, or something more specific, such as assembly instructions or a positional sketch. Whatever you may be presenting, the ability to give an oral presentation is a key skill. It is also a skill that can be developed and improved.

P **1** **Look at the pictures above and describe them using the words below.**

> to present • meeting • flipchart • graph • chart • laptop • preparation • to explain • sales pitch • audience • projector

P **2** **For what reasons might you have to give a presentation? Write a list.**

3  **With a partner, decide upon a final list and share it with the class.**

4  **With the same partner brainstorm what you think is important to remember when giving a presentation. Write your answers in a word web like the one below.**

A | Preparing a presentation

1 **In the following table are words which are linked to presentations. Match the English words (1.–10.) with the appropriate German words (a.–j.).**

1. audience	a. Augenkontakt
2. prompt cards	b. beschreiben
3. body language	c. Zusammenfassung
4. eye contact	d. visuelle Hilfsmittel
5. handout	e. Publikum
6. to prepare	f. Schaubild
7. graph	g. Stichwortkarten
8. visual aids	h. Körpersprache
9. to describe	i. vorbereiten
10. summary	j. Informationsblatt

M **2** KMK II **Fassen Sie den folgenden Text über die Vorbereitung einer Präsentation unter Beantwortung folgender Fragen auf Deutsch zusammen.**

1. Warum soll eine Präsentation nicht schriftlich ausformuliert werden?
2. Wie soll eine Präsentation gegliedert sein?
3. Was ist „signposting"?
4. Welche Vorteile bieten visuelle Hilfsmittel?
5. Wie müssen Präsentationsfolien aussehen, damit sie wirken?

How to make a presentation

You have been asked by your boss to give a presentation? Here are a few tips:

- → Do not write out your presentation in full. Instead, use numbered prompt cards with key words – they are the best way to remember important points.
- → Remember: your presentation needs to have an introduction, a main part, and a conclusion.
- → Begin by giving a brief overview of the points to be covered.
- → Use "signposting" phrases to lead through your presentation, e.g.:

  I would like to begin by … • Let me start by showing you … • Next, I would like to say something about … • Another important point is … • Finally, I will talk about … • In conclusion, …

- → Always finish with a conclusion.

Visual aids

You can use visual aids, such as Powerpoint, to help reinforce what you say. Visual aids help you explain complicated ideas or technical details more easily and hold the interest of your audience. They also make your presentation look more professional.
If necessary, you can print them out and use them as a handout for the audience. Visual aids could include graphs, pictures, plans, diagrams, or short texts. However, if you do use your visual aids to show text, then follow these guidelines:

- → Limit the text to six lines.
- → Try to use no more than six words per line.
- → Print the text in large letters, using upper and lower case letters.
- → Use dark colours, such as black, red, blue, or green. Light colours are difficult to read.

WORD BANK

assembly – Montage
positional sketch – Technologieschema

3 Match the visual aids (1.–6) with the pictures below (a.–e.).

1. plan 2. pie chart 3. line graph 4. bar chart 5. diagram 6. table

a.

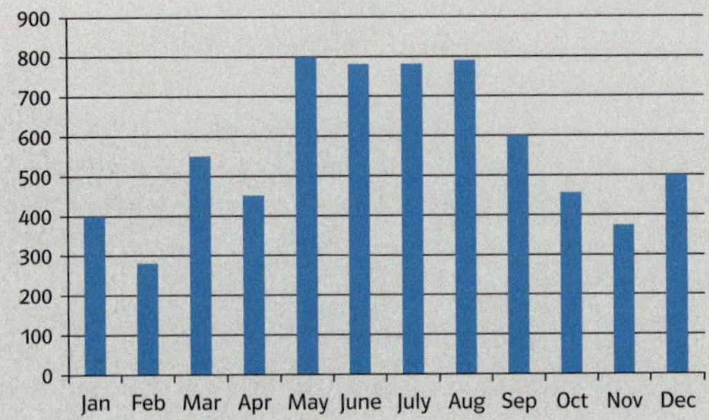

b.

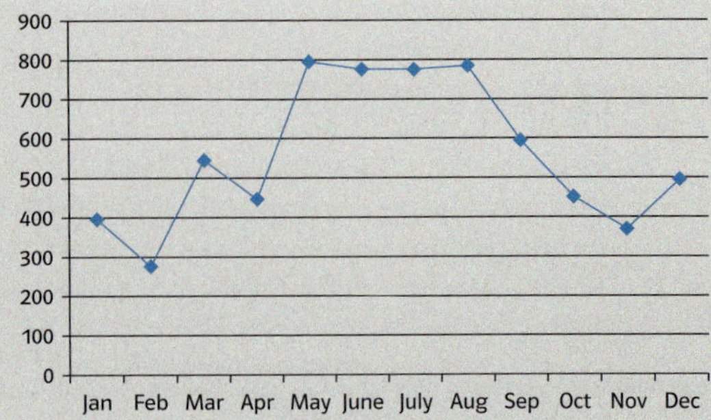

c.

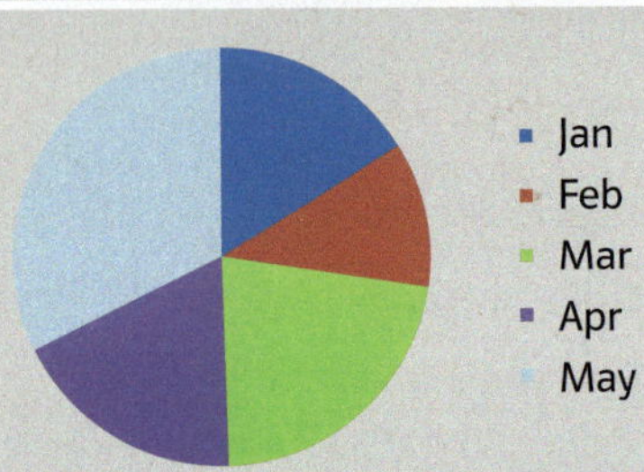

d.

2012		
Jan	$1,256	-6%
Feb	$1,477	+4%
Mar	$1,288	-5%
Apr	$1,543	+9%

e.

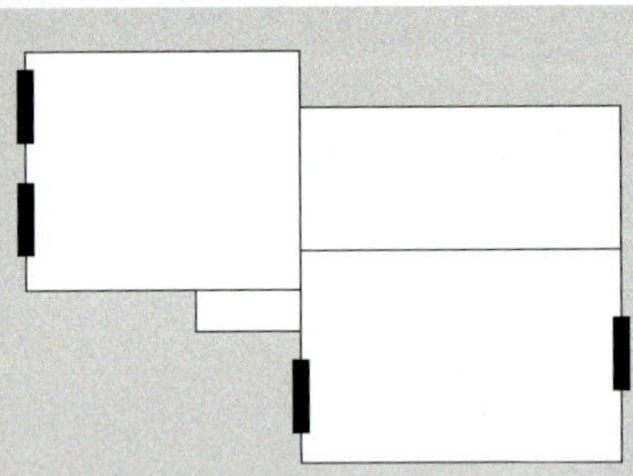

f.

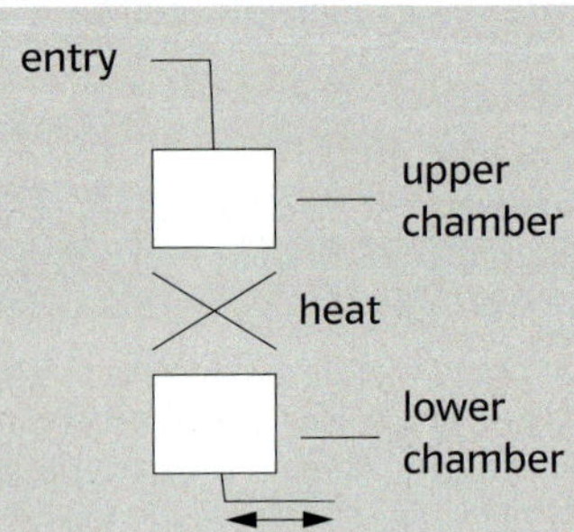

B | Describing materials and products

P **1** Think of something that you use often and describe it by using the terms in the box to help you. Don't name the item you are describing. Try and write 3 to 5 sentences.

I **2** Take it in turns to read your sentences to each other and see if you can guess what your partner is describing.

INFO BOX: Useful phrases for describing materials and products

It is a | strong · sturdy · rigid · flexible · lightweight · shiny · robust · matt | material.
The design is | modern · state-of-the-art · classic · elegant · old-fashioned.
It is | user-friendly · difficult to operate · reliable · innovative · hand-crafted.

C | Delivering a presentation

R **1**
A 1.6 **Max Wiesinger, a trained carpenter who works for a furniture design company, is presenting a new line of furniture at a trade show. Listen to the presentation and complete the following text.**

Good morning ladies and gentleman. Today **1** our new range of **2**, *Simply Wood*. The range, which is shown here on the first slide, includes chairs, a large table, a lounger, and benches. I would like to start by talking about the **3** used in the furniture. All of the *Simply Wood* range is made from single softwood timber and has been **4** by our highly-skilled carpenters and joiners. If you look at this picture, you can see that the benches and the seats are designed with a low back, deep seats and long arms to offer a great deal of comfort and convenience. Thanks to a special varnish, the furniture is 100% **5** and will not suffer from discolouring. **6** from this final slide, the furniture is also available in white, to give it a classic, timeless look. And do not worry, we have used a durable white polyurethane coating that is suitable for every environment. On your handout you will see more details about each piece, including the measurements. **7** this morning. Are there any questions? Yes …

P **2** **Now it's your turn. Work in small groups and design a chair, a pocket torch, or any other object of your choice. Present your ideas in class. Use the following words and phrases to help you:**

→ **PHRASES:** Presentations

We have designed a … • Our idea was to … • Our design is made of … • The advantage of the material we used is … • Its measurements are … • length • diameter • weight • width • height • rectangular • circle • circular • square • smooth edges • glued/screwed together • made out of one piece

M **3**
KMK I **Ihre Kollegin muss nächste Woche eine wichtige Präsentation halten und bittet Sie um Ihre Hilfe. Sie hat den folgenden Text gefunden, versteht aber leider nur wenig Englisch. Übertragen Sie den Text für sie sinngemäß ins Deutsche.**

7 Ways to Do it Right: Presentations

1. Keep it short and simple (KISS).
2. Do not use too many visual aids.
3. If you are presenting in a group, decide beforehand who will say what.
4. Practice at least once in front of an audience.
5. Do not read from your notes. Look at your audience.
6. Structure your presentation with phrases so your audience can follow more easily.
7. Tell the audience when they can ask questions – either during the presentation, or at the end.

WORD BANK

carpenter – Tischler(in) / Schreiner(in)
circle – Kreis
circular – kreisförmig
diameter – Dicke
furniture – Möbel
height – Höhe
length – Länge
rectangular – rechteckig
smooth – glatt
square – quadratisch
trade show – Messe
weight – Gewicht
width – Breite

WORD BANK

durable – haltbar
joiner – Tischler(in) / Schreiner(in)
polyurethane coating – Polyurethanbeschichtung
softwood – Weichholz
timber – Holz
varnish – Lack

08

NACH DIESEM MODUL:

- √ kenne ich wichtige englische Begriffe in der Webtechnologie,
- √ kann ich Internet- und Webtechnologien und die Entwicklung des Internets und des World Wide Webs auf Englisch beschreiben.

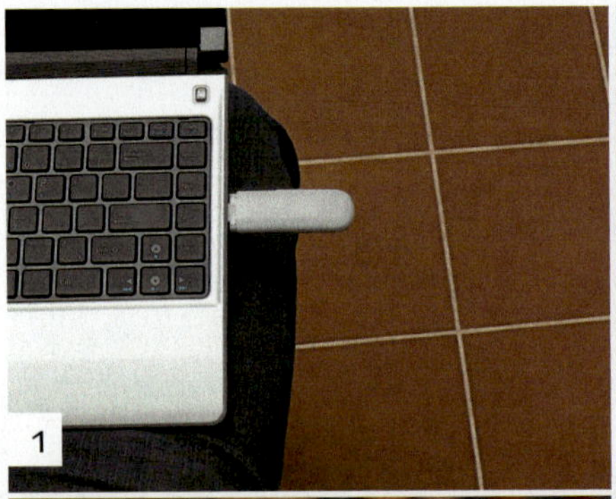
1

2

3

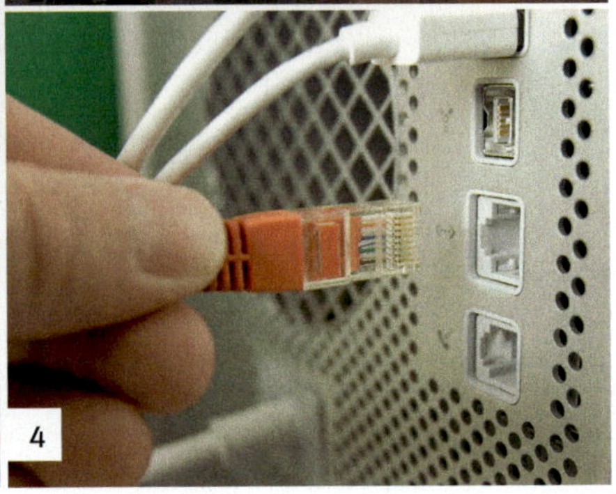
4

The Internet

The increasing popularity of the Internet has made it necessary to develop a range of ways to connect to the Internet according to users' demands.

I **1** **Look at the pictures above and discuss with your partner which technology you usually use to connect to the Internet. Report back to the class.**

P **2** **Describe the main advantages and disadvantages of the various types of Internet connections shown above. List them on a separate sheet of paper as shown below.**

	UMTS network	Fixed LAN connection	Wireless LAN connection	Satellite
+				*fast*
–	*slow*			

3 **Complete the following facts about the Internet by choosing the correct option.**

1. Early networks were created on the basis of research by …
   a. the Advanced Research Project Agency • b. Internet Service Providers • c. Domain Name System
2. In 1969 the first network connection was established between the University of California and …
   a. University of Paris • b. Harvard University • c. Stanford Research Institute

A | FAQs on Internet milestones

R **1** **Put the six milestones in the order according to the time they appeared first.**

FAQs: Internet milestones

???

1 What is the difference between TCP/IP and FTP?

With increasing numbers of network nodes a common protocol was needed to ensure a stable connection in the late 70's. The idea of a "Transmission Control Protocol/Internet Protocol" that enables a host to connect and transmit data finally reduced the role of the network to a minimum allowing more networks to connect. To transfer large files over a TCP/IP network a special application layer protocol, the File Transfer Protocol (FTP) was designed. For connecting home computers to the Internet over regular phone lines the Point-to-Point Protocol (PPP) is most commonly used.

2 When were domain names invented?

The Domain Name System was created in 1984 making Internet addresses more human-friendly. Compared to numerical IP addresses which can be used to locate a computer on the Internet, DNS servers allow users to type in an easy-to-remember domain name which the server automatically converts into an IP address.

3 Why is HTTP (Hypertext Transfer Protocol) necessary for surfing the web?

HTTP serves as a common code to transmit and receive information between servers and clients. Its invention by Tim Berners-Lee in 1989 led to the World Wide Web, a virtual space that uses the Internet as the network to distribute the information. From a single web page in 1991 it has increased to an estimated number of 20 billion web pages in 2011.

4 Who invented the e-mail?

E-mail as a way to exchange messages was invented by Ray Tomlinson who decided to use the "@" symbol in e-mail addresses to separate the user name from the computer name. The first e-mail client called MSG made e-mailing popular by the mid-70's. However, only with the introduction of the Post Office Protocol (POP) did sending and receiving e-mails become common.

5 Why do I need an ISP (Internet Service Provider)?

An Internet Service Provider (ISP) is a company that collects a fee in exchange for providing the subscriber with Internet access. The first commercial ISP, the World, appeared in 1990. The same year, Arpanet ceased to exist.

6 What is the ARPAnet?

In the late 50's the US Department of Defense founded the Advanced Research Project Agency that provided first designs for a network that should withstand nuclear strikes. However, only with the idea of dividing data into small packages (packet switching), developed by the Massachusetts Institute of Technology, first messages were sent through ARPAnet. In 1969, the first node-to-node message was sent from the University of California to the Stanford Research Institute, thus establishing a precursor to the Internet.

R **2** **Read the texts above again and match the numbers with the letters below.**

1. data is sent through a network
2. an e-mail address and its components
3. a way to ensure network stability
4. the necessity of the HTTP
5. the task of a DNS server within the Internet

a. username@computername
b. using a common protocol such as ICP/IP
c. converting a domain name into an IP address
d. serving as a common code to transmit and receive information between clients
e. packet switching

P **3** **Find out about recent developments in Internet technology and present them to the class.**

WORD BANK

application layer protocol – Protokoll auf Anwendungsebene
convert (v) – verwandeln, umwandeln
distribute (v) – vertreiben, verteilen
enable (v) – ermöglichen
node – Knotenpunkt
numerical – numerisch
packet switching – Paketaustausch
subscriber – Abonnent, Kunde
stable – stabil
transmit (v) – übermitteln

B | The future of the Internet and the World Wide Web

The Internet has become a location where an increasing amount of private, public and commercial data can be stored and processed.

R **1** Your company needs to restructure its IT system and has invited a system administrator. Listen and describe her proposal.
A 1.15

R **2** Listen again. Make a list of the advantages and disadvantages mentioned.
A 1.15

I **3** Discuss with your partner whether this alternative would be a solution for his/her company. Say why or why not.

→ **PHRASES:** Socialising

I **4** Discuss the following statement: "The web poses more dangers than benefits."

P **5** Read text A below and sum up the main idea of Web 2.0. Use as many of the following synonyms for the words in italics as possible.

dialogues • viewing • cooperation • content • application • group • participants

A In contrast to the passive *reception* of information (Web 1.0), everyone now has the opportunity to contribute to the web. The term Web 2.0 is linked with the idea of sharing, reprocessing and publishing *information* in *collaboration* with other Internet users. Web 2.0 *programs* allow *interaction* between *users*, especially in the field of social media, thus making the World Wide Web more user-centered. In this light, the web has turned into a virtual *community* whose users are able to redefine truth and reality. Features that play an active role in this process are social networking sites, wikis, blogs, video sharing sites and hosted web services.

M **6** Geben Sie den Inhalt des folgenden Textes sinngemäß auf Englisch wieder.

B Die Inhalte des World Wide Web können derzeit nur von Menschen verstanden und interpretiert werden. Die Entwicklung eines **Web 3.0** basiert auf der Vorstellung, Daten entsprechend ihrer Bedeutung in einem semantischen Netz zu strukturieren, welches schließlich Computern ermöglicht diese entsprechend ihrer inhaltlichen Bedeutung auszuwerten und neu zusammen zu stellen. Informationen über Orte, Personen und Dinge würden somit von Computern in Beziehung gesetzt, was die Informationssuche drastisch erleichtern würde. Somit liefere der Computer bei der Suche *„wo kann ich schnell und günstig essen gehen?"* die richtige Adresse – je nach Vorliebe, Budget und Position des Nutzers. Dafür sind jedoch noch eine Vielzahl von Problemen zu bewältigen.

C | Connecting to the Internet

M **1** KMK II

Ihr Vorgesetzter plant ein Netzwerk aufzubauen. Fassen Sie für ihn die wesentlichen Punkte des folgenden Internetartikels auf Deutsch zusammen.

WLAN – Yes or no?

The popularity of WiFi networks is due to the fact that cables are unnecessary and that users are not forced to stay in one spot once they have logged in to the WiFi access point. These access points are easy to install, whereas laying cables, especially in older buildings, may be quite expensive. The range of wireless networks can be expanded infinitely by repeaters – a possibility that airports and large companies take advantage of. However, wireless networks are still much slower than fixed LANs. You may save money on cabling, but receiving a WLAN signal requires wireless NICs that are still more expensive than the wired versions. Above all, data transmission over WLANs can always be intercepted. For this reason, encryption standards like WEP or WPA need to be installed and configured, and that requires time and know-how.

R **2** KMK II

Ihr Vorgesetzter beauftragt Sie, ein W-LAN Netz für ein Großraumbüro aufzubauen. Welches Produkt würden Sie empfehlen, wenn folgende Kriterien beachtet werden müssen: *große Reichweite, Kompatibilität mit unterschiedlichen Betriebssystemen, hohe Sicherheit, Preis.* Im Internet finden Sie folgende Produkte. Schreiben Sie eine kurze Notiz auf Deutsch für Ihren Chef. Begründen Sie dabei Ihre Entscheidung.

Netconnector N900 802.11n WiFi router
Price: 89.99 $

- Directs data packets from the Internet to your PCs at a speed up to 150 Mbps @ 2,4 GHz
- WiFi Protected Access – latest encryption standards (WPA2)
  Supports all current operating systems
  Provides four gigabit Ethernet ports
- ReadyShare Printer - enables USB printers to be accessed

Fastlink Repeater/Access point NL-320
Price: 59.99 $

- Excels in a speed of 150 @ Mbps for IEEE802.11n
- Extends your WiFi network by receiving and transmitting data
- Compatibility: Mac, Windows
- Uses up-to-date encryption standards
- Router function: connects you with your existing WiFi network

further info at: info@ITlinkk...com

P **3**

Schreiben Sie eine E-Mail, in der Sie höflich nach Rabatten, Zahlungs- und Lieferungsbedingungen fragen. Außerdem bitten Sie um die Zusendung eines Infokatalogs.

→ **PHRASES:**
Written communication

4 **UNDERSTANDING TECHNICAL ENGLISH**

Look up the following nouns in an English-German dictionary. Explain their technical meaning with the help of their original meaning.

trojan horse • web • cookie • tag • gateway • bookmark

5 **SAFETY FIRST** ⚠ – Wireless Networks

What do you have to consider when setting up a secure wireless network?

WORD BANK

access (v) – zugreifen
access point – Anschlussknoten, Zugangspunkt
bookmark – Lesezeichen
collaboration – Zusammenarbeit
cookie – Keks, Cookie
expand (v) – erweitern, vergrößern
feature (n) – Merkmal, Bestandteil
gateway – Eingangstor, Leitcomputer
intercept (v) – abfangen
reprocessing – Wiederaufarbeitung
tag – Etikett, Anhängeschild, Identifizierungskennzeichen

WORD BANK ◎

administer (v) – verwalten
authentication – Authentifizierung
custom-designed – anwendungsspezifisch
encryption standard – Verschlüsselungsstandard
heterogeneous – uneinheitlich
host (v) – beherbergen
maintenance – Instandhaltung
software suite – Anwendungssystem
streamline (v) – rationalisieren, vereinfachen

842j42

H

NACH DIESEM MODUL:

- ✓ kann ich auf Englisch auf Kundenbeschwerden reagieren,
- ✓ kann ich auf Englisch mit unzufriedenen Kunden umgehen.

1

2

3

4

Dealing with customers

The way a company deals with its customers is the key to its success. Whether you are arranging appointments, handling enquiries, or dealing with complaints, it is essential that you are able to express yourself clearly, confidently, and politely. And remember: the customer may not always be right, but they are very important.

1 Brainstorm words that describe what is shown on the photos above.

P **2** Compare your list of words with your partner and work together to describe the pictures. Use these words to help you:

complaint • hotline • builder • hard hat • building site • meeting • customer • plans • mechanic • explain • repairs • bonnet • overalls • engine

3 Which of the customers do you think are happy, and which are unhappy? Explain your answer.

P **4** In what situations do you deal with customers in your job? Copy and complete the word web below to brainstorm reasons for talking to customers.

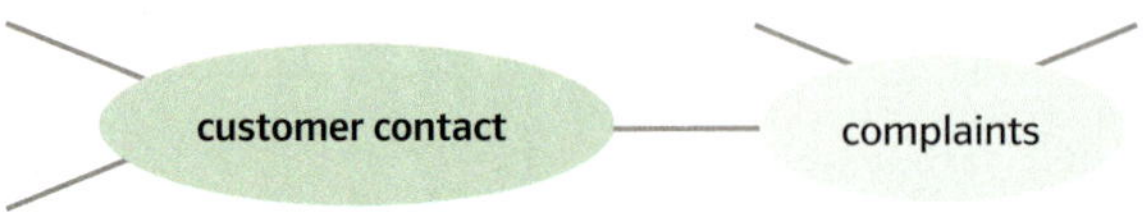

A | Complaints

1 Match the common causes for complaint on the left with the suggested solutions on the right. Several options may be appropriate.

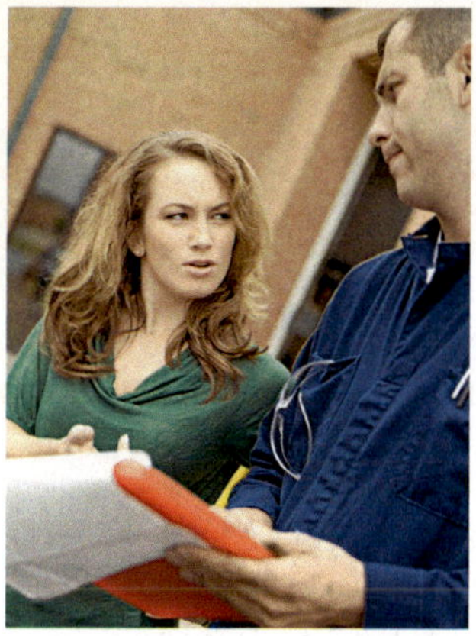

1. delay in delivery	a. offer a price reduction
2. faulty goods	b. improve the service
3. damaged goods	c. repair the goods
4. unsatisfactory services	d. replace the goods
5. wrong goods	e. send the goods by air freight
6. too many / too few goods received	f. send the missing goods
7. too early delivery	g. take the goods back
	h. collect the surplus goods
	i. send a credit note

P **2** What about your industry? Which are the most common reasons for complaints? Make a list and compare it with a partner. Be as specific as possible.

R **3** Which of the following phrases are used for making complaints and which ones for replying to complaints? Make a list.

→ **PHRASES:** Dealing with customers

1. This is very inconvenient for us because we need the goods urgently.
2. We are sorry for any inconvenience this has caused.
3. We will keep the damaged goods until we hear from you.
4. Please return the damaged goods at our expense.
5. We can assure you that this will not happen again.
6. Some items were badly damaged.
7. We regret to inform you that the order has not yet arrived.
8. We think the damage may have occurred in transit.
9. We are experiencing difficulties with our new logistics software.
10. Could you please look into this problem immediately?
11. Please accept our apologies.
12. The reason for the mistake is that we are extremely busy at this time of the year.
13. Please send us replacements as soon as possible.
14. We hope that this proposal will find your approval.
15. We believe the problem is down to human error.

R **4**
KMK II
◎ A 1.7

You work for *Deutsches Netz*, an IT company in Hamburg. Your boss, Mr Bauder, receives a voicemail message on his mobile phone from Mr Jenkins, owner of *New Wave Marketing*, a subsidiary of an English marketing company based in Hamburg. Listen to the message and answer the following questions.

1. What did the technicians from Deutsches Netz do for New Wave Marketing?
2. What problems are the employees having (three things)?
3. What is the most serious problem?
4. Why is this a serious problem?
5. How should Mr Bauder contact Mr Jenkins?

WORD BANK

bonnet – Motorhaube
builder – Bauarbeiter
building site – Baustelle
hotline – Informationsdienst
repairs – Reparaturen
technician – Techniker(in)

P **5** **Mr Bauder asks you to respond to Mr Jenkins' phone call. He sends you the following email and asks you to draft a short email to the customer.**

→ **PHRASES:** Dealing with customers

Von: mailto:s.bauder@DNetz...de
An: mailto:info@DNetz...de
Betreff: Bitte an Herrn Jenkins schreiben (eilt!!)

... diese Firma ist ein sehr wichtiger Kunde von uns und wir wollen ihn **auf keinen Fall** verlieren!! Bitte sagen Sie ihm folgendes:

- Es tut uns sehr leid, dass es diese Probleme gegeben hat.
- Wir verstehen völlig, dass es jetzt sehr ungelegen und ärgerlich ist.
- Wir vermuten, dass das Problem durch menschliches Versagen verursacht wurde.
- Wir werden sofort jemanden schicken, um das Netzwerk zu reparieren. (selbstverständlich auf unsere Kosten!)
- Der Techniker wird um spätestens 17 Uhr dort sein.

Bringen Sie nochmals unser Bedauern für das Problem zum Ausdruck und versichern Sie ihm, dass sich dies nicht wiederholen wird.

Danke,
Bauder

M **6** **You work for a plumbing and heating installation company in Leipzig. Your supervisor, Mr Hüber, receives an email about a recent job done for an American family living in the area. Your supervisor does not speak very good English and asks you to read the email and to sum it up in German.**

Von: mailto:j.t.levine@kwq...net
An: mailto:info@sippelheizung_sanitaer...net
Betreff: Problems with the heating

Dear Mr Hüber,

I am writing in reference to the heating system installed by your company at my house last week. Unfortunately, my family and I have been having some problems. Firstly, the water in the bathroom takes a long time to warm up – sometimes over 5 minutes!

Secondly, the temperature in the house is too low, and I cannot make it warmer. Also, I cannot find the instruction manual – did your technician take it with him? My final problem is that the underfloor heating does not seem to be working in the bathroom. The tiles on the floor are still cold in the morning. Is something wrong?

As it is winter, and very cold, I would ask you to send someone to my house as soon as possible to find a solution to these problems. Please give me a call, or send me an email to confirm.

Thank you in advance,

John Levine

B | Customer service

P **1** What five tips would you give a colleague about dealing with unhappy customers?

2 Compare your list with a partner.

How to deal with unhappy customers

No company has happy customers 100 % of the time.
Things can always go wrong and customers can become unhappy – or worse, upset. Here are some tips on how to avoid making the situation worse.

Stay calm: The customer may be angry at somebody, but it does not help the situation if you get just as angry. The last thing you want to do is start an argument – that is very unprofessional and unhelpful. Try to calm the customer down.

Listen, listen, listen: You will only be able to understand what has upset the customer if you listen, and listen carefully. Before you start talking, listen actively to the customer until you fully understand why they are unhappy. If you don't know what's wrong, you will not be able to do anything about it.

The customer is king: Show the customer that they, and their problem, are important to you. Tell them quickly how sorry you are for their problem and reassure them that you will do everything you can to help them. And, always be patient and polite.

Stay positive: Do your best to stay positive at all times. Remember that your goal is to solve the problem and you can do this better if you have a positive frame of mind. Regardless of how negative and furious the customer gets, it is important that you do not let it affect your mood.

No excuses: No matter what the problem is, or who you think caused it, do not blame other people or try to make excuses. Instead, take the initiative and do whatever you can to solve the problem.

R **3** Find the synonyms in the text for the following words and expressions:

1. to stop sth. from happening
2. disagreement
3. to aim
4. to fix
5. attitude
6. very angry
7. reason
8. to take control

R **4** KMK II Sie lesen den oben stehenden Artikel im Internet. Beantworten Sie die folgenden Fragen dazu in ganzen Sätzen auf Deutsch.

1. Warum ist es wichtig zu wissen, wie man mit unzufriedenen Kunden umgeht?
2. Was sollte man tun, wenn der Kunde sehr verärgert ist?
3. Warum ist es wichtig, dem Kunden ganz genau zuzuhören?
4. Wie kann man einem Kunden zeigen, dass man sein Problem ernst nimmt?
5. Wann ist es gerechtfertigt, jemand anderem die Schuld für das vorliegende Problem zu geben?

I **5** Choose one of the problems you listed in exercise A1 and create a short role play. One of you should play the unhappy / angry customer and the other the employee. Act out your role play in front of the class.

WORD BANK

instruction manual – Bedienungsanleitung
plumbing and heating – Heizung und Sanitär
underfloor heating – Fußbodenheizung

09

NACH DIESEM MODUL:

- ✓ kann ich auf Englisch mit Schlüsselthemen in der Softwareentwicklung umgehen,
- ✓ kenne ich die gängigen Vokabeln in Bezug auf Entwicklungsumgebungen,
- ✓ kann ich Softwarefehler auf Englisch besprechen.

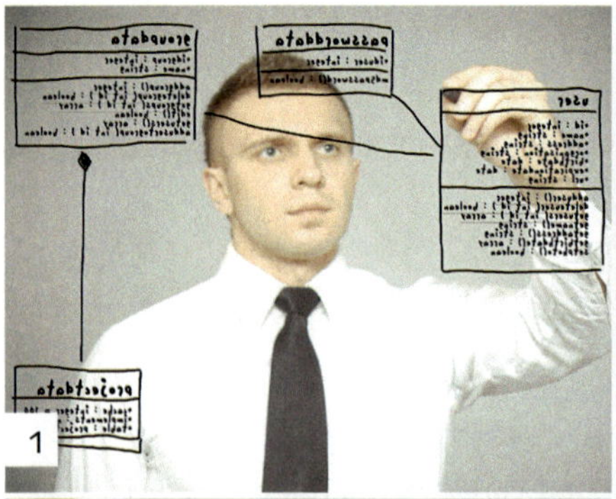

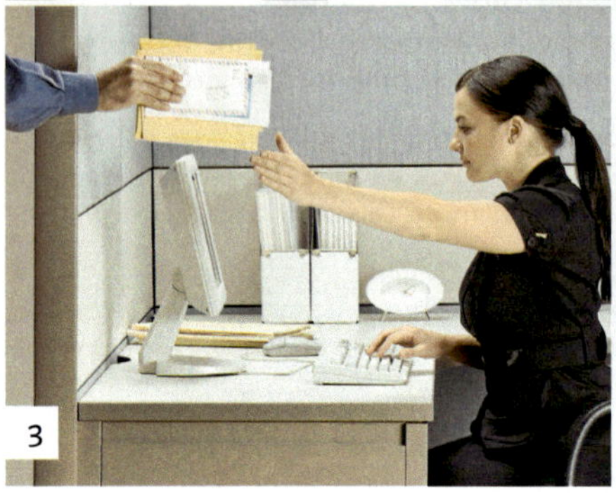

Writing software

Different types of software developers have different specialities. Before the first line of code is written, a lot of effort goes into modelling the software and dimensioning the data centre infrastructure which the new software will run in. Then as soon as you have the code, you need to test it.

1 Match the sentences with the photos.

1. A lead tester tests new software on lots of different computers to ensure that it is free of bugs and that it meets customer requirements.
2. Based on the software architect's model, a deployment specialist creates the right infrastructure in the data centre where the software is to be deployed.
3. Software architects create models based on customer requirements. They may use a computer, or draw a diagram on a whiteboard or on paper.
4. A programmer implements the functionalities the customer needs based on the specifications made by the software architect.

P **2** List the aspects of software development that you already know.

P **3** **UNDERSTANDING TECHNICAL ENGLISH**
Use a dictionary to find the general and technical German meanings of the terms.

1. operate   2. code   3. bug

A | Writing code: the IDE

No matter how much time and effort goes into software design and testing, the source code is at the heart of every software. Programmers use an integrated development environment (IDE) to write the source code. This tool helps programmers to reduce common problems, such as syntax and spelling mistakes, as well as to fix bugs.

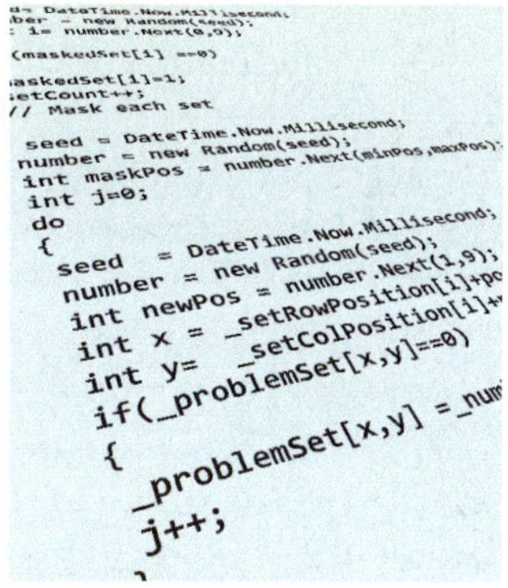

1 Complete the text using the words in the box.

> line • Java • debugging • application • compilation • key words • memory • syntax • mistakes • processor • source code • IDE • execution • fix • free of charge • modules

In theory, you could use a word processing program to write a **1**. However, this would not be practical and an integrated development environment **2** is a better tool. An example of such an environment is Eclipse. It is open source and may be used **3**. By using Eclipse you can write code in many languages such as **4**, C++ or PHP. An IDE contains several features and **5** that make it easier to create software applications. The source code editor automatically colours **6** to make it easier to read the code. The editor also checks for the correct **7** of the code. It can also detect and underline commonly made **8**. Once the code has been written, it is transformed into something a computer **9** can understand. This transformation process is called **10**. The compiler is part of the IDE. It goes through every **11** of code, and transforms and optimizes it. The IDE also helps with a process called **12**. After the source code has been compiled, the IDE starts the new **13** in debug mode. While it is running in this mode, the programmer can tell the IDE to pause the **14** of the program. This allows him or her to look at what is currently stored in the **15** area the program is using. This makes it easier to find and **16** errors, hence the term 'debug'.

P **2** Decide whether the statements are true or false. Correct the false statements.

1. The Eclipse IDE is limited to one language.
2. IDEs are meant to help the software developers with their work.
3. The source code editor of an IDE finds and fixes all of the errors that the programmer makes.
4. An IDE does not help the programmer to debug software.
5. It is possible to stop the program in debug mode.

M **3** Describe how an IDE works in German.

P **4** Outline which IDE you use and give its most useful features.

5 Create a table like the one below and add information about IDEs that you find in the Internet. Present your results to the class. → **PHRASES:** Presentations

IDE	Programming languages	Proprietary/Open source

WORD BANK

compiler – Compiler
data centre infrastructure – Rechenzentruminfrastruktur
debug mode – Debug-Modus
dimension (v) – vermaßen
IDE (integrated development environment) – Entwicklungs-umgebung
model (v) software – Software entwerfen
open source – Open Source
proprietary – proprietär
source code – Quellcode
word processing program – Textverarbeitungsprogramm

B | Debugging

When writing source code people try very hard not to cause mistakes or bugs. The process of fixing those mistakes is referred to as debugging.

R **1**
A 1.16 **Dan Rivers, an American, and the German Phillip Esser are game developers at Snowstorm Entertainment. Their team is responsible for the multiplayer modules of the game, 'Forge III', to be released in six weeks. Listen to the dialogue and answer the questions.**

1. What problem is Phillip working on?
2. What is the number of the issue the two developers are talking about?
3. Was Phillip able to compile the source code?
4. When was the bug discovered?
5. Does the problem related to the bug always occur?

R **2**
A 1.16 **Complete the documentation of the changes Phillip made in the code and then put the steps into the order you hear in the dialogue.**

1. As soon as X-Link have solved the problem with their ?, we will reset the timeout value with an update for the game.
2. The bug is not directly related to our software but is actually a problem with the X-Link firmware. The router sometimes takes too long to ? to our messages. X-Link is working on a ? of their own.
3. Rivers and Esser fixed bug # ?.
4. The bug causes the game to run into an exception when ? or more players try to connect to a game and one of the players is using an X-Link ?.
5. We have solved the problem for now by increasing the timeout value from 43 ms to ? ms (see line ?).

I **3**
Later that day Dan's supervisor, Tina, asks him to start work on another problem. Act out the dialogue in English.

Tina		Dan
Sagen Sie, dass es ein Problem mit dem Punkteverwaltungs-Modul *(ranking management module)* gibt.	→	Fragen Sie, ob das Problem bereits eine Nummer hat.
Verneinen Sie und weisen Sie Ihren Gegenüber an, das Problem im Projektmanagementsystem einzutragen und ihm die Nummer 44391 zuzuweisen.	↙ →	Sagen Sie, dass Sie im Moment an dem Fehler mit der Nummer 417 arbeiten. Fragen Sie, was Sie tun sollen.
Erwidern Sie, dass das neue Problem eine höhere Priorität hat und dass Ihr Gesprächspartner die Lösung des anderen Problems verschieben soll.	↙ →	Bitten Sie darum, noch ein oder zwei andere Teammitglieder zu Ihrer Unterstüzung einzuteilen, um mit der zusätzlichen Arbeit fertig zu werden.
Antworten Sie, dass das schwierig werden wird, aber Sie kümmern sich darum.	↙ ↘	Bedanken Sie sich.

4
Act out a call to a software company using the role cards for Speakers A and B in the Appendix.

C | Comments and documentation

In order to make source code easier to understand for other developers, its functionality is documented and comments are inserted into the code. A comment starts with /** and ends with */. For example, a comment can tell you that when a method is used, it loads data from a file.

M **1** KMK III **Sie arbeiten als Software Entwickler(in) in einer international tätigen Firma. Ihre Aufgabe ist es, in dem Projekt für eine verständliche und hochwertige Dokumentation zu sorgen. Nicht alle Teammitglieder können gutes Englisch. Daher müssen Sie gelegentlich Quellcode-Kommentare aus dem Deutschen ins Englische übertragen. Übertragen Sie folgenden Kommentar sinngemäß ins Englische. Die Sonderzeichen müssen Sie zum Bearbeiten dieser Aufgabe nicht übernehmen.**

```
/**
* Diese Methode lädt Daten aus einer XML Datei und macht diese
* für die Anwendung verfügbar.
* Beim Aufrufen dieser Methode muss ein Parameter „pathToXMLFile"
* übergeben werden. Dieser Parameter von Typ File gibt an, welche
* Datei geladen werden soll. Falls die Datei nicht gefunden werden
* kann, tritt eine Ausnahme vom Typ FileNotFoundException auf.
* Weiterhin kann eine Ausnahme vom Typ JAXBException auftreten,
* falls die Datei keine gültige XML-Datei ist.
* Projekt: Kundenverwaltungssystem
* Modul: loadData
* Autor: Ludwig Wieland
* Letzte Änderung am: 23. Mai 20…
* Version: 1.1.43.2
*/
    public void loadDataFromXMLFile(File pathToXMLFile)
            throws JAXBException, FileNotFoundException {
...
```

P **2** KMK II **Ihre Firma ist unzufrieden mit dem Kommentarstil einiger Mitarbeiter. Ihr Vorgesetzter hat ein Memo verfasst und bittet Sie, dies für die Mitarbeiter Ihrer Firma in den Niederlanden ins Englische zu übertragen.**

Memo

Von: Frank Walter, Qualitätssicherung, Generics IT AG
An: Ariel van Pelt, Leiter Software-Entwicklung, Generics IT Netherlands Ltd.

Ich möchte Sie darauf hinweisen, dass wir in der Zentrale Verbesserungsbedarf beim Kommentarstil Ihrer Abteilung sehen. Bitte nehmen Sie folgende Anregungen zur Kenntnis.

1. Die Kommentare sind auf Englisch zu verfassen.
2. Vor jeder Methode sollte ein Kommentar zur Funktion der Methode stehen. Diese Zusammenfassung gibt Aufschluss darüber, was der Code macht. Die Zusammenfassung enthält außerdem eine Beschreibung der Parameter, die die Methode annimmt.
3. Am Ende des Kommentars folgt der Name des Projektes, der Modulname, der Autor, wann die Methode zum letzten Mal geändert wurde und die aktuelle Versionsnummer.

WORD BANK

multiplayer module – Mehrspielermodul
ranking management module – Punkteverwaltungsmodul

WORD BANK ⊙

beta testing phase – Betatest-Phase
bug report – Fehlerbericht
compile report – Kompilierungs-Bericht
firmware – in Hardware-Geräte eingebettetes Betriebssystem
hotfix – Hotfix
multiplayer matchmaking – Mehrspielerspielvermittlung
patch – Aktualisierung, die einen oder mehrere Fehler behebt
reset (v) – zurücksetzen
router – Gerät, das es ermöglicht gemeinsam einen Internet-anschluss zu nutzen
run (v) into an exception – in einen nicht erwarteten Zustand geraten
timeout value – Zeitüberschreitungswert
tune (v) – fein abstimmen

10

NACH DIESEM MODUL:

- ✓ kann ich auf Englisch webbasierte Anwendungsprogramme erklären,
- ✓ kann ich Wege zur Systempflege und Datensicherung auf Englisch beschreiben.

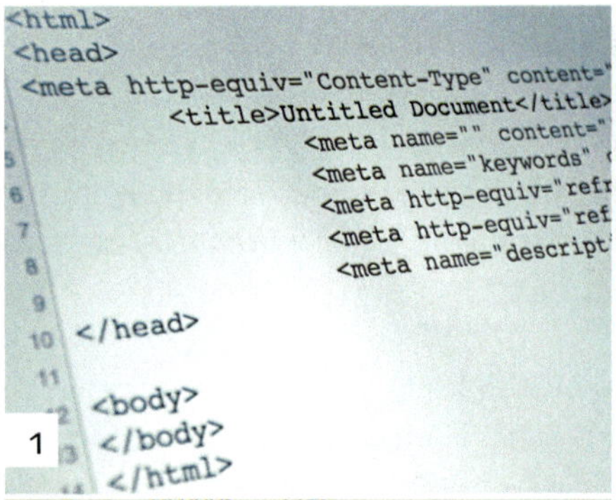

1

2

3

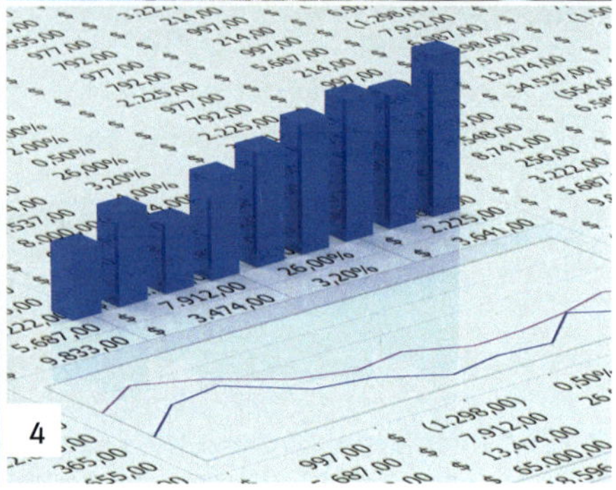
4

Tools and applications

System software coordinates and prepares the computing resources of a system to perform specific tasks. Tools and applications make use of these resources to enable the user to perform specific tasks.

1 Which tools and applications were most likely used for the tasks shown in the pictures above?

2 Which other programs exist for the tasks shown in the pictures? Brainstorm their advantages and disadvantages with a partner. Present your ideas to the class.

3 Match the types of application software on the left with the definitions on the right.

Application software	Definitions
1. Media development software	a. enables the user to create and manage information by editing text, calculating numbers and displaying information.
2. Information worker software	b. is mainly used to access content without editing it.
3. Simulation software	c. is usually interactive educational software.
4. Enterprise infrastructure software	d. supports enterprise software systems by managing databases, networks and security.
5. Entertainment and educational software	e. simulates developments for research, training or entertainment.
6. Content access software	f. is used to generate multi-media content for others to consume.

P **4** Which other types of application software do you know?

A | Web-based application software

The spirit of the Internet has always been access to information anytime, anywhere. Now, increasingly, the Internet also offers the possibility of storing and sharing personal files online, and of processing the data using online or "web-based" software applications.

I **1** **Make a survey. Find out which is the most popular word processing, spreadsheet or presentation software in your class. Give reasons.**

R **2** A 1.17 **Listen to the dialogue. Which type of application software are John and Sue talking about? Make a list of the advantages and disadvantages mentioned.**

R/P **3** A 1.17 **Listen again and describe the icons below.**

Example: Icon 3 aligns the text to the right.

4 **Here are the step-by-step instructions for two separate web-based word processing functions, a web clipboard for copying and pasting, and a web translator. Unfortunately the instructions have got completely mixed up. List the instructions in the correct sequences on a separate sheet of paper as shown below.**

a. Right click und scroll down the list of languages into which you would like to translate the passage.
b. *Select what you want to copy.*
c. Select a format **(HTML, plain text)**.
d. Click on the **Clipboard icon** on your toolbar.
e. Left click on the tab **Tools** in the **toolbar menu** and select **Web translator**.
f. Go to your destination document and place the cursor where you want to put the content.
g. Click on the **clipboard icon** again.
h. Click on **Copy Selection to web clipboard**.
i. Select what you want to paste and choose a format for the content.
j. *Mark the passage that you want to translate.*
k. Choose a document in which you would like to insert the translated text.
l. Press **OK**.
m. Select a language.

Web clipboard menu	Web translator
1. (b) Select what you want to copy. 2. …	1. (j) Mark the passage that you want to translate. 2. …

P **5** **Give a presentation of a web-based application software of your choice. Include information such as general use, system requirements, (dis)advantages, price, source.**

WORD BANK

content access software – Zugangssoftware
educational software – Lernsoftware
enterprise – Unternehmen
entertainment software – Unterhaltungssoftware
information worker software – Datenverabeitungssoftware
media development – Mediengestaltung
toolbar – Symbolleiste

WORD BANK

redo (v) – etw. noch einmal machen
revision history – Überarbeitunghistorie
spreadsheet – Tabellenkalkulation
undo (v) – rückgängig machen
word processor – Textverarbeitungsprogramm

→ **PHRASES:** Presentations

B | Computer health maintanance

Depending on how you use your computer, you should maintain the health of your system to reduce the chances of crashes or data loss.

1 Discuss with your partner which problems may lead to error messages. How could you solve these problems? Report your ideas to the class.

P **2** Describe a software problem you have had and its effects on your computer. Which steps did you take to solve it?

R/P **3** A 1.18 In a podcast you learn about measures to maintain the health of your PC system. Listen to the different measures suggested, create a table as shown below on a separate sheet of paper, and fill in the columns a., b. and c.

Measures	a. Why is it necessary?	b. What is done?	c. When should you do it?

P **4** Work with a partner and take turns. Your partner has to deal with one of the three problems described below. Give advice on which measures you would take. Use the information table you created in exercise 3.

programs load really slowly • program suddenly shuts down • can't access the hard drive • computer refuses to start

5 Check the Internet and make a list of programs that you would recommend for disc cleaning and checking, defragmenting and registry cleaning. Compare your recommendations with those of your partner and give reasons why your choices are better.

M **6** **SAFETY FIRST ⚠ – Tips for backing up data**
Match the numbers with the letters. Then make a list of the tips in German.

1. You should remember to backup …
2. It is advisable to save the backup …
3. Keeping the data in a safe location …
4. Backup your personal data especially …
5. Name your backups wisely …
6. Change between a full backup and an incremental backup from time to time …

a. prevents the loss of the backup.
b. to save disc space.
c. before you start a complete reinstallation of your system.
d. your data regularly.
e. to be able to identify the backups.
f. on an external drive.

7 **UNDERSTANDING TECHNICAL ENGLISH: How to translate the German word "Fehler".**
In which contexts are the following words used? Work in groups and find examples.

error • mistake • fault • failure • lapse

C | Data backup methods and data recovery

M **1**
KMK III

Sie sind Auszubildender in der IT-Abteilung eines Dienstleisters, der Datensicherungssysteme vertreibt. Ihr Vorgesetzter beauftragt Sie, für eine Kundenpräsentation die gängigsten Datensicherungsmethoden gegenüberzustellen. Er gibt Ihnen dazu den folgenden englischen Text. Stellen Sie die Vor- und Nachteile der Datensicherungsmethoden auf Deutsch dar. Berücksichtigen Sie dabei die drei wichtigsten Faktoren der Datensicherung: Die Kapazität des Speichermediums, die verfügbare Zeit zum Speichern und die Zeit, die zur Verfügung steht, die Daten wieder aufzurufen.

Data backup methods

A FULL BACKUP:
A full backup includes all the files on your PC. These are copied to an external drive in each session. This is ideal protection because the backups are self-contained and restoration of the data is the fastest. But a lot of storage space is required and the time needed to create a full backup speaks against using this backup method on a daily basis. Full backups should be done on a weekly basis. You also need to consider the security aspects of this method, as each full backup contains a 1:1 copy of your data.

B INCREMENTAL BACKUP:
This backup method is a much quicker way of backing up data compared to full backups. This is because only the files that have changed since the last full backup are included. This reduces the time needed for backing up, but more time is needed for restoration, as you need to restore the full backup plus each individual incremental backup. On the positive side, you need less storage space than for any of the other methods. Incremental backups can and should be run on a daily basis.

C DIFFERENTIAL BACKUP:
In contrast to incremental backups, where the reference point is the last incremental backup, the reference point in differential backups is the last full backup. This means that restoration is quicker than from incremental backups, and backing up is quicker than for the full backup method. On the negative side, however, restoration is slower than from a full back up, and backing up is slower than for incremental backups. Storage space requirements are also halfway between the two other methods: higher than for incremental backups but lower than for full backups.

D MIRROR BACKUP:
A mirror backup means creating an identical copy of the selected files at a given reference time without any compression. No container file is created, so you can't track different versions of files. But since the destination becomes the mirror of the source, the files can be accessed by tools like the Explorer. This also makes it the fastest backup method with the quickest restoration time. But mirroring also has a drawback. It needs the greatest storage space of all methods, and password protection of your data is not possible.

WORD BANK

reference point – Bezugspunkt
restoration – Wiederherstellung
self-contained – unabhängig
storage space – Speicherplatz
track (v) – etwas verfolgen

WORD BANK ◎

disc defragmenter – Defragmentierungsprogramm
system registry – Systemregistrierung
temporary files – temporäre Dateien

P **2**
KMK II

Die externe Festplatte eines Kunden wurde durch einen Virus unbrauchbar gemacht. Auf der Festplatte liegen wichtige Daten, die er in der letzten Zeit angesammelt hat. Leider erfolgte nur zu Beginn eine vollständige Sicherung der Daten mittels der mitgelieferten Backup Software. Schreiben Sie eine E-Mail an den Kunden, in dem Sie Ihr Bedauern ausdrücken und Ihre Unterstützung bei der Datenrettung anbieten. Geben Sie Hinweise zur zukünftigen Datensicherung.

→ **PHRASES:** Written communication

11

NACH DIESEM MODUL:

- √ kann ich auf Englisch mit dem Thema Firmensoftware umgehen,
- √ kann ich Kundenanforderungen für Anpassungen von Firmensoftware auf Englisch erfassen.

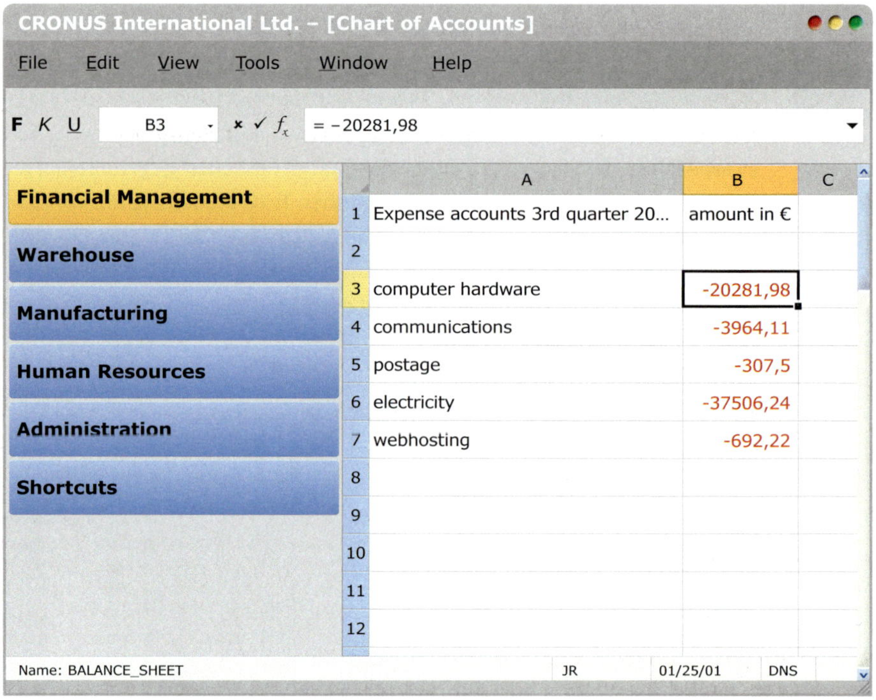

Enterprise software

Software can be divided into consumer software and enterprise software. But not all software used by enterprises or businesses is classed as enterprise software. A word processing program is used by businesses and consumers alike, but it is not considered to be enterprise software. All pieces of software target a certain use case. Some use cases like operating systems are generic or broad ranged. Other types of software such as video games are specific as is enterprise software. Good examples of this are enterprise resource planning or payroll systems. They help businesses to manage daily operations more efficiently and to speed up processes.

P **1** **Decide whether the statements about enterprise software are true or false. Correct the false statements.**

1. Enterprise software can make a company run more efficiently.
2. Video games are considered to be enterprise software.
3. All pieces of software are meant to be used by everybody.
4. Enterprise software is meant to help businesses with their daily work.

P **2** **Look at the screenshot and answer the questions.**

1. Which module is currently selected in the program?
2. What information does the module display?
3. Which module would you use to find out how much raw materials are in stock?
4. Which icon do you click on to change the settings of the program?

A | Enterprise resource planning

At the centre of a company's enterprise software you will find the enterprise resource planning system. This tool allows departments to efficiently use and manage the company's resources.

R/M **1** **Read the text and answer the questions in German.**

1. What does the term ERP describe?
2. Why is it not possible for every department to use the same ERP module?
3. What function does an ERP system try to offer?
4. What does the concept of "just in time" refer to?
5. Give examples of how departments can use an ERP system.

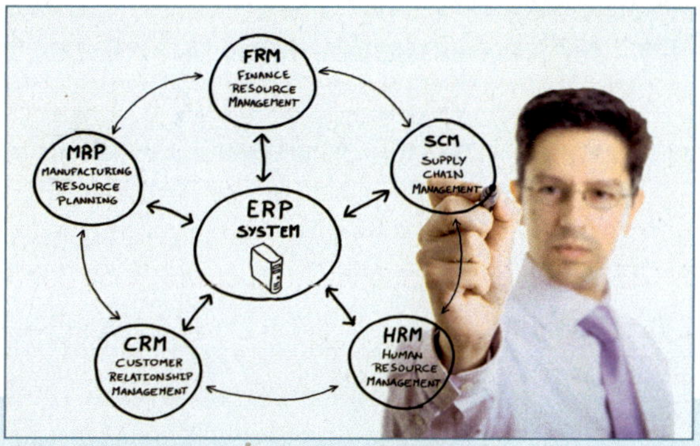

The term enterprise resource planning (ERP) was first used in 1990. Since then the term has come to describe one or a collection of software modules designed for an enterprise use case. The purpose of ERP is to make information, from both inside and outside of the company, available to employees. Each department uses a module of the system which is tailored to their needs. Specifically, the ERP maps the business processes which each department follows to modules in the system. These departments include: accounting, sales, customer relations, customer relationship management and manufacturing. For example, ERP keeps track of raw materials. As soon as stocks reach a certain value, ERP automatically orders new raw materials from the supplier. Car manufacturers rely heavily on this feature. Everything that is taken out of storage is registered with the ERP. Since most manufacturers nowadays operate just in time, they usually only have enough materials in stock to last for a couple of days or even hours. For this reason they need deliveries of raw materials almost every day.
By using ERP, the accounting department can automatically print invoices as soon as the product is ready for shipment. This makes accounting much easier. If the companies' books are always kept up to date, ERP also helps with the company's tax declaration, as the relevant data can usually be exported into the formats commonly used by software for tax advisors.

M **2** **Describe in German how the departments use an ERP system.**

P **3** **Correct the statement about ERP.**

ERP has been around since the 19th century, but not many people use it today. Basically an ERP is only useful if a company operates in the service sector and does not manufacture anything.

M **4** **UNDERSTANDING TECHNICAL ENGLISH**

1. **Find the general and technical meanings of the word 'process'.**
2. **Translate the sentence into German.**

The term 'business process' describes a collection of tasks related to a specific service or product whereas in IT, a process refers to an instance of a program executing concurrently alongside other instances.

WORD BANK

map (v) a process to a module – einen (Geschäfts)prozess in einem Modul abbilden
operating system – Betriebssystem
setting – Einstellung
use case – Anwendungsfall

B | Business intelligence

Business intelligence software is complex but the idea behind it is simple. Almost everything a company does generates data. This can be analysed and the results viewed as reports. By interpreting the reports, companies make better decisions on how to improve efficiency in general and relationships with customers in particular.

1 Complete the text using the words in the box.

> data • related to • business • likely • term • decisions • statistics • quality assurance • generates • analysed • tolerance • email • support • reports • intelligence • human resources • complex • CRM

The term [1] intelligence was coined by German computer scientist Hans Peter Luhn in 1958. However it was not until the 1990s that the [2] came into widespread use. Businesses collect [3] on almost everything. A sales representative writes an [4] to a customer. Then he or she files a report in the customer relationship management system [5]. When a defective product is returned, [6] inputs the relevant data into the ERP so manufacturing processes may be improved. Every time an employee is paid or takes a day off, [7] update their data. Over time, this [8] a large amount of data which needs to be [9]. This is where business [10] software comes in. The goal of enterprise software is to help the people who run businesses make better [11]. Hence the term decision [12] system (DSS). The system looks at all of the data which the business generates before creating [13]. These could contain [14] on how many defective products were returned last month. If the number of returns is above a certain [15], such a report could indicate a problem in the manufacturing process. But BI also enables more [16] reports. For instance it is possible to see how a customer's orders are [17] how the sales representative interacts with the customer. The report could show that a customer is more [18] to buy a new product following a demonstration rather than in response to an email telling him or her about the product.

P **2** Compare the uses of ERP and BI. Write your ideas in a table.

P **3** Find out which companies develop enterprise software. Are there open source solutions available or not? Present your results to the class.

I **4** Michael Schlüter is a sales representative for KP-Software, a German company that develops enterprise software. He calls customers regularly to see if they are interested in buying more software products. Act out the phone call in English using the role cards for Speakers A and B in the Appendix.

→ **PHRASES:** Telephoning

R **5** Five days later Michael is at the headquarters of Entex in Leeds. Listen to the dialogue and answer the questions.
A 1.19

1. What do you see on the screen after logging in?
2. Why was Lisa thinking of using a software produced by a different company?
3. Why is the start screen empty?
4. Does Lisa have to configure the start screen herself?
5. What makes the new interface so special?

C | Customizing enterprise software

Enterprise software is targeted at businesses. But not every business works in the same way. That is why enterprise software often has to be customized to meet the customer's needs.

M **1** KMK II

Sie arbeiten in einem Unternehmen, das Firmensoftware anbietet. Das Gehaltsabrechnungsmodul muss für einen Kunden angepasst werden. Die Entwickler verteilen sich über verschiedene Länder. Als gemeinsame Sprache dient Englisch. Übertragen Sie die Anforderungen des Kunden sinngemäß ins Englische. Sie dürfen die einleitenden Aussagen ignorieren.

Von: liebermann@h2ic-solutions...net
An: johannes.strasser@kps-software-systeme...de
Betreff: Anpassungen

Guten Tag Herr Strasser,

wir sind schon sehr zufrieden mit den bisherigen Anpassungen. Es müssen allerdings noch einige Dinge an unsere Anforderungen angepasst werden:

1. Die Schriftart auf der grafischen Benutzeroberfläche ist zu klein (jetzt Größe 12). Bitte 15.
2. Es soll möglich sein, das Passwort beim Login zu speichern.
3. Wenn man auf die Schaltfläche zum Löschen der Daten klickt, muss noch ein Popup erscheinen in der Art: Sind Sie sicher?
4. Wenn man auf die Schaltfläche zum Speichern der Daten klickt, muss ebenfalls eine Abfrage erscheinen (siehe oben).
5. Der Daten-Export muss angepasst werden, damit wir die Daten an den Steuerberater weiterleiten können. Das XML Schema wird Anfang nächster Woche geschickt.

Mfg,
Andrea Liebermann

M **2** KMK II

Einer der Entwickler hat Ihnen nun Rückfragen zu den Anforderungen geschickt. Übertragen Sie diese nun sinngemäß ins Deutsche, damit der Kunde dazu Stellung nehmen kann.

From: anandi.chandramouleeswaran@kps-software-systems...in
To: johannes.strasser@kps-software-systeme...de
Subject: Questions on customer requirements

Dear John,

1. Should it be possible to change the font size or should it always be size 15?
2. How does the user save the password? Should he/she click on a checkbox (I recommend that option)? Should there be a yes/no message asking if he/she wants to save the password?
3. I'm afraid that the information regarding the data export is of no use to us. If the customer tells me what software their tax adviser uses, I will find the relevant specifications myself.

Best regards,
Anandi

WORD BANK

computer scientist – Informatiker(in)
configure (v) – konfigurieren
decision support system – Entscheidungsfindungssystem
interface – Schnittstelle, Interface

WORD BANK ◎

menu bar – Menüleiste
performant – leistungsfähig

12

NACH DIESEM MODUL:

- ✓ kann ich Arten schädlicher Software, Firewalls und Antivirusprogramme auf Englisch beschreiben,
- ✓ kann ich auf Englisch helfen, Einrichtungsprobleme von Firewalls zu beheben.

1

2

3

4

Computers in danger

Computers are everywhere today. Computerization has made many things faster and easier, but relying on computers can be dangerous, for instance when malware (software with malicious intent) comes into play.

1 Why might a hacker be interested in infiltrating the systems shown above?

2 Look at this list of systems. Discuss how your life could be affected if a hacker manipulated them successfully. Rate the systems (a. – j.) from 1 (It wouldn't affect me) to 10 (My life would be seriously affected).

a. Nuclear power plants
b. Military weapons systems
c. Telecommunication networks
d. Emergency services
e. Bank systems
f. Public transport
g. Power grids
h. Home computer networks
i. Public radio and TV networks
j. Navigation systems (GPS)

3 SAFETY FIRST ⚠
Put the jumbled safety measures into the correct order. Work in pairs and find other safety measures. Make a list.

1. use • Always • your password • letters • for • and digits
2. down • password • Never • write • your
3. frequently • programs • Update • security • your

A | Types of malware

Harmful applications called malware may wipe out information on your hard drive, block network traffic or simply spy on you. Nowadays the Internet has become the biggest distributor of malware.

WORD BANK

buffer overflow – Pufferüberlauf
infect (v) – infizieren
macro – kleiner Programmcode
redirect (v) – umleiten
self-replicate (v) – selbstreplizieren

1 Have you ever been a victim of malware? What happened?

P **2** Explain the five types of malware below in your own words.

Types of malware

1. **Virus:**
A computer virus may modify computer functions and can self-replicate. It requires a host program that executes infected files by the user.

2. **Trojan:**
A Trojan horse is a program that appears harmless but hides malicious functions. The user (un)consciously has to download and install an .exe file first.

3. **Worm:**
Spreading itself automatically through computer networks by e-mail, a computer worm does not require a host program to infect and manipulate systems.

4. **Denial of Service-Attack (DoS):**
A PC may deny its service or a server becomes unavailable when a network of infected computers trigger multiple requests addressing this system.

5. **Spyware:**
Spyware is often installed unintentionally and collects information on your Internet surfing habits and may redirect your Web browser activity.

R **3** Match the 'Top five digital menaces' with the types of malware above.

Top five digital menaces

a. **Top 1:**
"Storm worm": Via e-mail and fake links about weather disasters in 2007, curious users were fooled into downloading and installing a READ MORE.exe. It didn't show any news but the program sent spam mail across the Internet.

b. **Top 2:**
"Code Red": In 2011 this malware caused a buffer overflow on Win 2000 and NT systems that made them unavailable. Most seriously, all infected computers contacted the White House web server at the same time, overloading the machines by this distributed attack.

c. **Top 3:**
"I LOVE YOU": In the year 2000 ten percent of all Internet users fell victim to a catchy e-mail attachment called LOVE-LETTER-FOR-YOU.txt… that automatically turned into a malicious program that stole password information.

d. **Top 4:**
"Melissa": After opening a Word document that reached Office users, a macro initiated a self-replication of the file and automatically sent it to the top 50 people of a user's Outlook address book.

e. **Top 5:**
"CoolWebSearch": After an unintended drive-by installation, this program hijacked Web browsers by changing their homepages to coolwebsearch…com, spying on surfing habits and redirecting users to other websites.

4 Search the Internet for five more major computer menaces that have already occurred.

B | Remedies for computers in danger

Malware can be blocked by various firewalls. One tool can be a firewall program already integrated in the system software of the computer.

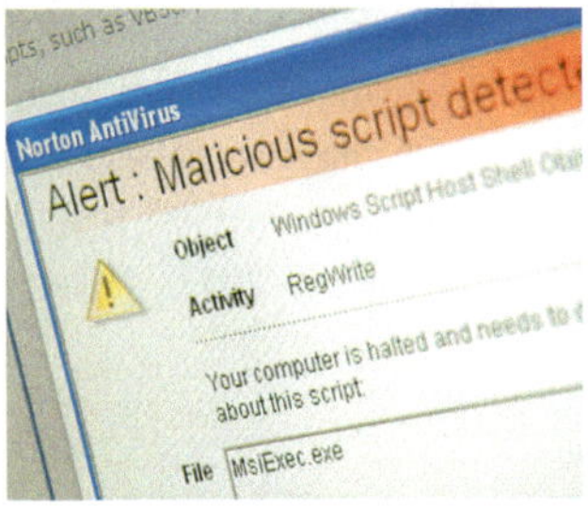

1 Ask your partner whether his / her computer has an integrated firewall. Report to the class.

R **2** ⊙ A 1.20 A customer enquires about firewall software. Listen to his phone call with a sales assistant and describe the assistant's first and second suggestions.

R **3** ⊙ A 1.20 Listen again. Make a list of the advantages and disadvantages of integrated firewalls.

I **4** Ask your partner which kind of firewall he / she would recommend for a) a home computer and b) for an office PC. Report to the class.

P **5** Use the phrases from the dialogue and write a similar enquiry in a dialogue.

→ **PHRASES:** Written communication

I **6** Study these different types of virus scanners that are available from Global Computers. Which features would your partner need at home or at work? Why?

Virus Scanners

Antivirus Edition	Standard	Professional	Small Business	Office Edition
System scanner (stops viruses, worms and trojan horses)	✓	✓	✓	✓
AntiAd/AntiPhishing (blocks unwanted pop-ups and spam)	✓	✓	✓	✓
PC speed tune-up (boots your PC more quickly)	✓	✓	–	–
Parental Time-limit Control (monitors children's Internet access time)	–	✓	–	–
Disaster recovery (backs up data)	–	✓	✓	✓
Real time virus scanner (monitors PC's activities permanently)	–	✓	✓	✓
Personal firewall	–	✓	–	✓
Restrictive URL Filter (blocks access to inappropriate websites)	–	–	✓	✓
Real time support	–	–	–	✓
Mail server protection (scans all incoming and outgoing mails)	–	–	✓	✓
File server protection (supports Windows, Linux and Novell servers)	–	–	–	✓
→ Price per license	29.99 $	49.99 $	129.99 $	149.99 $

R **7** Decide which version provides the best value for the following users:

1. users who want to restrict their daughter's use in social networks
2. users who want to restrict their staff's internet use
3. users whose computers are already infected by a virus and need help immediately
4. users who share data on a server and need to speed up their PC(s)
5. users who exchange mail professionally but are in need of a firewall

I **8** Make a telephone enquiry using the phrases for an enquiry and role cards A and B in the Appendix. Act out the role play.

C | Setting up a firewall

1 UNDERSTANDING TECHNICAL ENGLISH

While using a software firewall the following error message appeared. Rewrite the message in plain, understandable English using suitable grammar and vocabulary.

> **Error**
>
> Lest you modify Firewall regulations Internet circulation will be blocked due to disagreeing rule politics.

WORD BANK

deny access (v) – Zugriff verbieten
import (v) – importieren
phishing – Identitätsdiebstahl
recovery – Wiederherstellung
restrictive – eingeschränkt, restriktiv
shield (v) – abschirmen, schützen

WORD BANK ⊚

configure (v) – aufbauen, gestalten, konfigurieren
on board – integriert

M **2** KMK III **Die Software Firewall GuardD soll auf dem deutschen Markt angeboten werden. Vorab sind Sie beauftragt worden, Auszüge aus dem Benutzerhandbuch zu übersetzen. Zur Vorbereitung dieser Aufgabe machen Sie sich Notizen zu dem nachfolgenden Abschnitt in deutscher Sprache (in ganzen Sätzen).**

Firewall rules control how Firewall GuardD shields your computer from malicious programs and unauthorized access. All traffic that comes in or out of your computer is permanently checked against these rules by the firewall. Two kinds of firewall rules can be distinguished and both kinds of rules can be enabled at the same time:

Program rule: Supervises network access for programs on your PC.
General rule: Supervises all the incoming and outgoing network traffic.

Firewall GuardD processes General rules before it processes Program rules. Consider the situation when there is a Program rule that allows your Internet browser to access the Internet using port 80 with TCP protocol and a customized General rule that blocks TCP communication via port 80 for all applications. In this particular case, the browser application cannot contact the Internet as long as the Firewall Guard gives precedence to customized General Rules over Program rules.
Within the list of General rules, rules are processed according to their order of appearance, from top to bottom. That means rules that appear higher in the list override the rules appearing lower in the list. Program control entries are not processed in order. The rules within each Program control entry, however, are processed in order of their appearance, from top to bottom. The key to shielding your system and still enjoying flexibility is done by shifting individual rules to the top. The 'Default' setting for Program rules is to deny all access attempts by the user's programs.That is why it is advisable to modify all rules before first use:

> Settings window > click 'Network' Tap > click 'Advanced Setting' > click 'Modify' General Rules pane (left) > check 'Default General Rules' box > OK.

> Settings window > click 'Network' Tap > click 'Advanced Setting' > click 'Modify' Program Rules pane (right) > customize 'Program Rules' → check 'Allow' for each Program rule → uncheck 'Import previous rules' > OK.

NOTE:
The firewall settings for programs are automatically imported from previous versions of Firewall GuardD.

P **3** KMK III **Als Programmierer von GuardD sollen Sie einem Kunden erklären, warum die Verbindung von Programmen mit dem Internet eingeschränkt sein kann. Geben Sie Hinweise zur Lösung des Problems.**

13

NACH DIESEM MODUL:

- ✓ kann ich Regeln im internationalen Kundenkontakt anwenden und auf unterschiedliche Kundentypen eingehen,
- ✓ kann ich einige Strategien zur Fehlerfindung und -behebung auf Englisch benennen.

Customer support

Providing support to customers requires not only good communication skills, but also experience with the software and hardware in use.

I **1** What trend in customer support is shown in the photo above? Discuss its pros and cons in class.

P **2** Describe two examples of customer support you have experienced. Explain why you were satisfied / unsatisfied.

I **3** There are different ways of getting support. List advantages and disadvantages of these ways on a separate sheet of paper as shown in the example below.

	1. Telephone support	2. Internet forums	3. On site service support	4. Written correspondence	5. Friends
+		*quick answers*			
–	*long wait period*				*make things worse*

4 Unscramble the definitions of two other ways of giving support.

1. User manuals • guides • that • with • new products • come along • are • written
2. Remote desktop applications • to remote control • allow • via • a computer • a network

A | Saying the right things on the phone

Successful communication is all about using the right tone and language. Other important factors include what you are talking about and the person you are talking to.

I **1** Brainstorm behaviour that a.) creates or b.) destroys a relaxing atmosphere. Check with your partner afterwards and report to the class.

R **2** Match the jumbled rules for successful communication with the consequences.

Rules for successful communication on the phone:	Konsequenzen für das Gespräch:
1. Say good-bye politely and ask if the caller has any further questions. 2. After the description of the problem ask close-ended follow-up questions, which can be answered with "yes" or "no". 3. Repeat the content of what the customer has explained. 4. Do not interrupt the customer during his/her description of the problem. 5. Listen actively to the customer during his/her description of the problem. 6. Determine what the customer knows about computers in a sensitive manner. 7. Ask for permission to transfer the customer to an expert. 8. Address the customer with his/her name.	a. Der Kunde erkennt durch das Weiterleiten an einen Experten Ihr Interesse an der Problemlösung. b. Die Klärung der Computerkenntnisse wird bei der Problemlösung helfen. c. Der Kunde wird Sie in guter Erinnerung behalten. d. Durch die Ansprache mit dem Namen entsteht eine persönliche Beziehung. e. Den Kunden ausreden lassen verhindert Spannungen und zeigt Respekt. f. Durch die Wiederholung des Gesagten kann überprüft werden, ob die Nachricht richtig verstanden wurde. g. Durch geschlossene Fragen erhält man spezifische Informationen. h. Rückfragen können durch aktives Zuhören vermieden werden.

M **3** Translate the consequences above (a.–h.) into English.

I **4** Giving support over the telephone follows certain phases, such as:

1. Greeting the customer
2. Determining the problem
3. Solving the problem
4. Finishing the call

Discuss which of the communication rules as described in task 2 apply to which phase (1.–4.).

5 Check the Internet and find further rules for effective telephone communication.

R **6** Listen to a podcast from a communications expert. Describe his main advice in English.
A 1.21

R **7** Listen again. Describe the types of customers mentioned and how to deal with them.
A 1.21

B | Troubleshooting and troubleshooting software

Troubleshooting is the process of searching for and solving problems. In the field of IT this is often aided by specialized software designed to speed up the process.

I **1** Make a survey in class. Find out how many people have had problems with any of the items from the list below in the last year. Discuss the problems in class.

A. Hardware:	B. Software:	C. Network:
Input/Output devices	System software	Internet
System devices	Application software	Other networks

2 Complete the following descriptions using the words from the box below.

newsgroups · settings · scratch · functionality · application · record · outcome · symptoms · cables · cause · trial and error · peer · components

Troubleshooting strategies

"At first it is essential that you <u>find out</u> what is actually going wrong. Gather information and keep a **1** of all **2**." Once you have understood the problem, <u>set up</u> an action plan. Here you decide which steps you will take and the expected **3** of each step. Next you should <u>narrow down</u> the **4** of the problem by using **5** methods. Simply exchanging some **6** might <u>work out</u> but very often it is necessary to rebuild the system from **7**. Make sure that all **8** are connected properly before switching on the machine! If it is a software issue, you can attempt to reproduce the symptom by using another **9** with similar **10**. <u>Pick out</u> the best solution for your problem by testing different **11** in the application or by choosing the most suitable device. If you can't <u>sort out</u> the problem after all, don't despair. <u>Check out</u> online forums or **12** that offer **13** support for common problems.

3 Now replace the underlined phrasal verbs above with the words in the box.

try · develop · choose · limit · solve · be successful · investigate

M **4** Write a short note in German informing your boss about QuickView.

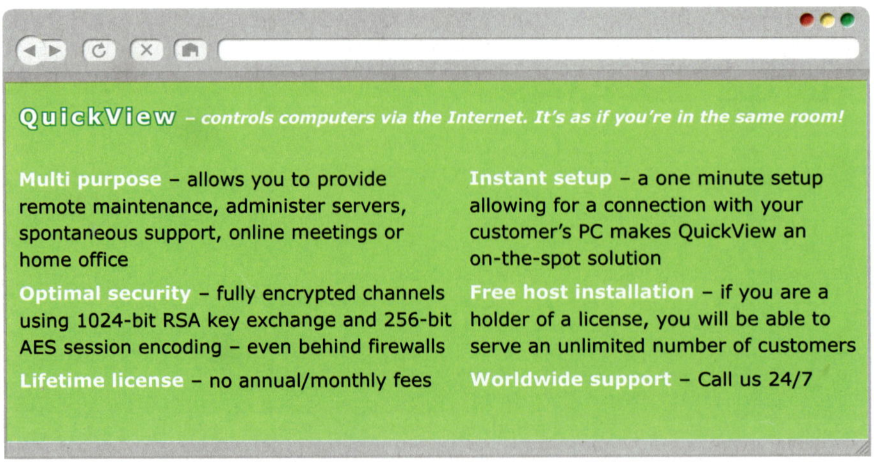

C | Intercultural communication

In all forms of business, intercultural communication involves adapting your communication style to your business partner.

I **1** Discuss how Germans tend to behave in greetings, general communication or when taboos are mentioned. Which specific feature might be peculiar to foreigners?

M **2** KMK III Ihr Chef bittet Sie, folgenden Internetartikel für Ihn tabellarisch auf Deutsch zusammenfassen. Gehen Sie dabei schwerpunktmäßig auf die Punkte „Treffen und Begrüßungen", „Kommunikationsweise" und „Tabus" ein.

A Guide to Intercultural Customer Communication

A. North America Greetings may be quite casual and often only the first name is used in introductions. A firm handshake upon greeting and leaving is standard – an embrace is only custom among good friends. Usually smiling and small talk questions, e.g. "How was your flight?" are common ways of breaking the ice and establishing a promising relationship. Your business partners are said to be direct and to the point which may be seen as rude and aggressive. Speaking about problems directly ("That's not the right way!") is seen as an efficient way to get things done. Avoid jumping in queues, close body contact and if you get into a conversation, stay away from topics such as sex, war, or terrorism.

B. Asia When it comes to meeting and greeting give a handshake accompanied with a nod or even a bow, but avoid touching. Also, you should be well dressed and arrive on time. Let your highest ranked representative make the presentation by mentioning name, position and title. The exchange of business cards should be acknowledged and treated with respect (never write on a card you have received!). During your communication use formal titles and be aware that your business partner has a reputation of being 'indirect'. This often means that wishes are expressed discreetly by respectful phrases. When talking to Asian partners, saying "No" is something to avoid as it can cause embarrassment and a loss of face. A "No" is often expressed by "Yes, probably". Taboos you should avoid are a prolonged eye contact, close body contact and talking about issues such as politics and human rights.

C. The Middle East Customary meeting and greeting situations involve a handshake along with a hearty smile and eye contact. However, once a relationship has developed it is common to kiss on one cheek and then the other even between persons of the same sex. Also, during communication be aware that touching among members of the same sex is common and moving away is a sign of distance. When speaking you might encounter not only deep eye contact, but also a long-winded and flattering language which is expected to be returned as a sign of great respect. This all means that discussions can take a long time, so patience is necessary. Gift giving is a very common and effective way of establishing a good relationship. But be careful! Small gifts should respect religious conventions. When making conversation, avoid religious topics or comments on the situation in the Middle East.

I **3** Do you agree with the texts? Are they helpful or do they just enforce prejudices and stereotypes? Discuss in class.

WORD BANK

AES – Advanced Encryption Standard
encrypted – verschlüsselt
newsgroup – Nachrichtenforum
remote maintenance – Fernwartung
troubleshooting – Fehlersuche und Fehlerbehebung

V1 Company tour

lingua tv
we watch languages!

Before watching

1. Describe the photo.
2. Who do you think the men in the picture are?

While watching

3. Watch the film and find out the following:
   a. the number of countries SAND Machinery delivers to.
   b. the names of three departments that the men have visited.
   c. the number of people who work for the company.
   d. whether SAND Machinery has other sites and if so, where they are.
4. Watch the film again and answer the questions.
   a. What will Mr Kramer's main tasks be during the internship?
   b. What is made at the company's production site?

After watching

5. Explain the sentences from the clip in your own words.
   a. "I'm eager to get in and get my feet wet."
   b. "… around the globe, around the clock."

V2 Telephoning

lingua tv
we watch languages!

Before watching

1. Describe the photo.

While watching

2. What problem does Ralf have at the beginning of the call?
3. Watch the film again and answer the questions.
   a. Who is calling?
   b. Who does he want to speak to?
   c. What is the purpose of his call?
   d. Why can Ralf's boss not contact the caller until the 15th of the month?
4. Find out the following technical information about the vehicle in question:
   a. the engine size
   b. the top speed
   c. the distance that can be travelled on a single charge.

After watching

5. Use the information in parts 3 and 4 to write a short memo for Ralf's boss explaining who called and what the call was about, and giving other key information.
6. How does Ralf handle the phone call? Discuss what he did well and what he could improve.

V 3 Job interview

lingua tv – we watch languages!

Before watching

1. Describe the photo.

While watching

2. Write down three of the questions that the interviewer asks.
3. Watch the film again and answer the questions.
   a. What is the applicant's name?
   b. What position is he applying for?
   c. What position did the applicant hold in his last job?
   d. According to the applicant, what is his greatest strength?
   e. What is the applicant's weakness?
   f. What questions does the applicant ask the interviewer?

After watching

4. Do you think the applicant will get the job? Give reasons for your answer.

V 4 Technical support

lingua tv – we watch languages!

While watching

1. What does 'rebooting the system' mean?
2. Watch the video again and decide whether the following statements are true or false.
   a. The caller cannot connect to the Internet.
   b. He has been having problems for two days now.
   c. He has tried rebooting the system.
   d. Turning the modem on and off did not help the problem.
   e. The scanner is not connected to the caller's computer.
   f. The technical support employee is unable to solve the problem with the scanner.

After watching

3. Make a list of problems that employees may have with their computers.
4. Record the call by copying the headings onto a sheet of paper and filling in the information.

   Name of caller • Problem(s) • Solution(s) • Further action necessary: Yes/No

V 5 Waste – the future's most valuable resource

2DF.enterprises

Before watching

1. What things do you recycle every day, and how?
2. How many different waste bins does your city or community provide per household?

While watching

3. Watch the film and find out the following information:
   a. How many tons of rubbish does Germany produce each year?
   b. What nations are eager to pay for our rubbish?
   c. What metal is particularly desirable for recycling?

4. Watch the film again and answer the following questions:
   a. How many tons of copper were stolen in Germany?
   b. How much heat can one ton of residual waste produce?

After watching

5. Explain these phrases/sentences from the film in your own words.
   a. “modern urban warfare”
   b. “Our waste is getting a second lease on life.”

V 6 Pipe inspection

2DF.enterprises

Before watching

1. What do pipelines transport?

While watching

2. Watch the film and find out the following information:
   a. What is the inspection device called?
   b. How long is it?
   c. How fast does the device travel?
   d. How many days does it take to inspect 300 km of pipeline?

3. Watch the film again and answer the following questions:
   a. Where are the data analyzed?
   b. How accurate is the data grid?
   c. What does the device use to identify defects?

After watching

4. What may cause defects in or damage to pipelines?

V7 High voltage work

ZDF.enterprises

Before watching

1. What do you think the men in the steel basket are preparing to do?

While watching

2. Watch the film and find out the following:
   a. what weather conditions are necessary for repairing overhead power lines.
   b. how many volts of electricity high-voltage lines carry.
   c. how the repairmen get to the damaged lines.
   d. what safety measures are taken.

3. Watch the film again and answer the following questions:
   a. How long does the job shown in the film take?
   b. Where is the electricity switched off and on?

After watching

4. Why is it important that the men work quickly?
5. Explain in your own words: "A power cut can quickly bring an entire city to its knees."

V8 Ras Laffan

ZDF.enterprises

While watching

1. Watch the film and find out the following:
   a. where Ras Laffan is located.
   b. what is processed there.
   c. how much is processed each year.
   d. how large the Ras Laffan industrial region is.

2. Watch the film again and answer the following:
   a. What problems do the construction workers face?
   b. How is the concrete cooled, and why?
   c. Why is the gas cooled?

After watching

3. Explain the phrase "liquid gold".

V9 Pipelines

ZDF.enterprises

Before watching

1. Name some things which are transported in pipelines.

While watching

2. Watch the film and find out the following:
   a. what alloy is popular for making long-distance pipelines.
   b. how thick are the steel plates that are formed into round pipes.
   c. the welding technique used in the factory shown.
   d. what the expander is for.

3. Watch the film again and answer the following:
   a. What conditions do offshore pipelines have to cope with?
   b. Why do they have an additional outer casing of concrete?

After watching

4. Explain why quality-control checks are important in the production of pipelines.

V10 Robots in the hospital

ZDF.enterprises

While watching

1. Watch the film and find out the following:
   a. What hospital is shown as an example? Which parts of the hospital do we see?
   b. How many robots do they have?
   c. What powers the robot couriers and how do they navigate?
   d. What is a 'lift-and-tunnel system'?

2. Watch the film again and answer these questions:
   a. What metal in the plates keeps the food warm?
   b. Do the robots distribute the food to the patients?
   c. How many containers are used to transport food?
   d. How does the hospital director feel about using robots to transport patients?

After watching

3. What else do you think the robots transport in the hospital?
4. Where else might transportation robots be used?

V11 Portable power stations

BBC Motion Gallery

Before watching

1. Think of situations in which a portable power station like the one in the photo could be useful.

While watching

2. Watch the film and list the uses of electrical power 'out in the open' that the reporter mentions.

3. Watch the film again and answer the following:
   a. What supplies the power for the 12-volt portable power station?
   b. Why are batteries not such a good choice?
   c. Where was the portable power station invented?

After watching

4. Do you think the inventor will be able to sell his power station in Germany? Where might the need for it be greater?

V12 Car speed control

BBC Motion Gallery

Before watching

1. What speed limit is acceptable
   a. on city streets?
   b. on the motorway?

While watching

2. Watch the film and find out the following:
   a. how many people die in road accidents in the UK every year.
   b. what the MIRA is working on.
   c. what the satellite positioning system does.

3. Watch the film again and answer the following:
   a. Is speed control popular with car manufacturers? Why or why not?
   b. Do speed cameras have any effect on driving habits?
   c. How is the speed-control system being tested?

After watching

4. Would you buy a car with a speed-control system? Give reasons for your answer.

KMK-Prüfungssätze (Stufe II und III)

Sie arbeiten für die Firma *RestAssured*, einem internationalen Beratungsunternehmen mit dem Spezialbereich Netzwerksicherheit und Datenrettung.

1 Hörverstehen / Rezeption (Anrufbeantworter) **8 VP**

⊙ A 6.4 **Ihr Vorgesetzter bittet Sie, den folgenden Anruf abzuhören und ihm folgende Fragen auf Deutsch zu beantworten. Sie hören die Aufzeichnung zweimal.**

1. Wer ist der Anrufer, was für eine Firma vertritt er und welche Funktion übt er bei seiner Firma aus? *(1 VP)*
2. Was ist der Anlass für die Nachricht? *(1 VP)*
3. Warum kann Ihr Kunde den Angriff nicht selbst untersuchen? *(1 VP)*
4. Was erwartet der Anrufer von Ihrer Firma? *(1 VP)*
5. Wie ist der Name des Mitarbeiters, den der Anrufer schicken wird und was wird er mitbringen? *(1 VP)*
6. Nennen Sie die Flugdaten. *(1 VP)*
7. Worum bittet der Anrufer Ihre Firma in Bezug auf den Mitarbeiter? *(1 VP)*
8. Gibt der Anrufer Ihrer Firma die Schuld an dem Vorfall bzw. was ist seine Erklärung für den Vorfall? *(1 VP)*

2 Hörverstehen / Rezeption **12 VP**

⊙ A 6.5 **Ihr Vorgesetzter, Herr Lindenmüller, hat einen englischsprachigen Podcast heruntergeladen und ihn nicht ganz verstanden. Beantworten Sie bitte seine Fragen:**

1. Welche Ports werden laut Podcast einfach durch Konvention festgelegt und welche Funktion haben sie? *(1 VP)*
2. Was leistet das Netfilter-System von Linux? *(2 VP)*
3. Was genau leisten die *iptables*? *(2 VP)*
4. Wie konfigurieren die User die Firewall? *(2 VP)*
5. Welche fünf Front-Ends werden angeboten und was leisten sie? *(5 VP)*

3 Produktion **30 VP**

Das Material Ihres englischen Kunden ist inzwischen eingetroffen und Ihr Team hat es sich sofort angesehen. Herr Lindenmüller bittet Sie, noch vor der endgültigen Auswertung eine E-Mail an Mr. Lassiter zu schicken.
Schreiben Sie, dass Ihr Team die Protokolldateien teilweise wiederherstellen konnte. Jedoch waren viele Datenblöcke auf der Festplatte nicht wiederherzustellen. Eine Analyse mit den firmeneigenen Tools ist nicht möglich. Sie werden diese Analyse nun per Hand durchführen, was einige Zeit dauern kann. Schreiben Sie, dass Sie den zeitlichen Ablauf der Attacke zusammenfassen werden und hoffen, auf folgende Fragen eine Antwort geben zu können:

- Wann begann der Angriff?
- Wie erhielt der Angreifer Zugriff zum Netzwerk?
- War es tatsächlich eine Sicherheitslücke, an der Ihre Firma die Schuld trägt?
- Auf welche Daten wurde zugegriffen?

Unterzeichnen Sie mit Ihrem Namen als Herrn Lindenmüllers Assistent(in).

4 Mediation

30 VP

Wie in der E-Mail versprochen, untersuchen Sie die Protokolldatei nach folgenden Fragestellungen:

- Wie ist der zeitliche Ablauf, wann begann der Angriff?
- Wie erhielt der Angreifer Zugriff zum Netzwerk?
- War es tatsächlich eine Sicherheitslücke an der Ihre Firma die Schuld trägt?
- Auf welche Daten wurde zugegriffen?

Hinweis:
Sie dürfen zwischen folgenden beiden Varianten als Aufgabenstellung wählen.

Variante 1: **Schreiben Sie die Antworten auf diese Fragestellungen stichwortartig auf Deutsch für Herrn Lindenmüller. Dieser Abschlussbericht soll die Grundlage für sein Schreiben an Herrn Lassiter sein.**

Variante 2: **Schreiben Sie die Antworten auf diese Fragestellungen stichwortartig auf Englisch als Hilfestellung für Herrn Lindenmüllers E-Mail an den Kunden.**

02:35:17	Incoming connection from 84.220.256.101
02:45:18	Connection accepted
02:46:43	Logon Request for User root, Password root
02:46:44	Bad username or password, logon request denied
02:47:22	Logon Request for User root, Password toor
02:47:23	Bad username or password, logon request denied
02:47:58	Logon Request for User root, Password god
02:47:59	Bad username or password, logon request denied
02:48:37	Logon Request for User guest, Password guest
02:48:38	Bad username or password, logon request denied
02:49:01	Logon Request for User debug, Password debug
02:49:02	Bad username or password, logon request denied
02:49:03 – 03:01:45	Data missing or corrupted
03:01:46	Security system engaged, reason: too many bad usernames or password requests from 84.220.30.101, blacklisting 84.220.256.101, connection terminated
03:01:47	initiating 5 min security lockdown, accepting no connections for 5 minutes
03:01:48 – 03:05:48	IDLE
03:06:30	Incoming connection from 84.220.256.101
03:06:31	Connection refused, reason: connection source matches blacklist entry
03:10:11	Incoming connection from 82.198.40.256
03:10:12	Connection accepted
03:10:23	Malformed / illegal packet received on port 80 from 82.198.40.256, packet dropped
03:10:27	Malformed / illegal packet received on port 8080 from 82.198.40.256, packet dropped

▶

03:10:34 Malformed / illegal packet received on port 3128 from 82.198.40.256, packet dropped
03:10:41 Malformed / illegal packet received on port 25 from 82.198.40.256, packet dropped
03:10:48 Malformed / illegal packet received on port 119 from 82.198.40.256, packet dropped
03:10:50 – 03:17:23 Data missing or corrupted
03:17:49 Security system engaged, possible buffer overflow / underrun or flooding attack detected, reason: too many malformed / illegal packets received from 82.198.40.256, blacklisting 82.198.40.256, connection terminated
03:17:50 initiating 5 min security lockdown, accepting no connections for 5 minutes
03:17:51 – 03:22:50 IDLE
03:22:58 Incoming HTML request from 86.256.173.68 for /webpages/staff/lassiter.html
03:35:55 Incoming connection from 86.256.173.68
03:35:56 Connection accepted
03:36:28 Logon Request for User lassiter, Password edward
03:36:29 Bad username or password, logon request denied
03:36:34 Logon Request for User lassiter, Password drawde
03:36:35 Bad username or password, logon request denied
03:36:42 Logon Request for User lassiter, Password edward1954
03:36:43 User lassiter logged on

User activity log lassiter commands issued during last session

```
cd home/lassiter
ls -al
cd currentprojects
ls -al
cd ..
tar -zcvf currentprojects.tar.gz currentprojects
ftp 86.256.173.68 user admin pass xxxxxxxx
upload /home/currentprojects.tar.gz     /homerun
download /homerun/tools/cleanerscript.sh
sh cleanerscript.sh
- LOGGING INTERRUPTED, REASON TIME OUT
```

5 Leseverständnis / Rezeption **20 VP**

Sie dürfen zwischen den Varianten 1 und 2 als Aufgabenstellung wählen.

Variante 1: **Sie erhalten immer wieder Kundenanfragen zur *Cloud*, dem von Internetfirmen progagierten Outsourcing der Speicherung von firmeneigenen Dateien im Netz.**

Folgender Text aus dem *Manchester Guardian* betrachtet die rechtliche Seite dieser Angelegenheit. Herr Lindenmüller hat folgende Fragen:

1. Welches rechtliche Problem gibt es, wenn Datenspeicherung ausgelagert wird?
2. Was tun beispielsweise US-Firmen und welche Konsequenzen können ihre Praktiken unter Umständen haben?
3. Wo sehen europäische Anwälte, vor allem Guillaume Seligmann von der Firma CVML, das Problem?
4. Welche sechs kritischen Punkte möchte die Firma CVML berücksichtigt wissen?

Catching the Cloud

How to guarantee the safety of your data in the cloud

A growing number of companies and individuals handle their data to a remote infrastructure offering little hope of any legal leverage. The Cloud is the ultimate form of the outsourcing cascade. A US-based company rents capacity wherever electric power is cheap, connections reliable, and climate friendly to server farms cooling towers. [...] Data centres are sprinkled over a number of countries and workload moves from one server farm to another as capacity management dictates. At this point, no company knows for sure where its data reside. This raises further legal hurdles as Cloud operators might be tempted to deploy data centres in less stable but cheaper countries with even looser contractual protections.

European lawyers are beginning to look at better ways to protect their clients' interests. [...] I discussed the legal implications of cloud computing with Guillaume Seligmann, the lead tech attorney at the law firm Cotty Vivant Marchisio Lauzeral. [...] "When it comes to cloud computing, the relationship between the service provider and the customer is by nature asymmetrical," he says. "The former has thousands if not millions of customers and limited liability; in case of litigation, it will have entire control over elements of proof. [...] The customer bears the risk of having his service interrupted, his data lost or corrupted – when not retained by the supplier, or accessed by third parties and government agencies."

In theory, the contract is the first line of defense. "It is, except there is usually little room for negotiation on contracts engineered by expert American attorneys, based on US legislation and destined to be handled by US judges. Our conclusion is that solely relying on contracts is largely insufficient because it may not offer efficient means of sanctioning breaches in the agreement."

The CVML partner then laid out six critical elements to be implemented in European legislation. These would legally supersede US contractual terms and, as a result, better protect European customers.

1 / Transparency. Guillaume Seligmann suggests a set of standard indicators pertaining to service availability, backup arrangements and pricing – like in the banking industry for instance. [...]

2 / Incident notifications. Today, unless he is directly affected, the customer learns about outages from specialised media, rarely though a ▶

detailed notification from the service provider. Again, says Seligmann, the cloud operator should have the obligation to report in greater details all incidents as well as steps taken to contain damage. This would allow the customer to take all measures required to protect his business operations.
3 / Data restitution. On this crucial matter, most contracts remain vague. In many instances, the customer wanting to terminate his contract and to get back his precious data, will get a large dump of raw data, sometimes in the provider's proprietary format. "That's unacceptable", says the attorney. "The customer should have the absolute guarantee that, […] he has the right to get the latest backed-up version of his data, presented in a standard format immediately useable by another provider." […]
4 / Control and certification. Foreign-headquartered companies […] create a chain fraught with serious hazards. The only way to mitigate risks is to give customers the ability to monitor at all times the facility hosting their data. Probably not the easiest to implement for confidentiality and security reasons. At least, says Guillaume Seligmann, any Cloud provider should be certified by a third party entity in the same way many industries […] get certifications and ratings from specialized agencies […].
5 / Governing laws. […] According to Seligmann's proposal, the end-user should have the option to take his case before his own national court and the local judge should have the power to order really effective remedies. […]
6 / Enforceability. The credibility of the points stated above depends on their ability to supersede and to render ineffective conflicting contractual terms imposed by the service provider. In that respect, the European Union is well armed to impose such constraints, as it already did on personal data protection. In the US, imposing the same rules might be a different story. […]

From www.guardian.co.uk, Monday 18 July 2011; text by Frédéric Filloux.

***Variante 2:* Soziale Netzwerke interessieren Sie und Ihre Kollegen besonders. Im Urlaub in Irland haben Sie folgenden Artikel gelesen. Ihre Kollegen stellen sehr kritische Fragen bezüglich solcher Netzwerke. Beantworten Sie folgende Fragen auf Deutsch.**

1. Welches sind die eher positiven, welches die negativen Seiten von Twitter und ähnlichen sozialen Netzwerken? *(2 VP)*
2. Wie sah die rechtliche Situation bei sozialen Netzwerken insgesamt im letzten Jahr aus? *(2 VP)*
3. Die Beschwerden gegen Twitter sind zwar geringer als gegenüber anderen sozialen Netzwerken, aber wie sieht die Prognose hier aus? *(2 VP)*
4. Welcher Fragestellung und welchen neuen Problemen sieht sich die Polizei gegenüber? *(2 VP)*
5. Wie verhält sich Twitter gegenüber Menschen, die auf dieser Webseite verunglimpft werden? *(3 VP)*
6. Inwiefern stellen die Ratschläge von Twitter kaum eine Lösung für die Betroffenen dar? *(3 VP)*

7. Wie ist dagegen die Reaktion von Twitter, sobald dessen Geschäftspartner angegriffen werden? Geben Sie auch das Beispiel aus dem Text wieder. *(4 VP)*
8. Welche Konsequenzen hat nach Ansicht der Psychologin Maria Gardner die Anonymität auf solchen Seiten für das Verhalten der User? *(2 VP)*

The dark side of Twitter

This is the dark side of Twitter. Beloved by celebrities and ordinary people alike, the site has become part of the daily life of tens of millions of users around the globe. Yet along with the useful, informative and banal come also the hurtful, libellous and down-right illegal. Last year in Britain at least 14,000 alleged crimes specifically linked to social media are estimated to have been reported to police. Stuart Hyde, the chief constable of Cumbria constabulary and spokesman on e-crime for the Association of Chief Police Officers, said his force dealt with "around 700 offences where Facebook is the primary location" last year and that across the country the figure would be at least 20 times greater.

Complaints of abuse on Twitter were far fewer but are growing, and Hyde said he "would not rule out" the possibility the amount of crime carried out on the site would eventually overtake Facebook if it continued to grow at an exponential rate.

This social media explosion poses new challenges for the police and the legal system alike, which are struggling to keep up with the realities of the information age.

Should more police be taken off the street and made to walk the virtual beat? And are our existing laws adequate to deal with the cyberbullies once they have been caught?

And what of Twitter itself? As the provider of the platform on which such messages are carried, should it not be doing much more to monitor what is said within the confines of those 140 characters? [...]

The company takes a [...] robust view of those who complain it should do more to police the hurtful and sometimes defamatory or illegal comments that permeate the Twittersphere.

"As a policy, we do not mediate comment, including potentially offensive comment," it said in a statement. "We understand that everyone has different levels of sensitivity towards content ... If there is something you don't agree with, or find insulting, it's best to block that user."

Which, of course, is only a partial solution for those who find themselves in such a situation: while you may no longer be able to see the "offensive" things being written about you, everybody else still can – unless you embark on a further course of trying to prove abusive behaviour.

This laissez-faire approach has not prevented Twitter from intervening in defence of its "corporate partners": the site became embroiled in controversy last week after suspending the account of a California-based British journalist who had criticised the American network NBC's coverage of the Olympics and tweeted the email address of one of NBC's presidents.

▶

Although Twitter reinstated the account – after it was pointed out the address was a corporate one already in the public domain – the damage was done, especially since it later transpired Twitter had tipped off NBC and encouraged it to complain.
"One of the appeals of Twitter is its anonymity," said Maria Gardner, a psychologist and senior consultant at Criterion Partnership, who advises jobseekers on how to manage their exposure on social media.
"People use it almost like a stream of consciousness and this can lead to them sometimes being very funny, sometimes boring and sometimes offensive. Also, because the people they are communicating with on the site are in some ways dehumanised for them, they sometimes say things that they would not say if the person was sitting in front of them."

(580 words)

From The Sunday Times *(Ireland), August 5, 2012, Excerpt from the article "Tweet This! Is it Time to Tame Twitter" by Kevin Dowling and John Harlow; thesundaytimes.ie/news.*

Role cards

Module 9 Writing software, B 4

→ **PHRASES:** Telephoning

Speaker A

Jessica / Chester Adams places a call to Intelsio Software Solutions in Pforzheim to complain about the fact that an update that was to be released yesterday has not been made available for download yet. He / she is very angry. He / she accuses Intelsio of putting bugs into the software on purpose so people have to depend on them for updates. He / she says that the company is only interested in saving money and increasing profits and does not spend enough time and effort on testing and quality control. He / she believes that the company only fixes bugs if the number of people affected is large enough. He / she demands to know when the update will be available, because the problems are affecting his / her work. He / she apologizes for being so angry at first and thanks the other person for offering to call when the update is ready.

Module C Telephoning, B 3

→ **PHRASES:** Telephoning

Speaker A

Give your partner the following information:

1. The room is 54 m^2.
2. The wire needs to be 128.5 cm long.
3. The doors are 80 cm x 220 cm.
4. Each of the components weighs around 0.75 kg.

Module 11 Enterprise software, B 4

→ **PHRASES:** Telephoning

Speaker A

Lisa / Sam Horton from Entex Medical Supplies in Leeds receives a call. Prepare and act out the call using the key words and ideas.

1. answer phone
2. explain / now not the best time
3. interested in software / but busy
4. request / demonstration / new software / next week
5. will mail caller / time and date / for appointment
6. thank / caller

Module C Telephoning, B 3

→ **PHRASES:** Telephoning

Speaker B

Give your partner the following information:
1. The table is 2 m x 3 m.
2. The engine runs at 7500 rpm.
3. 220 V sockets are standard in Germany.
4. The customer would like the work surface to be 24 mm thick.

Module 12 Computers in danger, B 8

Speaker B

Salesman, Mr. Dyson is the general sales manager of Global Computers in Berlin.
1. He offers the customer two business products that meet his needs.
2. For the cheaper product there is a discount for a purchase of 15 licenses.
3. For the more expensive product there is a discount of $ 50 for each of the ten licenses.
4. He asks for the name and email address.

Module 9 Writing software, B 4

→ **PHRASES:** Telephoning

Speaker B

Michaela / Michael Haubert at Intelsio Software Solutions in Pforzheim receives a call. He / she apologizes for the fact that the update is not available yet. He / she is very patient with the caller and explains that the constant changes in the world of IT make it very difficult to create software that is absolutely bug free. He / she explains that they plan and model their software very thoroughly. He/she says that they also take testing and quality very seriously and that they care about every one of their customers. He / she tells the caller that they are sorry for the inconvenience and that the update should be ready to download in three hours. He / she thanks the caller for the feedback and promises to call as soon as the update is ready.

Module 11 Enterprise software, B 4

→ **PHRASES:** Telephoning

Speaker B

Michael / Michaela Schlüter from KP Systeme calls Entex Medical Supplies in Leeds.

Prepare and act out the call using the key words and ideas.

1. give name / name of company
2. want to talk about new business software / understand if an inconvenient time
3. offer / send / most important details by email
4. agree / demonstrate new software
5. agree
6. thank / person

Module 12 Computers in danger, B 8

Speaker A

Customer Mr Riley is the manager of Travels4you.de, a German start-up company.

1. He needs help to recover data after a virus hit the company network.
2. He also needs a tool to make the Internet use by his staff safer and to avoid viruses.
3. He needs software for at least 10 PCs.
4. He wants the cheapest software possible.
5. He asks for quantity discounts and the final price.

Phrases

A | Meeting people

Formal greetings	Formelle Begrüßung
Good morning / afternoon / evening, Ms Robinson / Mr Jones.	Guten Morgen / Tag / Abend, Frau Robinson / Herr Jones.
Good morning / afternoon / evening, ladies and gentlemen.	Guten Morgen / Tag / Abend, meine Damen und Herren.
Informal greetings	**Informelle Begrüßung**
Good morning, Susan / James.	Guten Morgen, Susan / James.
Hi / Hello / Morning, Karl.	Tag / Morgen, Karl.
Hi everybody!	Tag zusammen!
Formal goodbyes	**Formelle Verabschiedung**
Goodbye! It's been nice / pleasant meeting you.	Auf Wiedersehen! Es war nett / angenehm, Sie kennen zu lernen!
Thank you for your help / your time. Let's keep in touch.	Danke für Ihre Hilfe / Ihre Zeit. Wir bleiben in Kontakt.
Informal goodbyes	**Informelle Verabschiedung**
Bye!	Tschüss / Ciao!
See you later!	Bis später!
See you around!	Wir sehen uns!
See you tomorrow / on Monday / next week!	Bis morgen / Montag / nächste Woche!
Formal introduction	**Formelle Vorstellung**
May I introduce myself?	Darf ich mich vorstellen?
Hello, my name is / I'm Lukas Hansen from ATW Shipping.	Hallo, mein Name ist / ich heiße Lukas Hansen von ATW Shipping.
Pleased to meet you. / Nice to meet you. / How do you do?	Angenehm. / Sehr erfreut.
It's a pleasure to finally meet you in person.	Es freut mich sehr, Sie endlich einmal persönlich kennen zu lernen.
Informal introduction	**Informelle Vorstellung**
Hi. I'm Peter, Peter James.	Hi. Ich bin Peter, Peter James.
Hello, my name is Sarah O'Neill.	Hallo, ich heiße Sarah O'Neill.
Hi Sarah. Nice to meet you.	Hi Sarah. Freut mich, dich kennen zu lernen.

Introducing others (formal)	Andere miteinander bekannt machen (formell)
Have you met our managing director?	Haben Sie schon unsere Geschäftsführerin / unseren Geschäftsführer kennen gelernt?
Ms Hall? May I introduce you to Christian Eriksen, our new intern? Christian, Georgina Hall from our sales department.	Frau Hall? Darf ich Sie Christian Eriksen, unserem neuen Praktikanten, vorstellen? Christian, das ist Georgina Hall von unserer Verkaufsabteilung.
Introducing others (informal)	**Andere miteinander bekannt machen (informell)**
Here's someone I'd like you to meet.	Ich möchte euch gerne jemanden vorstellen.
Christian, this is Joe. Joe, Christian.	Christian, das ist Joe. Joe, das ist Christian.
Let me introduce you to the team.	Darf ich dich dem Team vorstellen?
Use of first names	**Verwendung von Vornamen**
Please call me Martin.	Bitte nennen Sie mich ruhig Martin.
My name's Marianne.	Ich heiße Marianne.
My first name's Andrew, but everybody calls me Andy.	Mein Vorname ist Andrew, aber alle nennen mich Andy.
May I call you Anna?	Darf ich Anna zu Ihnen sagen?

B | Your company

Introducing the company	Die Firma vorstellen
Our company was founded in 1997.	Unsere Firma wurde 1997 gegründet.
In 2005 we were taken over by ...	2005 wurden wir von ... übernommen.
We are a leading manufacturer of engines.	Wir sind ein führender Hersteller von Motoren.
We are a medium-sized family firm.	Wir sind ein mittelständisches Familienunternehmen.
We are a manufacturer of industrial cleaning machines specializing in high-pressure cleaners.	Wir sind ein Hersteller von industriellen Reinigungsgeräten und sind auf Hochdruckreiniger spezialisiert.
I work for a major construction company.	Ich arbeite bei einem bedeutenden Bauunternehmen.
We are a subsidiary of ...	Wir sind eine Tochtergesellschaft von ...
We are a chain of electronics suppliers.	Wir sind eine Kette von Elektronik-Anbietern.
Describing the company's products / services	**Die Produkte / Dienstleistungen der Firma beschreiben**
We offer sustainable solutions.	Wir bieten nachhaltige Lösungen an.
Our products are environmentally friendly.	Unsere Produkte sind umweltfreundlich.
Our products are well-known in Europe.	Unsere Produkte sind europaweit bekannt.
Our components are both reliable and long-lasting.	Unsere Komponenten sind zuverlässig und haben eine lange Lebensdauer.
Our software is adapted to suit your requirements.	Unsere Software wird Ihren Bedürfnissen angepasst.
We manufacture high-tech shock absorbers.	Wir stellen High-Tech-Stoßdämpfer her.
Our products are designed using the latest CAD technology.	Unsere Produkte werden mit der neuesten CAD-Technologie entworfen.

Describing the job	Den Beruf beschreiben
I'm training to become a …	Ich mache eine Lehre / Ausbildung zur / zum …
I am a bricklayer / carpenter / technician / plumber / joiner.	Ich bin Maurer(in), Zimmermann / Zimmerin, Techniker(in), Klempner(in), Schreiner(in).
I work in the automotive industry.	Ich arbeite in der Automobilindustrie.
I work with automated machines.	Ich arbeite mit automatisierten Maschinen.
Describing the workplace	**Den Arbeitsplatz beschreiben**
I work on an assembly line / a machine.	Ich arbeite am Fließband / an einer Maschine.
I work in a large warehouse / factory.	Ich arbeite in einem großen Warenlager / einer großen Fabrik.
I work in a garage / workshop.	Ich arbeite in einer Autowerkstatt / Werkstatt.
I work on a building site.	Ich arbeite auf einer Baustelle.
Talking about tasks and responsibilities	**Über Aufgaben und Zuständigkeiten sprechen**
I am responsible for programming the machines.	Ich bin für die Programmierung der Maschinen zuständig.
I report to the foreman.	Ich bin dem Meister / Vorarbeiter unterstellt.
I work shifts.	Ich mache Schichtarbeit.
I often have to do overtime.	Ich muss oft Überstunden machen.
I repair electrical devices.	Ich repariere elektrische Geräte.

C | Telephoning

1. Answering the phone	Sich am Telefon melden
Introducing yourself	**Sich vorstellen**
Smart EDV GmbH, good morning. Hendrik Klopp speaking.	Smart EDV GmbH, guten Morgen. Hendrik Klopp am Apparat.
Offering help	**Hilfe anbieten**
How may I help you? / Can I help you?	(Wie) kann ich Ihnen helfen?
What can I do for you?	Was kann ich für Sie tun?
Asking for details	**Nach Details fragen**
Who's calling, please?	Wer ist am Apparat, bitte?
May I / Can I ask who's calling, please?	Darf ich fragen, wer anruft?
May I / can I take your name, please?	Könnten Sie mir bitte Ihren Namen nennen?
Could you spell that please?	Könnten Sie das bitte buchstabieren?

Connecting	Verbinden
One moment, please. I'm putting you through now.	Einen Moment bitte, ich verbinde Sie.
Shall I put you through to …?	Soll ich Sie mit … verbinden?
Hold the line, please. I'll put you through.	Bitte bleiben Sie am Apparat. Ich verbinde.
Your boss is not available	**Der / die Vorgesetzte ist nicht zu sprechen**
I'm afraid Mr Deschler is not in the office at the moment.	Es tut mir leid, Herr Deschler ist z. Zt. leider nicht in seinem Büro.
… He is on a building site.	… Er ist auf einer Baustelle.
… He has a visitor with him.	… Er hat Besuch.
… He is out at lunch.	… Er ist in der Mittagspause.
Offering to call back	**Einen Rückruf anbieten**
Shall I ask her to call you back?	Soll ich sie bitten, Sie zurückzurufen?
Can she call you back this afternoon?	Kann sie Sie heute Nachmittag zurückrufen?
Does he have your telephone number?	Hat er Ihre Telefonnummer?
Can I just confirm your number?	Kann ich Ihre Nummer nochmals überprüfen?
I'll just repeat that.	Ich wiederhole.
Taking a message	**Eine Nachricht aufnehmen**
Can I take a message?	Kann ich etwas ausrichten?
Can I give him a message?	Kann ich ihm etwas ausrichten?
Would you like to leave a message?	Möchten Sie eine Nachricht hinterlassen?
Can I just confirm that?	Kann ich das kurz überprüfen?
So that's twenty-four square metres, isn't it?	Das sind also vierundzwanzig Quadratmeter, oder?
I'll make sure he gets the message.	Ich werde mich darum kümmern, dass er die Nachricht bekommt.
I'll tell her as soon as she comes back.	Ich sage ihr Bescheid, sobald sie zurückkommt.
Problems	**Probleme**
Sorry, I didn't quite catch that. Could you repeat it more slowly, please?	Es tut mir leid, das habe ich nicht verstanden. Könnten Sie es bitte etwas langsamer wiederholen?
I'm afraid I didn't catch the telephone number. Could you repeat it, please?	Leider habe ich die Telefonnummer nicht mitbekommen. Würden Sie sie bitte wiederholen?
I'm sorry, but we are having a bad connection. Could you repeat that, please?	Es tut mir leid, aber die Verbindung ist schlecht. Könnten Sie das bitte nochmals wiederholen?
Ending the call	**Das Telefongespräch beenden**
You're welcome.	Bitteschön. / Gern geschehen.
Thanks for calling.	Vielen Dank für Ihren Anruf.
Goodbye.	Auf Wiederhören.

2. Making a call	Jemanden anrufen
Introducing yourself	**Sich vorstellen**
This is … from Fertighaus Henke.	Hier spricht … von Fertighaus Henke.
My name's … I'm calling from Smart EDV.	Mein Name ist … . Ich rufe von der Firma Smart EDV an.
Asking to speak to somebody	**Nach jemandem fragen**
Could I speak to Ms Sheringham, please?	Könnte ich bitte Frau Sheringham sprechen?
Could you put me through to Mr Ferguson?	Könnten Sie mich mit Herrn Ferguson verbinden?
Could you give me his / her extension number, please?	Könnten Sie mir bitte seine / ihre Durchwahl geben?
I'd like to speak to someone from the production planning department.	Ich möchte mit jemandem in der Fertigungsplanung sprechen.
Spelling your name	**Den Namen buchstabieren**
It's S-C-H-N-E-I-D-E-R. Schneider.	Das ist S-C-H-N-E-I-D-E-R. Schneider.
Giving your phone number	**Die Telefonnummer nennen**
It's 0049 for Germany, then 0391 458 547.	Das ist die 0049 für Deutschland, dann 0391 458 547.
It's 0391 458 547.	Das ist die 0391 458 547.
Leaving a message	**Eine Nachricht hinterlassen**
Yes, please. Could you tell him that …?	Ja bitte. Könnten Sie ihm ausrichten, dass …?
Thank you. I'll ring back later.	Danke sehr. Ich rufe später zurück.
I'm afraid I won't be in the workshop this afternoon. I'll give you my mobile number.	Leider bin ich heute Nachmittag nicht in der Werkstatt. Ich gebe Ihnen meine Handynummer.
Ending the call	**Das Telefongespräch beenden**
Thank you very much for your help.	Vielen Dank für Ihre Hilfe.
Goodbye.	Auf Wiederhören.

D | Written communication

Salutation	Anrede
Dear Sir or Madam	Sehr geehrte Damen und Herren
Dear Mr … / Dear Ms …	Lieber Herr … / Liebe Frau …
Dear Peter	Lieber Peter
Complimentary close	**Schlussformel**
Yours sincerely / Yours faithfully (rarely used)	Mit freundlichen Grüßen / Hochachtungsvoll (selten benutzt)
Best regards / Kind regards / Best wishes	Schöne Grüße / Herzliche Grüße

Enquiries	Anfragen
We have visited your website and …	Wir haben Ihre Webseite besucht und …
Your services have been recommended to us by …	Ihre Dienstleistungen wurden uns von … empfohlen.
We are a well-established manufacturer of …	Wir sind ein gut etablierter Hersteller von …
Our firm is a leading importer of …	Unsere Firma ist ein führender Importeur von …
Could you please let us have a brochure and a price list?	Wir bitten um einen Prospekt und eine Preisliste.
Please send us a quotation for …	Bitte machen Sie uns ein Angebot über …
Please quote your lowest prices for …	Bitte nennen Sie uns Ihre günstigsten Preise für …
We would be grateful for information on your terms of payment and delivery.	Wir bitten um nähere Angaben zu Ihren Liefer- und Zahlungsbedingungen.
A visit by your representative would be appreciated.	Wir wären dankbar für einen Besuch Ihres Vertreters.
We look forward to hearing from you.	Wir freuen uns darauf, bald von Ihnen zu hören.
Offers	**Angebote**
Many thanks for your enquiry of 30 May about our new range of …	Wir danken Ihnen vielmals für Ihre Anfrage vom 30. Mai wegen unseres neuen Sortiments von …
As requested, we are sending you enclosed our latest catalogue and price list.	Wie gewünscht fügen wir unseren neuesten Katalog und unsere Preisliste bei.
We can offer a 10% quantity discount on orders of at least 500 units.	Für Aufträge über mindestens 500 Stück wird 10% Mengenrabatt gewährt.
We take pleasure in submitting the following cost estimate:	Wir freuen uns, Ihnen folgenden Kostenvoranschlag zu unterbreiten:
Our usual terms of payment are: – cash with order – cash on delivery – 30 days net, 10 days 2% – by irrevocable letter of credit	Unsere üblichen Zahlungsbedingungen lauten: – Barzahlung bei Auftragserteilung – Barzahlung bei Lieferung – 30 Tage netto, 10 Tage 2% Skonto – durch unwiderrufliches und bestätigtes Akkreditiv
The delivery period is 6 weeks.	Die Lieferzeit beträgt 6 Wochen.
We look forward to welcoming you as our customers.	Wir freuen uns darauf, Sie als Kunden begrüßen zu dürfen.
Orders	**Bestellungen**
Please supply the following items on the terms stated below:	Bitte liefern Sie uns folgende Positionen zu den unten genannten Bedingungen:
As agreed, we will effect payment by bank transfer 30 days from date of invoice.	Wie vereinbart werden wir die Zahlung 30 Tage nach Rechnungsdatum per Banküberweisung vornehmen lassen.
Please note that the goods must reach us by 1 March at the latest.	Wir weisen darauf hin, dass die Ware bis spätestens 1. März hier eintreffen muss.
Please acknowledge this order promptly.	Bitte bestätigen Sie diesen Auftrag umgehend.
We look forward to receiving the goods in time and to doing further business with you.	Wir freuen uns, die Ware rechtzeitig entgegennehmen und weitere Geschäfte mit Ihnen machen zu können.

E | Applications

Mentioning the source of the advertisement	Die Quelle der Anzeige nennen
I would like to apply for the job / work placement which you advertised in the … of … / on the … website.	Ich möchte mich auf die in der … vom … / auf der … Website ausgeschriebenen Stelle / Praktikumsstelle bewerben.
I saw your advertisement for a … (job / work placement) in the … of … / on the … website and would like to apply for the position.	Ich habe Ihre Anzeige für eine Stelle / Praktikumsstelle in der … vom … / auf der … Website gesehen und möchte mich auf die Stelle bewerben.
I am writing in response to your advertisement of … in the … / on the … website for a … (job / work placement).	Ich melde mich auf Ihre Anzeige vom … in der … / auf der … Website für eine Stelle / Praktikumsstelle.
Introducing yourself	**Sich vorstellen**
I am particularly attracted to this position as …	Ich bin an dieser Stelle besonders interessiert, weil …
I am currently doing a one-year / two-year … apprenticeship at a vocational college in … (town), Germany.	Ich mache zurzeit eine ein-/zweijährige … Ausbildung an einer berufsbildenden Schule in …, Deutschland.
I am in the second year of an apprenticeship in …	Ich bin im zweiten Jahr einer Ausbildung als …
At present I am working as a … with … (company).	Zurzeit arbeite ich als … bei der Firma …
After completing my apprenticeship / At the end of the apprenticeship I will be a qualified (job title).	Nachdem ich meine Ausbildung beendet habe / Mit Abschluss meiner Ausbildung bin ich eine qualifizierte / ein qualifizierter (Berufsbezeichnung).
Talking about yourself and saying why you are a good applicant	**Über sich sprechen und begründen, warum man ein guter Bewerber / eine gute Bewerberin ist**
As you will see from my CV …	Wie aus meinem Lebenslauf zu ersehen ist, …
I have a good knowledge of …	Ich verfüge über gute Kenntnisse in …
I am motivated / reliable / hard-working / keen to learn / friendly / open / a good communicator.	Ich bin motiviert / zuverlässig / sehr fleißig / lernwillig / freundlich / aufgeschlossen / ein kommunikativer Mensch.
I have previous work experience as …	Ich verfüge bereits über Berufserfahrung als …
I have a wide range of interests including …	Ich bin vielseitig interessiert, u.a. an …
I am familiar with this kind of work, because …	Mit dieser Tätigkeit bin ich vertraut, da …
I would very much welcome the opportunity to work in …	Über die Möglichkeit, in … zu arbeiten, würde ich mich sehr freuen.
I believe that I would be a valuable / enthusiastic employee.	Ich bin überzeugt, dass ich ein(e) nützliche(r) / engagierte(r) Mitarbeiter(in) wäre.

Finishing the letter	Den Brief beenden
I hope that you will consider my application.	Ich hoffe, dass Sie meine Bewerbung in Betracht ziehen werden.
Thank you in advance for considering my application.	Ich danke Ihnen im Voraus, dass Sie meine Bewerbung in Betracht ziehen.
I look forward to hearing from you (soon).	Ich freue mich auf eine (baldige) Antwort.

F | Socialising

Ice breakers	Eisbrecher
How was your weekend? – Good, thanks. How about yours?	Wie war dein / Ihr Wochenende? – Gut, danke. Und bei dir / Ihnen?
Did you see the game last night? – Of course! It was unbelievable. What did you think about the red card / winning goal?	Hast du / Haben Sie das Spiel gestern abend gesehen? – Natürlich! Es war unglaublich. Was halten Sie von der roten Karte / vom Siegtor?
Quite cold / warm today, isn't it?	Ziemlich kalt / warm heute, oder?
I really like your watch. Where did you get it?	Ihre / deine Uhr gefällt mir wirklich gut. Woher haben Sie / hast du sie?
Did you read the story about … in the newspaper this morning?	Haben Sie heute Morgen den Bericht über … in der Zeitung gelesen?
Ah! I see you are also in need of a coffee / cup of tea.	Ah! Wie ich sehe brauchen Sie / brauchst du auch einen Kaffee / eine Tasse Tee.
Is this your first time in Germany?	Sind Sie / Bist du zum ersten Mal in Deutschland?
The food is pretty good here, isn't it? – You can say that again!	Das Essen hier ist ziemlich gut, oder? – Das können Sie / kannst du laut sagen.
Keeping the conversation going	**Das Gespräch in Gang halten**
Really? Is that right? You're joking!	Wirklich? Ist das wahr? Sie machen / du machst Scherze!
That's brilliant / hilarious / fascinating!	Das ist brilliant / sehr lustig / faszinierend!
And what happened then?	Und was passierte dann?
No, unfortunately I missed it. What happened?	Nein, leider habe ich es verpasst. Was ist passiert?
It's interesting you should say that, because …	Interessant, dass Sie das sagen, weil …
Talking about food, have you already tried the new Italian restaurant in the city centre?	Wo wir gerade über Essen sprechen: Haben Sie schon den neuen Italiener in der Innenstadt ausprobiert?
Changing the subject	**Das Thema wechseln**
I think it's best if we don't talk about politics.	Ich denke, es ist das Beste, wenn wir nicht über Politik sprechen.
If you don't mind, I'd rather not talk about that.	Wenn es Ihnen nichts ausmacht, würde ich lieber nicht darüber sprechen.
Yes … By the way, have you read …	Ja … Übrigens, haben Sie … gelesen?

Ending the conversation politely	Die Unterhaltung höflich beenden
Well, it's been good talking to you.	Nun, es war schön, mit Ihnen zu sprechen.
I suppose it's time to get back to work. See you around.	Ich denke, dass es Zeit ist, zur Arbeit zurückzukehren. Man sieht sich!
Excuse me, but I have just seen someone I need to speak to. It was nice talking to you.	Entschuldigen Sie, aber ich habe jemanden gesehen, mit dem ich sprechen muss. Es war nett, mit Ihnen zu reden.
Eating out	**Essen gehen**
Talking about preferences	**Über Vorlieben sprechen**
Do you eat meat / seafood / fish?	Essen Sie Fleisch / Meeresfrüchte / Fisch?
Do you like spicy food?	Mögen Sie scharfes Essen?
I'm a vegetarian / vegan.	Ich bin Vegetarier / Veganer.
I'm allergic to nuts.	Ich bin allergisch gegen Nüsse.
I'd prefer something light; I'm on a diet.	Ich würde etwas Leichtes bevorzugen – ich bin auf Diät.
I don't drink alcohol.	Ich trinke keinen Alkohol.
Talking about the menu	**Über die Speisekarte sprechen**
It's sweet / savoury / sour.	Es ist süß / herzhaft / sauer.
It's a starter / main dish / dessert.	Es ist ein(e) Vorspeise / Hauptgericht / Dessert.
What's in it?	Was ist da drin?
It's made of …	Es wird aus … gemacht.
It's boiled / fried / baked / roasted / filled with …	Es ist gekocht / gebraten/gebacken / geröstet / gefüllt mit …
Ordering	**Bestellen**
Are you ready to order?	Sind Sie bereit zum Bestellen?
As a starter, I'll take the … and then …	Als Vorspeise nehme ich …, und dann …
I'd like a side order of rice, please.	Ich hätte gerne (eine Portion) Reis als Beilage.
Shall we share a bottle of wine?	Sollen wir uns eine Flasche Wein teilen?
How do you like your steak? – Rare / medium / well-done, please.	Wie möchten Sie Ihr Steak? – Englisch / medium / durch, bitte.
What kind of wine / beer do you have?	Welche Weine / Biersorten haben Sie?
Talking about the food	**Über das Essen sprechen**
Enjoy your meal.	Guten Appetit!
How's your meal?	Wie ist Ihr Essen?
What's your … like?	Wie ist Ihr …?
The meat is very tender / a little tough.	Das Fleisch ist sehr zart / etwas zäh.
It's not as sweet as I expected.	Es ist nicht so süß, wie ich gedacht habe.
Excuse me, but my soup is cold.	Entschuldigen Sie, aber meine Suppe ist kalt.

Asking for the bill	Nach der Rechnung fragen
Excuse me, could we have the bill, please?	Entschuldigen Sie, könnten wir bitte die Rechnung haben?
Do you accept credit cards?	Akzeptieren Sie Kreditkarten?
This one's on me!	Das geht auf mich!
Shall we split the bill 50-50?	Sollen wir die Rechnung 50-50 teilen?

G | Presentations

Beginning the presentation	Die Präsentation beginnen
I should like to start by telling you about my company.	Zunächst möchte ich Ihnen etwas über meine Firma sagen.
My presentation will deal with …	Meine Präsentation behandelt …
I intend to keep my presentation as brief as possible.	Ich möchte meine Präsentation so kurz wie möglich halten.
I would welcome any questions at the end of my presentation.	Ich wäre gern bereit, etwaige Fragen am Ende meiner Präsentation zu beantworten.
The handout summarises the main points and gives an overview of the relevant figures and statistics.	Das Handout enthält die Hauptpunkte und gibt einen Überblick über die entsprechenden Zahlen und Statistiken.
Structuring the main part of your presentation	**Den Hauptteil der Präsentation strukturieren**
Now my second point is …	Ich komme nun zu Punkt 2 …
Thirdly, let me give you some basic statistics.	Drittens darf ich Ihnen ein paar grundlegende Statistiken zeigen.
I should now like to move on to the next topic.	Ich möchte nun gern zum nächsten Thema übergehen.
An excellent example of this is …	Ein hervorragendes Beispiel dafür ist …
I should like to give you an example to illustrate this point.	Ich möchte diesen Punkt mit einem Beispiel erläutern.
Concluding your presentation	**Die Präsentation beenden**
To sum up we can say that …	Zusammenfassend kann man sagen, dass …
I should like to finish by saying / thanking the organisers / pointing out …	Ich möchte schließen mit der Bemerkung / dem Dank an die Organisatoren / dem Hinweis …
Are there any questions?	Gibt es Fragen?
Thank you for your attention.	Vielen Dank für Ihre Aufmerksamkeit.

H | Dealing with customers

Making a complaint	Eine Beschwerde / Reklamation vorbringen
We are writing with reference to our order no. ...	Wir nehmen Bezug auf unseren Auftrag Nr. ...
On unpacking the cases our Incoming Goods Control discovered that 15 items are missing.	Beim Auspacken der Kisten stellte unsere Warenannahme fest, dass 15 Positionen fehlen.
We are afraid that several units are - seriously damaged / defective. - broken / badly scratched / stained.	Leider sind mehrere Teile - schwer beschädigt / schadhaft. - zerbrochen / stark zerkratzt / verschmutzt.
We are sorry to point out that the repair work has been poorly executed.	Wir müssen leider darauf hinweisen, dass die Reparatur schlecht ausgeführt wurde.
We believe the damage may be due to rough handling in transit.	Wir glauben, dass der Schaden auf unsachgemäße Behandlung beim Transport zurückzuführen ist.
This is very inconvenient for us because ...	Dies kommt uns sehr ungelegen, da ...
We would ask you to - replace the faulty goods at your expense. - grant us a price reduction of 10 %. - cut the price to € 550.	Wir möchten Sie bitten, - die mangelhafte Ware auf Ihre Kosten zu ersetzen. - uns einen Preisnachlass von 10 % zu gewähren. - den Preis auf € 550 zu senken.
We will keep the damaged goods until we hear from you.	Wir werden die beschädigten Waren behalten, bis wir von Ihnen hören.
Responding to a complaint	**Auf eine Beschwerde / Reklamation antworten**
Thank you for your email drawing a serious problem to our attention.	Danke für Ihre E-Mail, mit der Sie uns auf ein ernstes Problem aufmerksam gemacht haben.
We wish to apologise for this mistake.	Wir bitten für diesen Fehler um Entschuldigung.
We are extremely sorry for the poor service you have received.	Es tut uns außerordentlich leid, dass Sie einen unzureichenden Service erhalten haben.
We will investigate the matter thoroughly and inform you of the steps taken.	Wir werden die Angelegenheit gründlich untersuchen und Sie über die Schritte informieren, die wir unternommen haben.
Please return the faulty items at our expense.	Bitte senden Sie die mangelhaften Artikel auf unsere Kosten zurück.
We are prepared to reduce the price by 10 % if you decide to keep the goods.	Wir sind bereit, den Preis um 10 % zu senken, wenn Sie sich entschließen, die Ware zu behalten.
We hope that this proposal will find your approval.	Wir hoffen, dieser Vorschlag findet Ihre Zustimmung.

Audioscripts

⦾ A 1.8 Modul 1 People and jobs in IT, B 1, 2

Ian: Good morning, you must be Michael. I'm Ian MacIntosh, your tutor for the next three months. Welcome to Scotland.

Michael: Good morning, Mr MacIntosh. Pleased to meet you. I'm glad to be here.

Ian: Just call me Ian, here at Computech we aren't that formal. Let me start by telling you a bit about our company and your future workplace.

Michael: Oh yes, please do, I'm really curious.

Ian: Well, first of all you need to know that we are organised into five departments and that we work in two major fields. First, there is our shop, where we sell computers and accessories, and then we also design and develop private and corporate networks.

Michael: Who are your typical customers?

Ian: Well, they're mostly small and medium-sized enterprises who come to us for help with their networks, and they usually buy the hardware here as well. In the shop, the customers are also private people who come in to get information and buy their computers from us. Also, Andy Jones, the head of the shop, is responsible for the repair orders taken there. From there they are passed on to the workshop, which is where I work. I'm actually the head of the workshop.

Michael: Will I be working there?

Ian: Yes, the plan is that you'll be working in the workshop for the first part of your stay here.

Michael: What happens in the workshop?

Ian: Well, one part of the job is diagnosing and repairing faulty devices that customers bring in. Also, you'll be joining one of our field service technicians. They go out to the customers, either to solve computer problems on their premises, or to install, commission and service networks.

Michael: Are these the networks designed by Computech?

Ian: Yes. Usually, when a customer wants a network installed, he is referred to Fiona Fraser's department, Project Management. There, Fiona and her colleagues find out what this specific customer needs, and then plan the network together. Once they have come up with a design, it's up to my department to implement it. You see, there's lots of interesting work here.

Michael: Oh yes, I'm sure. What other departments are there?

Ian: There are two more, both of which you won't have too much to do with. First, there is Human Resources, with Linda Donaldson at the top. Their responsibilities include hiring and, unfortunately, occasionally also firing staff members. Also, they do the holiday planning and the wage accounting. Last but not least they are responsible for the training of our apprentices, who you'll meet tomorrow. Actually, you should go and see Linda soon to get all your paperwork done.

Michael: I'll do that. Which is the last department then?

Ian: Oh, I see you're paying attention. The remaining department is Accounting. They are concerned with stock keeping, purchases and sales. They also do most of our business correspondence, you know, writing enquiries, orders, offers and the like. In addition, they take care of payments and of our reminder mechanism. As you can imagine, they have to keep in close contact with all the other departments, but Shaun Higgins, their head, does a really good job.

Michael: I hope I won't have to work there. I mean, I'm an IT-specialist.

Ian: No, don't worry. We have a little meeting arranged for tomorrow, where our Managing Director, Mr James MacPherson, will welcome you along with our new trainees and other new colleagues. You'll find out then exactly what plans we have for you. Jane Russell, Mr MacPherson's assistant, will tell you the details. Look, there she is over there. Let's go and talk to her. Hi Jane, let me introduce you to Michael Petersen. He's from our German partners, and he will be here …

A 1.1 Modul A Meeting people, A 1, 2

Dialogue 1

Mr Neureuther: Neureuther, good morning.
Ms Hornbach: Good morning, Mr Neureuther.
Mr Neureuther: Good morning Ms Hornbach.
Ms Hornbach: Mr Neureuther, the young man you were expecting from Denmark is here.
Mr Neureuther: Ah yes, please send him in. And Ms Hornbach, give Mr Dachs a call, will you please?
Ms Hornbach: I've already called him.
Christian: Hello, my name is Christian Eriksen. I come from Fanö in Denmark, and, uh, I'd like to work here as an intern for the next three months.
Mr Neureuther: Felix Neureuther. I'm the manager of the company.
Christian: Nice to meet you, Mr Neureuther.
Mr Neureuther: Nice to meet you too, Christian. I hope you had a pleasant trip.
Christian: Yes, it was fine, thank you. It's not far from Fanö to Kiel.
Mr Neureuther: Fine. Now, let me see, I guess you've handed all the necessary papers over to my secretary, Ms Hornbach?
Christian: Yes, I have.
Mr Neureuther: Oh good, Mr Dachs. I don't believe you've met Christian Eriksen. He'll be our new intern for the next three months. Christian, this is Mr Dachs, our personnel manager.
Mr Dachs: Nice to meet you Christian.
Christian: Nice to meet you too, Mr Dachs.
Mr Neureuther: Christian, Mr Dachs will take you to your team, so you can get to know them all. See you later, Christian.
Christian: See you later, Mr Neureuther.

Dialogue 2

Mr Dachs: Morning, everybody.
All of them: Good morning, Mr Dachs.
Mr Dachs: I'd like you to meet our new colleague. He'll be working with us for the next three months. He's in his second year of training. Christian, would you like to introduce yourself?
Christian: Hello, my name is Christian Eriksen. I come from Fanö, that's an island off the coast of Denmark. The company I work for is a bit smaller than yours; there's just the boss, a skilled worker and two trainees.
Silke: Hi Christian, nice to meet you. My name is Silke, and I'm also in my second year of training.
Christian: Nice to meet you too, Silke. I'm glad you speak English, because my German is not so fluent. But I'm doing my best to improve.
Silke: No problem, we'll manage.
Josef: Hello Christian, I'm Josef, but everybody calls me Joe. I'm your foreman. My English is not perfect, but Silke can always help. I've been here for quite a long time. Isn't that right, Mr Dachs?
Mr Dachs: Yes, Joe has been with us for over 20 years now. I think for the first few weeks you'll work with him. Well, let's get back to work now. If you have any questions, you can ask Joe, but you can always come to my office, too.
Christian: Thank you, Mr Dachs.

A 1.9 Modul 2 Computer hardware, B 1

A computer is of little use if you cannot see or hear what is going on, or give it instructions. In other words, the user needs to communicate with the machine. This is where external computing components, or peripheral devices, come in. These devices connect to the computer via different interfaces. The most common devices of this kind are the monitor, which allows you to follow on the screen processes going on inside the computer, a keyboard for inputting text, a mouse to help you navigate on the screen, ear-phones or speakers for acoustic output (although they are often integrated into the monitor), and a microphone for acoustic input. Some users prefer a head-set, a combination of microphone and earphones, which is often used for VoIP connections, e.g. in a call center or when working at a help desk. Even in private conversations or video-conferencing they come in handy. Finally, you need a printer to transfer what is on the screen to paper. Instead of having just a printer and a scanner, many people use a multi-purpose device integrating printer, scanner, photocopier and sometimes even fax.

Nowadays, an increasing number of people also use a webcam – which is generally integrated in the lid of mobile computers. The interface for most of these devices is USB, DVI for monitors and RCA (cinch) for acoustic devices. This list, however, is by no means complete, there are a number of other devices that can be connected to your PC to input or output data, – either with cables or without – via infra-red or Bluetooth connections.

A 1.2 Modul B Your company, A 4

Herr Kirchner: OK, so we've covered human resources, accounting, sales and marketing, and purchasing. Now we come to the more technical side of the company, and – of course – the area where you will be spending your time. OK, do you have any questions before we continue?

Sean: Yes, just a general question really. How old is the company?

Herr Kirchner: Older than you, Sean, that's for sure! Krone Elektronik was founded by Dr. Florian Krone in 1954, and is still a family-owned company to this day.

Sean: And is this the headquarters here in Bochum?

Herr Kirchner: Yes, it is. Krone has nine manufacturing plants and sales offices across Europe, but this is the largest. In fact, we also have two in the USA – in Chicago and Baltimore.

Sean: Are there any plants in Great Britain?

Herr Kirchner: No, there's not. But we are opening a new factory in South Korea next year.

Sean: And how many people work for Krone Elektronik?

Herr Kirchner: That's a good question, Sean. I don't know the exact number, but it is at least 10,000, if you include the USA. OK, let's go on with the tour, shall we? The building to your right is our research and development department. They are currently working on a new braking system for a major German car company.

Sean: And what goes on in the large building next to it?

Herr Kirchner: This is our main building, which has three functions. Firstly, it is where production planners work – and this is where you will spend most of your time. Their job is to optimize the manufacturing process by keeping production times and costs down. Secondly, as you can see, here are also the production halls, where you will start your internship.

Sean: You mentioned three functions. So what else happens over there? It's a really big place.

Herr Kirchner: Yes, it's over 6,000 square metres. Those people you can see over there are responsible for quality control. They test all of the components and devices before they go to the customer.

Sean: How many components are made here in Bochum?

Herr Kirchner: Well, one of the main components we produce here are the cylinder heads, and we make thousands of them every year. And each and every one of them must be inspected by the guys in quality control.

Sean: I guess that's an important job. I'm really looking forward to getting to work.

Herr Kirchner: That's great. I will introduce you to the foreman this afternoon. OK, finally, behind this building we have the IT department. At the moment, they are very busy dealing with the problems caused by our new operating system.

Sean: Oh, that doesn't sound too good. What exactly is the problem?

Herr Kirchner: I'm not sure exactly, some kind of interface difficulties, I think. OK, let's go into the canteen and have some lunch, shall we? Then I can answer some more of your questions.

A 1.10 Modul 3 Storing data, C 4

Don Clark: Hello everyone. My name is Don Clark and you are listening to our monthly IT expert exchange podcast. I am joined today by Michael Simon, Chief Technology Officer at CloudedJudgment Inc. Michael, thank you for coming on the show.

Michael Simon: Thanks for having me.

Don: So, Michael, a lot of people out there have heard of you, but for those who haven't tell us a little about yourself and give us the gist of what you and your company do.

Michael: Gladly. To cut a long story short, I've always been fascinated by vast amounts of data, and how we can use computers to analyze and store that data so businesses and scientific organizations can use it to make better decisions, or find the things they are looking for quicker. Working with such large amounts of data is difficult and requires a very powerful computer infrastructure, which not all companies can afford. CloudedJudgement Inc. was founded by Andrew Turner, Leah Phillips and myself to enable our customers to use our infrastructure and technology to process, analyze and store whatever big data they can't handle on their own.

Don: 'Big data', can you give us a definition? I mean, I know what it refers to, but if you would care to enlighten our listeners …

Michael: Sure. The term 'big data' can't be precisely defined, but briefly, it's an amount of data which can't be handled using standard technologies such as relational databases. Currently when we talk about big data we refer to data amounts in the area of several peta bytes. A peta byte is one thousand tera bytes. Ten years from now – or even sooner maybe – big data may refer to exa bytes, the next higher order on the scale.

Don: Several peta bytes. That sounds like a lot …

Michael: It sure is, Don. Let me give you two examples. The largest search engine in the world – we all know who I'm talking about, but we don't have to advertise here – currently gathers 24 peta bytes of data every day. They use this data to build their search index for the Internet. Another example of big data is the Large Hadron Collider experiment in CERN. The scientists there gather approximately 15 PB per year. Not as much as a search engine, but still, well, still big data. You can't very well store that much data in a simple relational database and run a search on it.

Don: And why is that?

Michael: Well, let's spare your listeners the painful details, but it is safe to say that the mathematical and computational foundations of such relational databases are not suited to handling data that large within a reasonable time frame. They are great for accounting and bookkeeping, or keeping an inventory of things you have in a warehouse. They may very well catch up one day, but until that day we need something else.

Don: And that something else for you and CloudedJudgement Inc. is Hadoop?

Michael: Well, not exclusively, but yes, Hadoop plays a large part in our daily operations.

Don: Let's tick one thing off our list: where did the name come from?

Michael: Ah, the name. Hadoop was created by Doug Cutting. He based his work on two papers published by Google Inc. about Google's technology called MapReduce. His son had a toy elephant he called Hadoop, so Cutting decided to name the new technology after the elephant. The mascot, by the way, is also a little yellow elephant.

Don: Who owns Hadoop?

Michael: No one owns Hadoop in the classical sense. It's open source. It was actively developed by the Apache Software Foundation. It was written in the Java programming language and anybody can download and alter the source code as long as he makes his alterations open source as well.

Don: So, tell us more about Hadoop and how your company uses it.

Michael: Hm, where do I begin? First of all it is not a software you can install and run just like that. Hadoop is a software framework. You can think of a framework as a toolbox which enables you to write more powerful software by using parts of that toolbox. With the Hadoop framework you can write software applications which run on not one but as many as 4,000 computers.

Don: If I may interrupt you there: how many machines do you have in your cluster right now?

Michael: I'm afraid I can't give you an exact number since machines die and have to be replaced regularly, but we usually have about 1,000 computers in our cluster. Anyway, using the framework, we have created our own software to run on the cluster. We can use the software to handle around 1 to 1.5 peta bytes per day.

Don: When you say handle, what do you mean by that?

Michael: Let's say you're a company that wants to use computers to read blog posts on the Internet. Not just a few, but all the blogs you can find on the Internet to see what people around the world are talking about: what kind of movies or products they are interested in, what political news items are they discussing most. So some form of market research, right? You can easily gather the data, right?

Don: Sure, you just crawl the Internet and download everything you can find.

Michael: Right. You get the data and now you want to know how many people have posted something about the elections in some country or see how many blog entries relate to a brand new car. If you were to store everything in a relational database and search for a certain keyword, it would take forever to go through all of the data in the database. What we do is this: we take all the data and, based on what our customer wants to know, restructure it into a form that is much faster to search through. We eliminate all the unnecessary information from the data and reduce it so that it only contains the information that the customer wants. So staying with the example of a car manufacturer, we first eliminate all blogs that don't deal with cars.

Don: How do you do that?

Michael: For example, if a blog post contains the words 'computer' 20 times, the word 'smartphone' five times and the word 'car' zero times, we can be pretty sure that this blog is not about cars, so we remove that blog entry from the data we have gathered. In the end, out of several million texts, we have maybe a couple of thousand left. Based on our customers' criteria, we can further eliminate data and "boil it down" to contain only what our client wants to know, say a specific manufacturer name or a certain model. In doing so, we will have reduced the big data to something that is much easier to handle than what you had at the beginning.

Don: Michael, I'm sure you could talk for hours on this new development and its implications. Unfortunately, we are running out of time again and have to make a cut here. Thank you so much for giving us some insight into this.

⊚ A 1.3 Modul C Telephoning, B 5

Alex: Fertighaus Henke, Alex Bauder.

Caller: Yes, hello. Do you speak English?

Alex: Er, yes, a little. How can I help you?

Caller: Well, my name is Matthew Reid and your company is currently building my house. I'm a little confused. I thought this was Mr Deschler's telephone number. He is the construction manager, isn't he?

Alex: Yes, he is, but unfortunately he is off sick today, so all of his calls are being diverted to me. Can I help you with something?

Caller: Well, I was calling to give Mr Deschler some changes to our house.

Alex: OK, and what was your name again, please?

Caller: Reid, Matthew Reid.

Alex: Could you possibly spell that please?

Caller: Certainly. It's R-E-I-D.

Alex: R-I-E-D.

Caller: No, R-E for England, I for India, D.

Alex: Sorry, R-E-I-D. OK, Mr Reid, and what is the address of the house?

Caller: Well, so far it is only a foundation pit, but it is Ringstrasse 26 in Lernsdorf.

Alex: Ringstrasse 26, Lernsdorf. Ah, yes, I know the site. We are scheduled to begin on your cellar next week, I think. OK, if you give me the information, I will pass it on to Mr Deschler. Let me just find a piece of paper ... OK, I'm ready.

Caller: First of all, in the kitchen we need to move the extractor fan twenty centimetres to the left, so that it is directly over the hob. And the hole needs to have a diameter of one hundred and eighty-four milimetres, and we also need ...

Alex: Sorry Mr Reid, but I am afraid any changes to your kitchen need to be discussed with the kitchen fitters. Are there any changes to the plans for any other part of the house?

Caller: Er, just a moment. Let me look at my list. OK, we need to change the height of the toilets in the bathroom. At the moment they are planned to be forty-five centimetres and we would like them to be fifty. Plus, we need to add another two hundred and twenty volt socket to the right of the bathroom mirror for my electric razor.

Alex: OK, anything else?

Caller: Yes, my wife and I have decided that we will need a larger carport. I have spoken to a friend and he says we should make it eight metres by six metres by three metres. Can you find out how much extra this would cost, please?

Alex: Of course. Let me just confirm, eight metres long by six metres wide. And how high should it be?

Caller: Three metres high. Of course, this means that we will have a smaller garden, but I think a carport is very useful. You can also ask Mr Deschler how big our garden will be with the new carport. It is currently one hundred and thirty-five square metres.

Alex: OK, I will ask him to adjust the plan and get in touch with you as soon as he is back in the office.

Caller: That's great. Oh, just one more thing. My wife wants to put larger windows in the living room. At the moment, they are one hundred and forty-eight centimetres by one hundred and eleven in the plan. She would like them to be one hundred and eighty-six by two hundred and twenty-two.

Alex: One eight six by two two two. OK Mr Reid, I will pass this information on to Mr Deschler and ask him to give you a call. Does he have your telephone number?

Caller: Yes, I think so, but let me give you my work number, too. It is 0391 587660... Thank you for your help Mr Bauder. Goodbye.

Alex: You're welcome Mr Reid. Goodbye.

A 1.11 Modul 4 BIOS and operating systems, C 1, 2

Robert: Hey Victor, how's it going?

Victor: Hi Robert. Fine thanks. I just have this web project I need to do.

Robert: What's wrong with that? You work on web pages all of the time.

Victor: Well, yes. But for this project we are supposed to plan everything including the web server and I need a model installation that I can present in class.

Robert: Good for you. You'll finally get to use a real operating system.

Victor: Very funny. Anyway. I downloaded the latest Cintrex Linux and installed it on my laptop.

Robert: And deleted mOS, I hope.

Victor: Of course not. I need that for my design applications. I installed it parallel to mOS. Everything worked fine.

Robert: So what's the problem?

Victor: Well, I didn't pay enough attention to the questions the installer asked me and I ended up overwriting the mOS bootloader.

Robert: Come on, the installer specifically asks you if you want to add other operating systems to the boot menu list.

Victor: Thanks for pointing that out. Can you help me?

Robert: Sure, what bootloader are you using?

Victor: I don't know. I didn't change any of the settings during the installation, so I guess it's the default bootloader.

Robert: Okay, so it's probably GRUB.

Victor: What is it?

Robert: GRUB, grand unified bootloader. Anyway, you will have to edit the configuration file for GRUB to add mOS to the boot menu list.

Victor: How do I do that?

Robert: Easy. Just type pico slash boot slash grub slash grub dot cfg and hit 'enter'.

Victor: Where do I type that?

Robert: Terminal...

Victor: Where is the terminal?

Robert: Don't tell me you installed a desktop environment for a server. You mOS users. Okay, not to worry. In the top left-hand corner of the screen you should see 'Applications'. Click on that and a menu shows up. There's an entry saying 'Accessories'. Navigate to that and you'll see another menu. Then click on 'Terminal'.

Victor: Hold on, I need to write that down.

Robert: Top-left corner, applications, accessories, terminal.

Victor: Got it. And then I enter pico slash boot slash grub slash grub dot cfg. By the way what does 'pico' mean?

Robert: That's just the standard text editor. You'll see the contents of the configuration file. You will have to manually create a menu entry for mOS. Just append it at the end of the file. Save the file using the key combination control O. Exit using control X and you're done.

Victor: How do I create the new menu entry?

Robert: No idea. I haven't used mOS in ages. Speaking of time. I have to go or I'll be late for class.

Victor: Wait. What about my problem...?

Robert: I'll call you when I get home and talk you through it step by step.

Victor: Thanks, Robert. Bye.

A 1.4 Modul E Applications, C 1

Andrea: Hi David, how are you doing?

David: Hi Andrea. I'm fine thanks. How are you?

Andrea: Yeah, I'm OK. Busy, but fine.

David: I heard that you were thinking about applying for a three-month internship in the Northampton branch. Is that true?

Andrea: Yes, that's right. I really want to spend some time in England. I guess it was the same with you and coming to Germany.

David: Exactly. I wanted to see how things worked over here. So, you want to spend some time with my old colleagues, eh? That's great.

Andrea: Well actually, I wanted to ask you for a bit of advice if that's OK with you?

David: Sure, what can I help you with?

Andrea: Well, I have to officially apply for the internship, which means a letter and a CV.

David: OK, would you like me to read your letter?

Andrea: Yes, that would be great. I am going to finish it this weekend, and then I will bring it to work on Monday. Thanks. But where I really need your advice is with the CV. I was wondering if you had any tips for me. I know there are some differences between German and English CVs.

David: Yes, there are, you're right. Hmm ... tips ... let me see. OK, the first thing to remember is that your CV should be no longer than two pages.

Andrea: Two pages, OK.

David: Also, make sure you use good-quality paper and never send your CV without a covering letter.

Andrea: OK ...

David: And don't forget to highlight your strengths and achievements. And when you talk about your work experience, start with your most recent job.

Andrea: Do I need to include a picture?

David: In England, a CV does not have a picture, but you can have one if you like. What is important is that you include the name and contact details of two references. These could be a supervisor, or maybe a teacher.

Andrea: OK, great. Anything else?

David: Yeah, make sure that everything you write in your CV is the truth. If you are asked to explain something during the interview and you can't, then it will be pretty embarrassing. Be confident and sell yourself, but don't lie. Er ... once you have finished the CV, read through it and check the spelling and the grammar. The best thing to do is to give it to a friend. And, when you send it, keep a copy for yourself to read before the interview.

Andrea: Thanks a lot for the advice, David. Thanks a lot, I'm really grateful.

David: Don't mention it, Andrea. Let me know if there is anything else I can do.

Andrea: Well ... you did say somebody should read over it and check everything – and who'd be better than a native speaker ...?

A 1.12 Modul 5 Types of computer, B1, 2

Sven: Hi, Naomi. Have you got a minute?

Naomi: Hello Sven. Of course.

Sven: I'm thinking of buying a new computer and I was wondering if you could give me some advice.

Naomi: Certainly. What do you want to use it for?

Sven: Well, just the usual things, I suppose. I'll need it to write e-mails, and to write and edit texts for school, and also to prepare presentations.

Naomi: OK, any standard machine with the appropriate software would do all of that for you. You'll need an e-mail programme, a word processing programme and a presentation programme. What else do you want to do with it?

Sven: Well, I have to do some calculating and I manage a library at school.

Naomi: So you'll also need a spreadsheet and a database programme. But don't worry, they're included in the standard packages. How about other activities such as surfing the Internet, watching movies, listening to music, playing games and the like?

Sven: That would be great!

Naomi: So we're talking about a multi-media PC. The flat desktop models with a monitor on top take up a lot of space on a desk. You could think about a tower chassis that leaves you more room for additional storage and other devices. Actually the big question is: Do you want your computer to be stationary or mobile?

Sven: I think I would prefer greater flexibility.

Naomi: Then a laptop or a notebook might be more suitable. They are small and, at less than 3 kg, lightweight enough to be carried around. They get their power from battery packs, but can also be plugged in to an external power supply. You also need the battery packs to re-charge the batteries regularly. An LCD screen in the lid folds down to protect the screen when the computer is transported. Laptops also have an inbuilt keyboard, an optical disc drive and a pointing device, such as a touchpad or trackball. Some users prefer to use a cordless mouse with their notebooks and connect it via USB. Another really useful feature is that modern notebooks all support wireless networking.

Sven: I've heard people talk about netbooks. What are they?

Naomi: Well, a netbook is a notebook with a smaller screen and keyboard, as well as reduced processing power. A netbook doesn't have an optical disc drive either. If you really want to be flexible, you could even consider a tablet PC. That's a portable PC without a keyboard. The touchscreen serves as the input device. Depending on the software, the tablet stores text as a picture or it turns your handwriting into regular text using handwriting recognition (HR). The tablets all have a virtual keyboard.

Sven: Well, that was quite a bit of information. I must think again about what I want the computer for and what I can afford, of course.

Naomi: Why don't you make a list and we can talk again?

Sven: That's what I'll do. Thanks Naomi.

Naomi: My pleasure. I've got to go now. See you later, Sven.

Sven: Bye, Naomi.

◎ A 1.5 Modul F Socialising, A 1

Fabian: Hi, I'm Fabian.

Jan: Hello Fabian, my name's Jan. I'm with the group from Warsaw, Poland.

Fabian: Welcome to our company. Is this your first visit to Germany?

Jan: Actually, I've been here before. But my German isn't very good.

Fabian: Don't worry, we can talk in English. I should really practice more anyway. How was your trip? Was it a long journey?

Jan: No, not really. We took the plane from Warsaw to Stuttgart. Then someone from your company met us at the airport.

Fabian: Jan, would you like something to drink: coffee, juice, lemonade?

Jan: Sure, a lemonade would be good.

Fabian: OK, let's go to our canteen and sit down for a while.

Fabian: Here we go; I hope it's cold enough.

Jan: Thanks. So, I guess that you are also a trainee. What year are you in?

Fabian: I'm in my third year. What about you?

Jan: I've just started. How many trainees are there in your company?

Fabian: Er ... about ten, I think.

Jan: That's quite a lot. There are only three trainees in our company, all in metal engineering. I think your company is much bigger than ours.

Fabian: Yeah, we even have our own football team. We don't play in a league; it's just for fun.

Jan: That sounds great! You should visit us in Poland one day. Maybe we could arrange a match.

Fabian: That's a good idea. Are you a football fan?

Jan: Yeah. I don't play myself, but I like to watch.

Fabian: Which team do you like?

Jan: Manchester United.

Fabian: Really? They're my favourite team, too! Well, apart from VFB Stuttgart, of course.

Jan: Do you live in Stuttgart?

Fabian: No, I live in a small town nearby. I have to take the bus every morning. But when the weather's good, I can take my motorbike.

Jan: Cool! Unfortunately I don't have a motorbike. I get a lift from a colleague who works in the same department as me.

Fabian: What do you do in your free time?

Jan: I like going to clubs, and sometimes I go fishing with my friends. What about you? Playing football, I suppose.

Fabian: Yeah, football and riding my motorbike.

◎ A 1.13 Modul 6 Networks, C 1, 2

Linda: IT helpdesk, Linda Stratton speaking.

Michael: Yes this is Michael Parker in the engineering department. I've just got a new laptop. It works fine, but I cannot access the company network or my company e-mail account.

Linda: I see, Mr Parker. I'm sure we can solve the problem. Could you check whether your ethernet cable is plugged into the computer and whether your Internet connection is set up correctly?

Michael: Of course, the cable is plugged in and the connection is fine. I have just downloaded what feels like a thousand updates for my operating system from the Internet. All my e-mail program does is give me a 'mail server not found' error.

Linda: Have you installed the VPN access software?

Michael: V what?

Linda: VPN, virtual private network. It lets your computer connect to our network over a secure connection.

Michael: Never heard of it. I didn't need that on my old computer.

Linda: Well, for five years now it has been impossible to access the company network without VPN.

Michael: Well I didn't install it, so it must have already been on the old laptop.

Linda: Yes, that's possible.

Michael: Why didn't you tell me I needed VPN beforehand?

Linda: Sir, no one told me you were getting a new laptop. It may be a good idea to call ahead next time. Now to the problem at hand. Please open your browser and type in westhamdrilling.co.uk/support/...vpn. From there you can download the VPN client installer.

Michael: I don't see it.

Linda: It's on the left-hand side, where it says 'click here to download'.

Michael: Got it. Downloading ... That was fast. What now?

Linda: Double click the file and then click on 'install'. The rest runs automatically.

Michael: Okay it's installed.

Linda: Please go to your desktop and look for an icon with Fresco Systems VPN client. Then double click on it.

Michael: OK. It says 'enter username and password'. What should I enter?

Linda: Let me check your account information on my computer. Your username is 'mparker'. The password is small x – capital Z – three – small k – nine – small o – capital L. Enter these and click 'connect'. Please be patient, the client takes about 45 seconds to connect to our network.

Michael: It says I'm connected. Let's see if I can check my e-mail… No, it still isn't working. This VPN thing is useless.

Linda: Let's check the settings of your e-mail client.

Michael: Fine.

Linda: Click on 'settings' in the menu bar. Select the mail server tab. What does it say in the IP address field?

Michael: It says 171 one dot 100 dot 100 dot 23.

Linda: That sounds about right.

Michael: Told you…

Linda: What does the data field for incoming mail server network port say?

Michael: I put in 25 just like for the outgoing mail server.

Linda: Ah, there we have it, network port 25 is just for sending mail, not for receiving mail.

Michael: That's stupid. Can't you make it use the same port?

Linda: I'm afraid not. Please enter 143 for the incoming mail server network port. Click 'save settings' and then check your e-mail again.

Michael: Hmpf, it's working now.

Linda: You're welcome.

A 1.6 Modul G Presentations, C 1

Good morning ladies and gentlemen. Today I would like to present our new range of wooden furniture, *Simply Wood*. The range, which is shown here on the first slide, includes chairs, a large table, a lounger, and benches. I would like to start by talking about the materials used in the furniture. All of the *Simply Wood* range is made from single softwood timber and has been hand-crafted by our highly-skilled carpenters and joiners. If you look at this picture, you can see that the benches and the seats are designed with a low back, deep seats and long arms to offer a great deal of comfort and convenience. Thanks to a special varnish, the furniture is 100% weather proof and will not suffer from discolouring. As you can see from this final slide, the furniture is also available in white, to give it a classic, timeless look. And do not worry, we have used a durable, white polyurethane coating that is suitable for every environment. On your handout you will see more details about each piece, including measurements. Thank you for your attention this morning.
Are there any questions? Yes …

A 1.14 Modul 7 Telecommunications, B 1, 2

Jo: Sorry, Andrew, I respect your opinion but you're wrong. Wired communication is not a thing of the past.

Andrew: Well, then it should be. The concept of connecting two points on earth with a wire is so outdated. The telegraph was great but its time is long gone. Wireless is the way to go.

Jo: So you think that all of the Internet should be wireless?

Andrew: Of course, cell phones have been around for two decades.

Jo: That's true, but how do you connect to the Internet?

Andrew: I use my cell phone. If I need Internet on my PC, I connect my cell phone to it.

Jo: Okay, what technology do you use?

Andrew: HSDPA. That's based on UMTS, isn't it?

Jo: Right.

Andrew: It provides a bandwidth of 7.2 Mbit/s. That's enough for me.

Jo: Yes, it's enough for one user. I can explain better if I draw a telecommunication network. What provider are you with?

Andrew: Komtel.

Jo: Okay, Komtel is a Tier 1 provider. Look, here is what their network could look like. This symbol represents your cell phone. Now you need something that provides access, an access node, or AN for short. I'll colour the access node green.

Andrew: That would be a cell phone tower in my case.

Jo: Exactly. Your device connects you to the provider's access network. That's sometimes referred to as MAN, which is short for metro area network.

Andrew: See, wireless communication is not a big deal, since…

Jo: Hold on, I'm not finished. The MAN can cover a large area, even a whole city. Your signal is in the MAN now, but it's not in the Internet yet. To get there, it has to go through several transport nodes. We'll colour them blue. Your data travels through the MAN towards the WAN, that's short for wide area network. The wide area network is also called the core network. On the edge of the WAN, or core network, there is a service node, SN. This is where your data enters the WAN.

Andrew: Yes, I know that. All the core networks together make up the Internet. You still haven't given me a good reason why we need wires.

Jo: Okay, you would like to make all of the communication wireless.

Andrew: That's what I just said. I see no reason why the transport and service nodes couldn't be wireless.

◎ A 1.7 Modul H Dealing with customers, A 4

Answering machine: *Guten Tag. Sie sind mit Stefan Bauder verbunden. Leider bin ich im Moment nicht erreichbar. Bitte hinterlassen Sie eine Nachricht nach dem Ton. Danke!*

Brian: Hello Mr Bauder, this is Brian Jenkins calling from New Wave Marketing in Hamburg. I am calling about the new IT network that your technicians set up last week. Unfortunately, we have been experiencing some problems. Since your technicians were here, some employees have had difficulty connecting to the Internet, and others have no access to our network at all and cannot even log on to their computers! However, the worst thing is that some important files and documents seem to have been lost as a result of the migration to the new software. One of these files was a presentation for a very important client. This is a particular problem for us because we have a meeting with this client on Monday, and we need the presentation and do not have enough time to redo it. Could you please look into this problem for us urgently as time is running out? If we do not hear from you by the end of today, we will have to look elsewhere. I will be in meetings this afternoon, but you can contact me per e-mail under B dot Jenkins at NWM.de. Thank you.

◎ A 1.15 Modul 8 The Internet, B 1, 2

Pauline: Hello, my name is Pauline Smith, senior IT-manager of IXcell Ltd. First of all, thank you for this opportunity to present the architecture of our IT solution and its advantages. Have you ever wondered where all the money goes when you expand your IT? Yes, purchasing a computer always means paying for software licences and maintenance, too. Now, our service offers you a cheaper alternative. Instead of installing a software suite for each new computer, your employees will only need one software suite which they load from custom-designed interface software. This software enables you to log into our web-based service, which hosts all the programs you need. This solution is called cloud computing, and it works like this. A cloud computing system is divided into two sections: the front end, which is made up of the client's computer or network; and the back end, where the data is processed. With a suitable web application on the client computer, you will gain access to your data via the world wide web anywhere and at any time. The storage space and software doesn't exist on your computer but on our cloud. This minimizes costs for high-end devices. The cloud, also called the back end, is made up of a control node which acts as a central server. Its task is to administer the cloud by means of software protocols called middleware. Each of the applications you need has its individual application server wherever the necessary data is saved on our data storage servers. In case of a breakdown, you can be sure that all your data can be retrieved from additional backup servers. Another advantage is of course the minimized costs for support, as only our servers need to be maintained. As you know, a new streamlined hardware system has fewer problems than an old network of heterogeneous machines… Now, I know you may have concerns about security, privacy and service in the event of a breakdown. Let me assure you that our business model stands or falls on our reputation. That's why it's in our own interest to offer you only the highest encryption standards not to mention authentication techniques. Finally, it's the experience of many years of research that makes us confident that we can serve all your needs. We look forward to welcoming you soon as a new customer. Thank you.

⦾ A 1.16 Modul 9 Writing software, B 1, 2

Dan: Good morning Phil. When did you get in?
Phillip: Hi Dan. I've been here all night debugging.
Dan: Do you mind if I take a look at your code?
Phillip: Be my guest.
Dan: Okay, what am I looking at?
Phillip: This is the source code for the next hotfix for the multiplayer matchmaking.
Dan: Ah, the one that was to be completed yesterday?
Phillip: Yes, that's the one. I've fixed all the bugs except for issue number 44376.
Dan: I thought that 44376 was fixed two weeks ago.
Phillip: It was but it had to be rescheduled.
Dan: What does the compile report say?
Phillip: That's the problem; it compiles without any errors.
Dan: So, what causes the module to run into an exception?
Phillip: I don't know. When there are just two players trying to create a game, everything works fine. As soon as there are more than two players, that's when a problem can arise. But it's not directly connected to the number of players because it doesn't always happen when there are more than two players.
Dan: And this is something that the automated tests didn't catch?
Phillip: Exactly. We discovered it during the beta testing phase when the game was open to the public.
Dan: And the players' bug reports are useless as always, right?
Phillip: I haven't had time to look at all of them.
Dan: Why don't you go home, take a nap, and come back in say four hours? Meanwhile, I'll look at the bug reports from the beta testing phase.
Phillip: Thanks, Dan. …
Dan: Hi there, Phil. Are you feeling better?
Phillip: Much better, thanks. Have you found anything?
Dan: I think so. First I went through the reports related to this issue.
Phillip: All 2,317 of them?
Dan: Some of the team helped. Anyway, the problem only seems to arise when people use an X-Link DSL router. I've already spoken to someone at X-Link. It looks like it's a problem with their firmware. The router sometimes takes too long to respond to some of our module's messages. None of this is official of course. They're working on a patch, but that won't be released until three weeks after we ship our game.
Phillip: You can't be serious! At least 10% of the DSL routers in the world are X-Link. Are we supposed to tell our players that they won't be able to play our game if they have an X-Link router?
Dan: Don't worry; I've already taken care of the problem.
Phillip: What did you do?
Dan: While debugging we determined that the X-Link router takes about 15–20 milliseconds longer to respond to our messages than the other routers.
Phillip: And?
Dan: And if our module doesn't get a response within 50 milliseconds while the session is created, we stop waiting and consider the session failed. Take a look at line 7231 of the source code. All I did was increase our waiting time from 43 ms to 63 ms.
Phillip: Hm, I don't really like doing that. We spent a lot of time tuning those numbers to make sure everything runs as efficiently as possible.
Dan: True, but look at it this way: We won't be able to fix all of the errors before we release the game, so there will have to be a patch after the release anyway. By that time X-Link will have fixed their routers. Then we just reset the timeout value to 43 milliseconds with the first patch and no one will ever know. We ship the game on time and X-Link won't be embarrassed. No one gets hurt.
Phillip: Except our pride.

⦾ A 1.17 Modul 10 Tools and applications A 1, 2

Sue: Hi John! Have you got a moment to tell me about the new tool you found on the Internet? What does it do again?
John: Sure! It's a web-based office suite that – once loaded – turns your web browser into a word processor, spreadsheet or presentation software. Then you can use it to write text documents, perform calculations or make diagrams or presentation slides. And it's free!

Sue: That sounds great! So I can save myself the high price of an office suite and simply work online?

John: That's right. But the main advantage is that you not only have access to your files anytime and anywhere but you can also work with other people on your files online in real time.

Sue: So does this online application also let me communicate with the other users when we're editing the file?

John: Of course it does! There's a chat function you can run for that. Unfortunately, the changes the other editors make during file-sharing are not highlighted in real time. You can only see them in the revision history. That keeps a record of the past edits, and you can use it to restore earlier versions.

Sue: And where are the files saved?

John: Well, you can save them on your hard drive, or online on your 1GB virtual space, which is commonly known as a 'data cloud'. You are granted copyright, but you have to be aware that your data may be intercepted…

Sue: … which makes this application unsuitable for government or commercial organisations. Is there anything else I need to know?

John: Well, apart from the fact that you have to submit personal information when you register, there is not much to worry about. The user interface is intuitive: for example the word processor lets you print, undo, redo, choose a font style and font size. You can write in bold, italics, underline or highlight text. It's just like a Word toolbar …

Sue: Wow, I must try it out! Can you send me the link?

A 1.18 Modul 10 Tools and applications, B 3

There are several ways to keep your system healthy. First, you can reduce the chance of system crashes or unwanted program errors by cleaning your system registry with a special system tool from time to time. The system registry is like a major database: it keeps a record of all your specific program settings. But it often fills up with invalid entries, especially after installations and major changes of the application software. The registry cleaning tool basically works by deleting or disabling these invalid entries.

Another system tool you should use from time to time is a disk defragmenter. When your computer saves your files, it fills up all the empty spaces on your hard drive, even if this means that a file is broken up into small fragments. The computer always knows where all the separate fragments are, but the head has to travel more to retrieve the fragmented data, and this will slow your system down. The defragmenting tool reorganises your hard drive so that all the fragments of your files are put back next to each other. This speeds up your PC.

Before you "defrag" your hard drive, you should first get rid of old, outdated files on your hard drive that are slowing down the performance of your entire system. The system tool for this is a disc cleaner, which deletes all the hidden temporary files or links on your hard drive. These are always created when you surf the web or work with your computer.

If you are having trouble accessing files on a hard drive, or you can't access the drive at all, you should use the check disc tool. Interruptions in the read and write process (like power cuts) may damage the structure of a file or even the drive. The check disc tool will find and repair any logical file system errors.

After doing all these things, you should set a system restore point. The system restore tool backs up system files with certain extensions (.exe, .dll, etc.) and saves them for later recovery and use. If anything goes wrong later, you will be able to roll back to a healthy configuration.

A 1.19 Modul 11 Enterprise software, B 5

Lisa: So Michael, forgive me if I get right to the point, but what is so great about your new business intelligence solution?

Michael: Well, I don't know where to start. But seriously, I have to say, KP-Systems BI 2 is not faster, not more performant and certainly not cheaper than BI 1.

Lisa: Interesting. Why would we want to buy it then?

Michael: Let me open the software and I'll show you why. Alright. You can see that the start screen of the software is still basically the same as in the previous version. You enter your username and password and click 'log in'. In BI 1 you had to manually select the department you wanted to analyze every time you logged in. Now the department is automatically selected based on the department you work in.

Lisa: And how can I analyze data for a department other than my own?

Michael: After you log in, you see the department screen. In the top right corner we have a 'change department option'. But Ms Horton, if you think about it, how often do you look at other department's data?

Lisa: Not that often, that's true. Show me more.

Michael: Right. So the department start screen is empty right now. In the past we had all the functions cluttered in one place.

Lisa: No need to remind me. To tell you the truth the old system was so complicated I was thinking of recommending that our company switch to NSoft DynamiX's solution.

Michael: I think you may change your mind once you have seen what BI 2 has to offer. So the start screen is empty because it hasn't been configured yet.

Lisa: I don't like what I'm hearing. Does that mean that I have to configure the screen to get all my old functions back?

Michael: Until you start using the system it is empty. But when you use the system, it configures itself.

Lisa: Explain!

Michael: You're the head of the sales department, right?

Lisa: Right.

Michael: Now all of the functions are still available in the menu bar at the top. What kind of analysis would you like to run?

Lisa: Well at least once a month I run an analysis on all of our sales to find out who our top ten customers are. Then I can make sure that they receive the attention they deserve.

Michael: Here, why don't you take the mouse and you can try out the software yourself?

Lisa: OK. What do I want to click now?

Michael: Could you click on 'sales' in the menu bar first?

Lisa: Hm, there is only one entry, 'new analysis'. That's not very convenient. I used to be able to select from a list of different options.

Michael: Bear with me, Ms Horton. Please click on 'new analysis'. You will see how BI 2 is better in a few minutes.

Lisa: Alright. Done. Ah I see, now I have all of the options. Let's see ... 'customers by revenue', there it is. So I suppose I click on that. Oh, that's nice, it allows me to specify how long I want the list of results to be. In the past I could either have the top ten, top one hundred or all customers. So let's say I want the top 15 instead of the top ten. Do I click on 'finish' now?

Michael: That's right. Now, if you remember, the system is empty. The code for the analysis has to be generated first. It shouldn't take longer than a minute or two.

Lisa: Does that have to be done every time?

Michael: No, only once. So now that it has been generated, let's look at the start screen.

Lisa: Oh, now that option is there for me to click on. So by using the system I customize the user interface to my needs. But what if I generate an analysis that I only need once? Will it be on the start screen forever?

Michael: No. You see, what makes the new interface so special is that it learns from the way you use it. You always have the functions you use the most at your finger tips. And if you only need some functions once in a while, you'll always find them in the menu bar.

Lisa: Well I have to say, I'm impressed. But I was a little disappointed when you said that the system wasn't faster or more performant.

Michael: Sorry Ms Horton, I was only joking. You see, every generation of software is technologically more advanced than the last, but what good is it if the software becomes more complicated to use? When we started working on BI 2, we decided that we could only set ourselves apart from other companies if we made our software simpler and more intuitive to use.

Lisa: Right.

Michael: Every department in your company knows how to do their job. Accounting knows how to keep the books in order, research and development knows how to come up with new products and manufacturing knows how to build them. Our aim is to give your people software to make their job easier. So our software shouldn't interfere, but behave the way the user needs it to. Isn't that what enterprise software is all about?

Lisa: It used to be in the past. And by the looks of it, it could be again. We still need to talk about pricing though.

Michael: Gladly.

◎ A 1.20 Modul 12 Computers in danger, B 2, 3

Helen Jones: Global Computers, Helen Jones speaking. How can I help you?

Tim Burner: Hello! My name is Tim Burner. I work for R&P Marketing Services. We are a small but growing company specializing in accounting. Your services have been recommended to us by one of our business partners and I'd like to know if you can help us make our network safer.

Helen: We certainly can. What exactly do you need?

Tim: We are interested in making the computers of our small network more resistant to hackers by a firewall. I know that our PCs are equipped with an integrated on-board firewall. Could you tell me if this is sufficient to protect our network?

Helen: Well, on-board firewalls have the advantage that they come along with the system software, and no separate installation or configuration is needed. That makes them easy to operate, which is useful especially for undemanding home users. Also, they are always compatible with the system software as both were programmed by one company.

Tim: Sounds great! OK, but what would we have to pay for that?

Helen: Nothing – in money terms. However, you have to be aware that on-board firewalls are often not complex enough to provide security for all computer operations. For example, data transfer within the network may be blocked as some on-board firewalls can't be correctly configured to open data ports. If configuration is possible, it is feasible only for IT specialists…

Tim: OK, setting up a firewall correctly is the key for a secure system.

Helen: Yes, but the lack of configuration options makes it difficult for the user to see which information is blocked, or not. In general, I would recommend using a hardware firewall, but that means replacing existing routers by routers which already include a firewall.

Tim: I guess that's because hackers have to get round the router first before they can enter the system. Er, … I doubt that this is an option as we already have functioning routers. Are there any other solutions on the market?

Helen: For businesses we offer several independent software firewalls such as the SoMoDo business solution, or the Fire IP one. They protect entire networks and are easy to configure. And they work instead of the on-board system firewall which is always a hacker's first target.

Tim: Well, we would require details of your prices and terms of payment. By the way, do you grant quantity discounts?

Helen: Usually yes, but it all depends on the program you choose. Could you give me your e-mail address?

Tim: It's RPmarketing@service….com. I look forward to hearing from you.

Helen: Got it. Thank you and have a nice day!

Tim: You too, bye-bye!

◎ A 1.21 Modul 13 Customer support, A 6, 7

Stanley: Hello. My name is Stanley Brown and you are listening to "The communicator" podcast, the podcast to enhance your business communication. Today we are going to focus on one particular kind of communication: communicative behaviour when giving support on the phone. That is not only the case in the field of IT support but can also be applied in other instances, for example explaining how a difficult process needs to be booked in a system. For good telephone service it is important to make the customer feel comfortable, of course. For this reason it is absolutely essential to establish a good rapport with customers. It's a fact that a relaxed customer is more likely to be able to explain the details of his problem. And once the problem has been identified, it is your turn to solve it. There are many different types of caller, and knowing how to handle them effectively will help you deal with the call successfully and quickly. Often you might have talkative customers who use a call to socialize rather than have a problem fixed. In these situations let the customer talk for a minute but then politely refocus the customer. To do this you may ask close-ended questions which can be answered by "yes" or "no". Also there are rude customers that complain and even use abusive language. Here you could at first try to contact the customer's favourite technician to see if they can take the call. If not, listen carefully so as not to make them repeat anything, express that you also want to solve the problem and apologize. When facing angry customers, sympathize with the customer's problem but avoid talking at length about the cause of the problem. If you have established a connection, focus on solving the problem but avoid transferring the customer or putting them on hold. Two other kinds of customers you might find are knowledgeable and inexperienced customers. Whereas the first one is impatient and tries to control the call, the latter can't describe the problem or follow directions correctly. In the first case you should transfer the customer to a more experienced level-two technician. If that's not possible, do not ask to check the obvious and avoid a step-by-step process. In the case of inexperienced customers you should avoid sounding condescending. The best is to speak in plain terms, avoid industry jargon and follow a step-by-step approach. OK, that should be it for now. Keep in mind that information is only half of the message! The bottom line is that your communication skills are sometimes just as important as your IT skills. Thanks for listening. Please comment, rate and subscribe!

Further reading

1 | The Internet and intercultural communication

R Read the following text and answer the questions below.

The Internet and intercultural awareness

Whether right or wrong, globalization, as one writer puts it sounds unstoppable. Mass tourism, the interdependency of world markets and the Internet with its cheap and instant links to even the remotest corners of the globe have all contributed to an upgrowth in intercultural communication. In the course of their daily working lives more and more people over the world are confronted with the task of communicating with people from cultures very different from their own. English, often not native to either speaker, is most frequently the language employed on the Internet, i.e. the lingua franca. Yet the language itself is almost the least of it; intercultural awareness and tolerance play a central role in making global communication work. How we express our needs, desires and feelings, however, is determined by the cultural context in which we operate. Caution is called for, though, in jumping to the conclusion that certain behavior is typically American, Malaysian or Swedish. We should also be aware that age, sex, regional differences, economic status and just plain personality differences also influence our communication patterns.

Certain core competences such as open-mindedness, respect, flexibility, and the ability to tolerate different habits can facilitate intercultural communication. More specifically, awareness and respect for the cultural differences in such areas as degree of formality, styles of addressing your counterpart, and time-management are helpful.

1. Does everyone agree on the import of globalization? If not, how do opinions differ? What do you, personally, think?
2. What factors have played a role in the spread of international contacts between people? What are the consequences? And for you personally?
3. What is meant by the term lingua franca?
4. Aside from being able to speak the other person's language, what do you need in order to deal with foreigners? Can you think of one example?
5. What factors determine how we speak to other people?
6. What makes it easier to talk to people from other parts of the world?
7. Can you think of any ways in which formality or style of address might differ from one country to the other?
8. In what way does the Internet influence intercultural communication?

2 | Computer viruses

P **1** **Read the following text and make up headings for the eight paragraphs.**

____

a

Analogous to biological viruses, a computer virus is a program that searches out and "infects" other programs. It does this by embedding a copy of itself in the boot sector of a disk or to other widely used programs such as spreadsheets or database software. The virus itself is executed when an infected file is activated or when the computer is started from an infected disk.

____

b

Viruses are increasing at a mind-boggling rate. Though there was only one known virus in 1986, only four short years later they were being discovered at the rate of one per week. Today computer viruses are on the rise with up to 15 new viruses flaming up daily and annual growth rates of more than 100 %. Naturally, an increase in the number of viruses at large in the computer world have led to a rapid spread in the rate of infections and the number of affected computers.

____

c

Originally viruses could not infect other computers without assistance. While disks were once the major source of infection, e-mail attachments soon replaced them as the bigger headache and were responsible for the sharp rise in infection rates. As opposed to diskettes, which are typical for boot-sector viruses, attachments are primarily responsible for the spread of macro viruses.

▶

d

For some time now worms are on the rise. A worm uses a network to send a copy of itself to another computer. In other words, worms can spread on their own and don't need human help. Unlike viruses which infect or corrupt files, worms affect the network itself. Internet worms, for example, take advantage of "remote vulnerabilities" (security holes in programs) which is now the way most viruses and worms spread.

---

e

What exactly do computer viruses and worms do? Some are relatively benign and may result in nothing worse than "funny" messages or graphics popping up unexpectedly. Others are anything but harmless and can cause extensive damage, wasting time, money and countless hours of manpower.

---

f

Particularly malignant viruses can delete or block access to a user's files and cause damage to software, while worms can seriously harm networks, if nothing else by consuming bandwidth. Virus hoaxes claiming to warn other users of some lethal virus on the loose are almost as bad. They jam e-mail networks and lead to lost productivity and downtime.

---

g

Understandably, people tend to react emotionally when their files or network are threatened. It's therefore important to remember a few points that run counter to the general myth building and media sensation surrounding viruses. Viruses don't infect write protected disks. With the exception of special types of hardware such as flash memory, they can't infect hardware.

---

h

Computer viruses can and do cause damage and call for effective countermeasures. Producing and peddling anti-virus software has become a lucrative business. Virus scanning and detecting can be done at intervals or each time a file is downloaded. As most people are aware, scanning e-mail attachments is also an important preventive measure.

R **2** Match the following virus terms to their descriptions below.

a. Trojan Horse b. Worm c. Benign virus d. Malignant virus e. Payload f. Macro virus g. File infectors h. Boot infectors i. Retro virus j. Virus hoax	1. are annoying false alarms that waste time and jam up your mailbox. 2. is a category of virus which damages a computer system by corrupting files or destroying data. 3. are viruses which either latch onto or replace .COM and .EXE files as well as other extensions. 4. are designed to attack anti-virus programs and wipe out anti-virus data files. 5. are programs with a nasty surprise designed to cause harm, in contrast to viruses they can't make copies of themselves. 6. affect the boot program of the hard drive when the system is rebooted with a infected bootable storage medium in the drive. 7. are script based viruses and are spread generally via e-mail attachments and Internet downloads. 8. are programs designed to copy themselves from one computer to another, not from file to file, via a network system – this means they don't need humans to help spread and are, therefore, especially dangerous. 9. is a category of virus which causes no significant damage. 10. is the part of the virus that triggers the actual events.

3 | The ABCs of entrepreneurship

1. An 'entrepreneur' is a person who embodies certain 'enterprise skills and attitudes'. The skills include the willingness to take risks on new products or processes and the ability to deal with uncertainty and change in a competent manner. Determination, self-confidence and a strong work ethic characterize the attitude of the entrepreneur. The Program for Entrepreneurship Teaching (PET) wants to root enterprise in schools, so that students can learn about it and practise it in realistic situations. PET was established by a group of educators and business people in New York in 1986 and now teaches over 150,000 people worldwide about entrepreneurship.

2. The first step in establishing a successful business is to come up with a profitable idea. This might be a new product, something

▶

which you have seen when travelling and think you can introduce in your own country, or you can even build on the back of something else (such as products to go with cell phones). A new business idea could also be the opportunity to buy into someone else's good idea through a franchise.

3. Research can help the budding entrepreneur to work out if the idea has potential. It is a support in understanding and assessing customers' needs. Research helps to break the market down into smaller parts, or segments, so that they can be more easily targeted. Entrepreneurs often use a SWOT analysis to evaluate new business ideas. This has a closer look at the Strengths and Weaknesses of the idea, and the external Opportunities and Threats. Students of PET workshops often come up with a wide range of business ideas. These are ideas for selling both goods and services – goods such as post-its and mousepads, and services such as setting up a swap shop so that other students in the school can sell and buy used text books at discounted prices.

4. When establishing a business one must differentiate between start-up costs, which only have to be paid initially, and running costs, which are needed to maintain the continued operation of the business. Running costs are usually further divided into direct costs, which are linked to output (such as material costs), and indirect costs – which are usually referred to as overheads (such as energy or interest rates). Entrepreneurs also need to estimate future cashflows using cashflow forecasts. They need to know if receipts will be greater than payments or if they will need to take out more in loans to make up for the deficit should payments be greater than receipts.

5. The students involved in PET projects are supported with a £50 loan to start the business. In normal businesses the most usual sources for start-up costs are owners' funds, i.e. the owners use their own savings or bank loans or overdrafts. Other possibilities are venture capital in which speculators risk their money by investing in businesses or so-called trade credit in which the new business pays for ordered goods at a later date.

6. The students report that they benefit enormously from their PET experiences. They feel they learn to work in teams, manage their time better and develop many other positive qualities. They feel that they would not have been able to develop many of these skills through the normal curriculum. In conclusion we can claim that PET helps young people to implement business ideas which use skills beyond those of the traditional curriculum. Students learn how to set up a business, manage market research, cash flow, work in teams and manage production, thus preparing them for the real world of business and work.

R **1** **Read the text above and choose the best title for each of the numbered paragraphs from the following list.**

A Students sell goods and services
B New ideas offer chances
C Stages in establishing a business
D Business person profile
E PET realizes business ideas
F Entrepreneurship is a global concern
G Students profit from project
H Calculating costs
I Student loans
J Initial capital vs overhead
K Financing a business
L Market analysis

R **2** **Using the information from the text complete each of the sentences (1.–4.) with a suitable phrase (a.–h.) from the list below.**

1. A SWOT analysis involves … 2. Through the project students felt they learned things that … 3. An entrepreneur needs to estimate costs in advance in order to be able … 4. To be successful a entrepreneur needs a good idea and, above all, …	a. a willingness to take chances, adapt to new situations and work hard. b. to distinguish between start-up costs and running costs. c. assessing the positive and negative aspects of a business idea. d. to know whether the business will make a profit. e. are not usually taught in classes. f. will help them find a job after completing the business curriculum. g. deciding which business ideas are good and developing strategies to deal with competitors. h. careful planning and new products ideas.

Grammar overview

Present Tense (Gegenwart)

Bildung: Present Tense (simple)		
Merke: Bei der 3. Person Einzahl *(he / she / it)* wird ein *s* an die Endung des Verbs angehängt.	I like / you like / he (she / it) likes we like / you like / they like	computer games.

Verwendung: Present Tense (simple)	
– bei allgemein bekannten Tatsachen und Aussagen	– Most cars run on petrol.
– bei regelmäßigen Handlungen: Schlüsselwörter: *usually, normally, always, never, sometimes, often…*	– I usually start work at 7 o'clock.
– bei Gewohnheiten	– He doesn't smoke.
– bei Fahrplänen, Öffnungszeiten etc. für die Zukunft	– My train leaves at 10 o'clock tomorrow morning.

Bildung: Present Tense (progressive)		
am / are / is + Infinitiv mit Endung *-ing*	I **am** / you **are** / he / she / it / **is** we **are** / you **are** / they **are**	work**ing** on a new project.

Verwendung: Present Tense (progressive)	
– bei Handlungen im Augenblick des Sprechens	– I am reading a manual at the moment.
– bei vorübergehenden Handlungen	– I'm staying at the Royal Excelsior Hotel.
– bei (fest) geplanten Handlungen in der Zukunft	– I'm meeting Ms Winter next week.
– bei gefühlsbetonten Aussagen mit *always* (negativ besetzt)	– He is always complaining about his boss.

Past Tense (Vergangenheit)

Bildung: Past Simple	
ed-Endung bei regelmäßigen Verben	I work**ed** in Munich last year.
2. Form bei unregelmäßigen Verben *(1. meet / **2. met** / 3. met)*	He **met** Mr Miller yesterday.

Verwendung: Past Simple		
bei Vorgängen, die in der Vergangenheit abgeschlossen wurden; oft mit Zeitangabe. Signalwörter u.a.: *yesterday, in (1990), two weeks ago, last year, last month, last week.*	I finished my studies	in 2008. 3 years ago. last week.

Present Perfect (Vollendete Gegenwart)

Bildung: Present Perfect (simple)		
have oder *has* + *ed*-Endung (bei regelmäßigen Verben)	I / you / we / they **have worked** He / she **has worked**	as a trainee.
	It **has** worked well for us.	
3. Form bei unregelmäßigen Verben *(1. see / 2. saw / **3. seen**)*	I have **seen** the new car.	

Bildung: Present Perfect (progressive)			
have / has + *been* + Infinitiv mit *-ing*	I / you / we / they He / she	**have** **has**	**been living** in Munich for 5 years.

Verwendung: Present Perfect (simple and progressive)	
– bei Handlungen in der Vergangenheit **ohne Zeitangabe**	– I have written three letters.
– bei noch andauernden Zeitbestimmungen	– We haven't had any complaints so far / today …
– bei Handlungen, die in der Vergangenheit begonnen haben, aber noch nicht abgeschlossen sind, wobei ***for*** bei Zeiträumen *(two hours / three weeks)* und ***since*** bei Zeitpunkten *(2001 / January)* benutzt wird	– I have been living in Stuttgart **for** 20 years. – I have been living in Stuttgart **since** 1982.
– Einige Verben werden in der Regel nicht in der Verlaufsform verwendet.	– I have **had** the car for five years. – I have **known** the company since 2010.

Future (Zukunft)

Bildung und Verwendung	
Shall / will drückt äußere Umstände aus.	Most of this year's teleworking jobs **will** be offered in autumn.
Will drückt die Bereitschaft oder Entschlossenheit aus, etwas zu tun, sowie Versprechungen.	I'**ll** do my best to get the job.
Will wird auch benutzt für eine spontane Entscheidung.	Wait a minute, I'**ll** help you!
Going to wird verwendet, um persönliche Planungen und Vorhaben auszudrücken.	I **am going to** apply for a job in teleworking. *(Ich habe vor…)*
Going to wird auch verwendet, wenn bereits Anzeichen dafür da sind, dass etwas eintreten wird.	Look at those clouds! It'**s going to** rain.
Present continuous wird verwendet um eine feste Vereinbarung (gewöhnlich mit Zeitangabe) mitzuteilen.	Jennifer is **meeting** her colleague this evening.
Present simple wird für die Zukuft verwendet in Verbindung mit Fahrplänen, Öffnungszeiten usw.	Jim's train **arrives** at 4.30 p.m. Our office **opens** at 9 o'clock tomorrow morning.

Comparison of adjectives (Steigerung des Adjektivs)

Bildung	
Einsilbige und zweisilbige Adjektive werden durch Anhängen von *-er* und *-est* (germanische Steigerung) gesteigert. Aus **y** wird *i*. Ein einzelner Endkonsonant wird nach einfachem betonten Vokal verdoppelt.	fast – faster – fastest easy – easier – easiest hot – hotter – hottest
Für die zweisilbigen gibt es keine eindeutigen Regeln. Gewöhnlich werden zweisilbige Adjektive, die auf *-y*, *-le*, *-er* oder *-ow* enden germanisch gesteigert, aber dies ist keine bindende Regel.	clever – cleverer – cleverest noble – nobler – noblest narrow – narrower – narrowest
Ebenfalls germanisch gesteigert werden zweisilbige Adjektive, wenn sie ihre Betonung auf der zweiten Silbe haben. Auch diese Regel ist nicht bindend. Daneben gibt es aber z. B. auch folgende Formen: *more / the most clever* oder *more / the most polite.*	polite – politer – politest sincere – sincerer – sincerest
Andere zweisilbige Adjektive werden in der Regel romanisch gesteigert.	nervous – more nervous – most nervous splendid – more splendid – most splendid
Alle drei- und mehrsilbigen Adjektive steigert man mit ***more*** und ***the most*** (romanische Steigerung).	expensive – more expensive – the most expensive beautiful – more beautiful – the most beautiful
Es gibt auch eine Reihe von unregelmäßigen Adjektiven.	good – better – the best bad – worse – the worst much / many – more – the most little – less – the least old – elder – the eldest (bei Familienangehörigen)

Verwendung	
Gleichheiten mit *as ... as*	He is **as** skilful **as** I. (so geschickt / fachmännisch wie ich)
Komparative mit *than*	Mike is **less** helpful **than** Tim. (weniger ... als)
Je ... desto...	**The** more I work with this machine **the** better I like it.
Superlativ beim Vergleich von mehr als 2 Objekten	The new electric drill is **the most** expensive tool in the brochure.

Adverbs (Adverbien)

Das Umstandswort (Adverb) dient zur näheren Beschreibung eines Eigenschaftswortes (Adjektives) oder eines Zeitwortes (Verbs).

Bildung	
Von der Wortbildung her unterscheidet man zwei Arten von Adverbien:	
1. ursprüngliche und durch Zusammensetzung gebildete Adverbien	often, quite, here, soon always, already, yesterday
2. durch Ableitung gebildete Abverbien: Hier wird an das Adjektiv ein *-ly* angehängt.	clear**ly**, usual**ly**, quick**ly**, easi**ly**, bad**ly**
Manche Adjektive und Adverbien sind	
– gleichlautend oder	daily, weekly, monthly, yearly, early, fast
– unterschiedlich.	good – **well**
Die Steigerung des Adverbs ist der Steigerung des Adjektivs vergleichbar.	carefully – more carefully – most carefully fast – faster – the fastest
Unregelmäßige Formen der Steigerung	well – better – best badly – worse – worst
y wird zu *i*	happy + -ly = happily
stummes *e* fällt weg	true + -ly = truly
Verdoppelung des Endkonsonanten	beautiful + -ly = beautiful**l**y

Verwendung	
Hier wird das Verb näher beschrieben.	The new machine **works well**.
Hier wird das Adjektiv *clear* näher beschrieben.	The small printer makes **remarkably clear** printouts.
Hier wird ein anderes Adverb *(quickly)* näher beschrieben.	Our new machine works **extremely quickly**.

Questions (Fragen)

Bildung: Alternative questions (Entscheidungsfragen)	
Entscheidungsfragen, die mit ja oder nein beantwortet werden können, werden im Englischen immer mit einem Hilfsverb oder einer Form von *to do* eingeleitet.	**Do** you smoke? **Did** you see Mr Miller yesterday?
Erstes Hilfsverb steht vor dem Subjekt.	**Have** you met Mr Miller?

Verwendung: Alternative questions (Entscheidungsfragen)	
Does Sally speak French?	Yes, she **does.** / No, she **doesn't.**
Can these tools be used in milling as well as in turning?	Yes, they **can.** / No, they **can't.**
Is the lathe set properly for this job?	Yes, it **is.** / No, it **isn't.**
Did he meet the chief executive at the fair?	Yes, he **did.** / No, he **didn't.**
Will you finish this job by Friday?	Yes, I **will.** / No, I **won't.**

Bildung: Questions with interrogatives (Fragen mit Fragefürwörtern)	
Die Fragen werden mit dem Fragefürwort eingeleitet. Vor dem Subjekt steht die Form von *to do (do / does; did)*, nach dem Subjekt steht das Vollverb im Infinitiv.	**How** do you **go** to work? **What** does she **do**?
Wird nach dem Subjekt oder einem Teil des Subjekts gefragt *(who, what, which, whose)*, so wird die Form von 'to do' nicht verwendet.	**What** is his job?

Verwendung: Questions with interrogatives (Fragen mit Fragefürwörtern)	
Fragewort ist Subjekt.	Who operates this machine? Which tools do you need for this job?
Fragewort ist nicht Subjekt.	Who / Whom did he meet at the exhibition? Which tool have you chosen for this job?

Word order (Wortstellung)

Bildung	
Die Wortstellung folgt im englischen Aussagesatz der Regel S – P – O: *Subject [They] – Predicate [have repaired] – Object [the broken tools]*	They have repaired the broken tools.
Dies gilt auch im Nebensatz (im Deutschen steht ja im Nebensatz das Prädikat am Ende).	I was told that they had repaired the broken tools.
Zeitbestimmungen stehen in der Regel entweder am Anfang oder am Ende des Satzes.	Yesterday they repaired the broken tools. They repaired the broken tools a week ago.
Mehrere Umstandsbestimmungen folgen gewöhnlich folgender Reihenfolge: *Manner – Place – Time* (Art und Weise – Ort – Zeit)	The mechanic repaired the tools in the shop yesterday. The mechanic repaired the tools quite skilfully in the shop last night.
Adverbien der Häufigkeit *(frequency)* können auch vor dem Hauptverb stehen: *always, ever, never, often, regularly, generally, rarely, seldom, occasionally.* Diese Adverbien stehen aber nach dem Verb *to be.* Bei Hilfsverben stehen die Adverbien der Häufigkeit zwischen dem Hilfsverb und dem Vollverb, bzw. nach dem Hilfsverb.	The service people **always** come on time. The service people **never** come without calling ahead. The service people **usually** check the machine in May. They are **generally** very reliable. The machine has **sometimes** had problems. With old machines you can **never** tell.

Defining relative clauses (Notwendige Relativsätze)

Ein Relativsatz ist notwendig, wenn die darin gegebene Information nötig ist, um deutlich zu machen, welche Person oder Sache gemeint ist.

Verwendung	
bei Personen ***who*** oder ***that***	The man **who / that** is operating the CNC machine usually works at the training centre.
bei Sachen ***which*** oder ***that***	The machine element **which / that** is moving the tool is the main spindle.
im Genitiv wird **whose** verwendet	Tom is an engineer **whose** skills are highly praised.
Das Relativpronomen als Satzobjekt kann weggelassen werden.	They called the technician (**who**) they saw standing at the milling machine. Sally read the operation plan (**which**) she had filled in this morning.

Non-defining relative clauses (Nicht notwendige Relativsätze)

Ein Relativsatz ist nicht notwendig, wenn die darin gegebene Information nicht nötig ist, um deutlich zu machen, welche Person oder Sache gemeint ist.

Verwendung	
Ein Relativsatz ist nicht notwendig, wenn die darin enthaltene Information nicht nötig ist, um zu erkennen, welche Person oder Sache gemeint ist.	**Sally's friend**, who is a skilled worker, **is doing his final exams this summer.** **The machine**, which is DEG's latest model, **works perfectly.**
Relativpronomen als Satzobjekt	**The three German apprentices**, who Sally met at the training centre, **are in their last year of training.**

Reported speech (Indirekte Rede)

Die indirekte Rede wird benutzt, wenn berichtet wird oder wurde, was jemand sagt oder sagte, bzw. macht oder machte (**Aussage**), wenn jemandem gesagt wird oder wurde, was geschehen soll (**Aufforderung**), oder wenn gefragt wird oder wurde, was geschieht oder geschah (**Frage**).

Bildung / Verwendung	
Steht das Wort, welches die indirekte Rede einleitet, in der Gegenwart, so ändern sich die Zeitformen der direkten Rede nicht.	"We **are measuring** this machined component." → Sally explains that they are measuring the machined component.
Steht das Wort, welches die indirekte Rede einleitet, in der Vergangenheit, so ändern sich die Zeitformen der direkten Rede wie folgt.	
Simple past und *present perfect* werden zu *past perfect*.	Sally **explained that they were measuring** the machined component. "The trainee **forgot** to set the revolution speed." → The master **noticed that the trainee had forgotten** to check the revolution speed.
Will wird zu *would*.	"The drilling operation **will** have to be prepared by marking out and centring." → Oliver **remembered** that the drilling operation **would** have to be prepared by marking out and centring.
Pronomen werden angepasst.	"**I can't** find the measuring equipment." → **Sally told** me that she **couldn't find** the measuring equipment.
Orts- und Zeitbestimmungen werden angepasst.	"**We** are seeing the other students **tomorrow**." → Oliver **added** that **they** were seeing the other students **the next day**. "I programmed the CNC machine **two days ago**." → He said that he had programmed the CNC machine **two days earlier**.
Aufforderungen werden in der indirekten Rede im Infinitiv wiedergegeben.	"**Use** HSS twist drills to drill metal stock." → The instructor **advised** Sally **to use** HSS twist drills to drill metal stock.
Bei Fragen wird die Wortstellung wie im Aussagesatz verwendet, d.h. am Anfang steht das Fragewort, dann folgen Subjekt, Prädikat und Objekt.	"Why has Oliver used the impact drilling function?" → The master **wanted to know why Oliver had used** the impact drilling function. "When did you sharpen the drill?" → He asked **when he had sharpened** the drill.
Die Umschreibung mit 'to do' wird nur bei Verneinungen angewendet.	"Why **don't** you call the salesman?" → She **asked** Sally why she **didn't call** the salesman.

Passive voice (Passiv)

Bildung	
Form von *to be* + *ed*-Endung (wie bei *simple past*) bei regelmäßigen Verben Form von *to be* + 3. Form bei unregelmäßigen Verben (*1. take / 2. took / 3.* ***taken***. Siehe Liste der unregelmäßigen Verben.)	The machine is equip**ped** with an emergency stop. He **is taken** to hospital.

Aktiv:	We *Subjekt*	recharge *Prädikat*	the batteries. *Objekt*
Passiv:	*Subjekt* The batteries	*Prädikat* are recharged	*Objekt (by-agent)* (by us).

Formen	
Present Tense (Simple)	The goods are transported every day.
Present Tense (Progressive)	The goods are being transported at the moment.
Past Tense (Simple)	The goods were transported yesterday.
Past Tense (Progressive)	The goods were being transported when the truck crashed.
Future 1 (will)	The goods will be transported next Monday, I promise.
Future 1 (going to)	The goods are going to be transported next month.
Present Perfect	The goods have already been transported.
Past Perfect	The goods had been transported before the order arrived.

Verwendung	
Das Passiv wird hauptsächlich verwendet, wenn der Ausführende (*by-agent*) unwichtig oder unbekannt ist oder nicht genannt werden soll. Deshalb wird der *by-agent* nur bei besonderer Betonung genannt.	The batteries **are recharged** (**by us**) when they are empty. A few years ago the first cars **were equipped** with airbags (**by the manufacturers**).
Die Passivkonstruktion wird besonders bei technischen Beschreibungen, Anweisungen in Handbüchern usw. verwendet. Bei der Umwandlung von Aktiv in Passiv wird das Objekt des Aktivsatzes zum Subjekt des Passivsatzes.	Aktiv: We recharge **the batteries.** Passiv: **The batteries** are recharged (by us).
Im Gegensatz zum Deutschen können bestimmte Verben im Englischen im Passiv verwendet werden. Die Übersetzung ins Deutsche erfolgt durch eine Konstruktion mit 'man'.	The fuel cell is considered to be a very promising invention. *(Man hält die Brennstoffzelle für eine sehr zukunftsweisende Erfindung.)*
Die Verlaufsform ist im Passiv nur im *Present Tense* und *Past Tense* gebräuchlich.	He **is being** taken to hospital. *(Er wird gerade ins Krankenhaus gebracht.)* He **was being** taken to hospital. *(Er wurde gerade ins Krankenhaus gebracht.)*

Gerund (Gerundium)

Wie im Deutschen kann man auch im Englischen aus einem Verb ein Substantiv machen. Beispiel: Durch häufiges **Messen** können Fehler vermieden werden.

Bildung		
Anhängen von *-ing* an den Infinitiv (Grundform) des Verbs	check + ing = checking drill + ing = drilling	
Verdoppelung eines Endkonsonanten (Mitlaut) nach einem Vokal (Selbstlaut)	put – putting control – controlling	travel – travelling refuel – refuelling
Stummes *e* fällt weg: aber: *agree – agreeing; see – seeing*	file – filing measure – measuring	

Verwendung	
Ein *gerund* kann Subjekt (Satzgegenstand) sein. Ebenso kann es die Funktion eines Objekts (Satzergänzung) haben.	**Filing** is rarely done by hand. He began **cleaning** the machine.
Nach Präpositionen (Verhältniswörtern) oder präpositionalen Ausdrücken steht ebenfalls das *gerund*.	He was afraid of **setting** the lever to a higher speed. They objected **to trying** the new software **without having** made a backup of the hard drive. The manager apologised **for being** late. They prevented the visitors **from entering** the production area without a hard hat. He was tired **of hearing** the same complaint.
Nach bestimmten Verben (Zeitwörtern) steht das *gerund*.	Try to **avoid overheating** the machine. The trainer **recommended turning** the machine off. We cannot **risk losing** this customer. Phillip **suggested using** a different production method.
Weitere Verben, die ein *gerund* nach sich haben.	enjoy, like, dislike, remember, stop He enjoys working in Italy.

Prepositions (Verhältniswörter)

Präpositionen geben das Verhältnis von Personen oder Dingen zueinander an (z. B. räumlich oder zeitlich).

Räumliche Präpositionen			
above	oberhalb	**into**	in … hinein
across	durch, quer durch	**off**	von … herunter, von … weg
at	neben, bei	**on, upon**	auf
opposite	gegenüber		

Räumliche Präpositionen			
behind	hinter	**out, out of**	aus, heraus
below	unter, unterhalb	**through**	durch
beneath	unter, unterhalb	**to**	zu, nach, in Richtung auf
beside	neben	**towards**	auf … zu (Richtung)
between	zwischen	**under**	unter
in	in	**within**	innerhalb

Zeitliche Präpositionen			
at	an, in	**from**	von
before	vor	**in**	am, im (Jahre)
between	zwischen	**on**	an, am
by	bis, bis spätestens	**since**	seit (Zeitpunkt)
during	während	**until, till**	bis
for	seit (Zeitraum)		

Modale Präpositionen und Präpositionen des Grundes			
according to	entsprechend, gemäß	**despite, in spite of**	trotz
because of	wegen	**with**	mit
besides	außer	**without**	ohne

Verwendung	
Laut Gebrauchsanweisung sollte **das Auswechseln** der Werkzeuge kein Problem darstellen.	**According to** the manual, there should be no problem **with** changing the tools.
… **hinten** im Raum … **unten** auf jeder Seite … **am** Eingang	The machine is **at** the back of the room. You'll find the number of the module **at** the bottom of every page. They were waiting **at** the entrance when it happened.
… ist **gegenüber / auf der anderen Seite** … rannte quer **über** die Straße	The printer is **across** the hall. The dog ran **across** the road.
… **zwischen** zwei Aktenmappen (räumlich) … **zwischen** 9 und 10 Uhr (zeitlich)	He found the letter **between** two folders. Why don't we meet **between** nine and ten?
… nur **während**	Smoking is allowed **during** the lunch break only!
… **von** … **bis**	He worked in Cardiff **from** December **until** January.
… **auf** der Straße	You should not park your car **in** the street.
… **bis** (spätestens)	You must be back **by** six o'clock at the latest.

Modal auxiliaries (Modale Hilfsverben)

Die modalen Hilfsverben werden im Englischen oft auch *defective* (d.h. unvollständige) *auxiliaries* genannt, denn sie können in der Regel nur das Präsens bilden. Für die übrigen Zeiten müssen Ersatzformen verwendet werden.

Bildung		
Hilfsverb	**Ersatzform**	**deutsche Bedeutung**
can	to be able to	können, fähig sein, in der Lage sein
can	to be allowed to	dürfen, die Erlaubnis haben
may	to be allowed to	dürfen, die Erlaubnis haben
must	to have to	müssen
mustn't	not to be allowed to	nicht dürfen
needn't	not to have to	nicht brauchen, nicht müssen

Verwendung	
Present Tense: You **must** read the installation instructions very carefully. After the installation is completed you **needn't reboot** your system.	**Simple past:** Yesterday he **had to** read the installation instructions twice because they were badly translated. I **didn't have to** reboot my system when I installed the screensaver the other day.
Present Tense: He **can** handle software problems quite well.	**Present perfect:** Up to now he **has been able** to handle software problems quite well.
Present Tense: You **must not smoke** in the office.	**Future:** You **will not be allowed** to smoke in the office.

Participles (Partizipien)

Bildung	
Present Participle Infinitiv + *-ing*	Wind turbines are a **promising** option.
Past Participle 3. Stammform: *damaged* (*ed*-Endung wie bei *simple past*); (3. Form bei unregelmäßigen Verben: *1. know / 2. knew /* ***3. known***. Siehe Liste der unregelmäßigen Verben.)	After the storm we had to replace three **damaged** solar panels.

Verwendung	
als Adjektiv	It is a **known** fact that solar power can be used as an alternative energy.
Partizipialkonstruktionen dienen zur **Verkürzung** von: 1. adverbialen Nebensätzen mit Konjunktion *(when, although, as, while,...)*	When **planning** to build a home, you should consider using solar energy to heat your water.
2. adverbialen Nebensätzen ohne Konjunktion	**Unlocking** the warehouse door, he smelled gas.
3. Relativsätzen	Wind farms **built** along the coast are most efficient.
Partizipialkonstruktionen zur **Verknüpfung** von zwei Hauptsätzen.	The guide led us through the factory. He warned us to stay away from the machines. The guide led us through the factory **warning** us to stay away from the machines.

If-clauses (Bedingungssätze)

Man unterscheidet drei Arten von Bedingungen:

1. erfüllbare Bedingungen
2. Bedingungen, deren Erfüllung unwahrscheinlich ist
3. Bedingungen, die überhaupt nicht mehr erfüllt werden können.

Zusätzlich zu den drei Typen gibt es noch einen weiteren Typ, der Regeln und Naturgesetze ausdrückt.

Bildung und Verwendung	
Type I (probable condition)	If you **lubricate** this machine regularly, it **will run** smoothly for a long time. *(Wenn man die Maschine regelmäßig ölt, läuft sie lange Zeit problemlos.)*
Type II (improbable condition)	If you **lubricated** this machine regularly, **it would** run smoothly for a long time. *(Wenn man diese Maschine regelmäßig ölen würde, würde sie für lange Zeit problemlos laufen.)*
Type III (impossible condition)	If you **had lubricated** this machine regularly, it **would have run** smoothly for a long time. *(Wenn man die Maschine regelmäßig geölt hätte, wäre sie lange Zeit problemlos gelaufen (jetzt läuft sie aber offensichtlich nicht mehr).*
Rules and laws of nature Hier handelt es sich im eigentlichen Sinne nicht mehr um eine Bedingung, sondern um ein Naturgesetz. Deshalb steht im Hauptsatz auch kein Futur, sondern ebenfalls das Präsens.	If you **heat** ice, it **melts**. *(Wenn man Eis erhitzt, schmilzt es.)*
Besonderheit bei Formen von *to be*	If I **were** you, I wouldn't use a combination spanner here.

Chronological word list

Videotraining: Englische Aussprache

Perfekte englische Aussprache leicht gemacht: Mit dem Lernprogramm zur englischen Lautschrift können Sie alle Laute einüben. Wählen Sie einfach in der Navigation rechts den entsprechenden Reiter (*Vowels* oder *Consonants*) aus und klicken Sie dann auf das gewünschte phonetische Symbol. Sprechen Sie die Wörter laut nach.

Unter www.klett.de geben Sie bitte den Code unter der Abbildung rechts ein.

n633sn

Abkürzungen und Zeichen

etw. = etwas
Pl. = Plural
jmdn., jmdm. = jemanden, jemandem
sb. = somebody
sth. = something
BE = britisches Englisch
AE = amerikanisches Englisch
◎ = Vokabeln zu den Hörtexten

Module 1 People and jobs in IT

responsibility [rɪˌspɒnsəˈbɪləti] Verantwortung
skill [skɪl] Fertigkeit
requirement [rɪˈkwaɪəmənt] Anforderung

A | Job descriptions

to apply [əˈplaɪ] anwenden
to design [dɪˈzaɪn] entwerfen, konstruieren
website [ˈwebsaɪt] Website, Internetseite
to integrate [ˈɪntɪgreɪt] integrieren
database [ˈdeɪtəbeɪs] Datenbank
focus [ˈfəʊkəs] Schwerpunkt
design [dɪˈzaɪn] Gestaltung, Design
to advise [ədˈvaɪz] beraten
functionality [ˌfʌŋkʃnˈælɪti] Funktionalität, Handhabbarkeit
option [ˈɒpʃn] Alternative, Möglichkeit
benefit [ˈbenəfɪt] Leistung, Nutzen
overall [ˈəʊvrɔːl] gesamt
suggestion [səˈdʒestʃn] Vorschlag
impact [ˈɪmpækt] Wirkung, Einfluss
performance [pəˈfɔːməns] Ergebnis, Erfolg
thorough [ˈθʌrə] gründlich
analytical [ˌænəˈlɪtɪkl] analytisch
verbal [ˈvɜːbl] mündlich
graphic [ˈgræfɪk] graphisch
to troubleshoot [ˈtrʌblˌʃuːt] Fehler beheben
maintenance [ˈmeɪntnəns] Wartung
LAN (local area network) [læn; ˌləʊkl‿eəriə ˈnetwɜːk] lokales Netzwerk
WAN (wide area network) [wæn; ˌwaɪd‿eəriə ˈnetwɜːk] Weitverkehrsnetzwerk
implementation [ˌɪmplɪmenˈteɪʃn] Einführung, Umsetzung, Implementierung
to recommend [ˌrekəˈmend] empfehlen
to schedule [ˈʃedjuːl] anberaumen
to handle [ˈhændl] umgehen mit
confidential [ˌkɒnfɪˈdenʃl] vertraulich
broad [brɔːd] breit angelegt
several [ˈsevrl] mehrere
to recognize [ˈrekəgnaɪz] erkennen, anerkennen

career [kəˈrɪə] Beruf, Laufbahn, Karriere
to outline [ˈaʊtlaɪn] umreißen, skizzieren
systems analyst [ˈsɪstəmz ˌænlɪst] Systemberater(in)
findings [ˈfaɪndɪŋz] Ergebnisse
job title [ˈdʒɒb ˌtaɪtl] Berufsbezeichnung
to swap [swɒp] tauschen

B | A new company

apprenticeship [əˈprentɪʃɪp] Lehre, Ausbildung
tutor [ˈtjuːtə] Klassenlehrer(in), Betreuer(in)
organigram [ɔːˈgænɪgræm] Organigramm

curious [ˈkjʊəriəs] neugierig
major [ˈmeɪdʒə] Haupt-, bedeutend
separate [ˈseprət] einzeln, gesondert
sheet [ʃiːt] Blatt
corporate [ˈkɔːprət] Firmen-, Unternehmens-
enterprise [ˈentəpraɪz] Unternehmen
actually [ˈæktʃuəli] eigentlich, tatsächlich
workshop [ˈwɜːkʃɒp] Werkstatt
faulty [ˈfɒlti] fehlerhaft, mangelhaft
to join [dʒɔɪn] beitreten, mitmachen, sich jemandem anschließen, mitkommen
premises [ˈpremɪsɪz] Firmengelände
to refer sb. to sb. / sth. [rɪˈfɜː tə] jmdn. an jmdn. / auf etw. verweisen
to implement [ˈɪmplɪment] ausführen, verwirklichen, realisieren
Human Resources [ˌhjuːmən ˈriːsɔːsɪz] Personalabteilung
accounting [əˈkaʊntɪŋ] Buchhaltung
stockkeeping [ˈstɒkˌkiːpɪŋ] Lagerhaltung

reminder [rɪˈmaɪndə] Erinnerung, Mahnung
to match [mætʃ] zuordnen
purchase [ˈpɜːtʃəs] Kauf, Erwerb
to assess [əˈses] bewerten, einschätzen, abschätzen
faulty [ˈfɒlti] defekt
customer field service [ˌkʌstəmə ˈfiːld ˌsɜːvɪs] Kundendienst
enquiry [ɪnˈkwaɪəri] Anfrage
order [ˈɔːdə] Bestellung, Auftrag
offer [ˈɒfə] Angebot
description [dɪˈskrɪpʃn] Beschreibung
stay [steɪ] Aufenthalt
organisation chart (org chart) [ˌɔːgənaɪˈzeɪʃn ˌtʃɑːt; ˈɔːg ˌtʃɑːt] Organigramm, Organisationsschema

Module A Meeting people

confident [ˈkɒnfɪdənt] sicher, selbstbewusst
appropriate [əˈprəʊpriət] angemessen, passend

A | Saying "hello" and "goodbye" and giving your name

existing [ɪgˈzɪstɪŋ] bestehend
trade fair [ˈtreɪd ˌfeə] Messe
job fair [ˈdʒɒb ˌfeə] Jobmesse

B | Intercultural awareness

politeness [pəˈlaɪtnəs] Höflichkeit
pleasantry [ˈplezntri] höfliche Floskel
profitability [ˌprɒfɪtəbɪləti] Rentabilität
to chat [tʃæt] sich unterhalten
health [helθ] Gesundheit
pleasant [ˈpleznt] angenehm
to waste time [ˌweɪst ˈtaɪm] Zeit verschwenden
impression [ɪmˈpreʃn] Eindruck
conference [ˈkɒnfrəns] Tagung
minutes [ˈmɪnɪts] Protokoll
polite [pəˈlaɪt] höflich
usual [ˈjuːʒl] gewöhnlich, üblich, normal
upset [ʌpˈset] verärgert
stranger [ˈstreɪndʒə] Unbekannte(r)
on the other hand [ɒn ðiˈʌðə ˌhænd] andererseits
in charge of [ɪn ˈtʃɑːdʒ‿əv] verantwortlich für
cash register [ˈkæʃ ˌredʒɪstə] Kasse
given name [ˌgɪvn ˈneɪm] Vorname
family name [ˌfæmli ˈneɪm] Nachname
to intend [ɪnˈtend] beabsichtigen

Module 2 Computer hardware

to refer to [rɪˈfɜː tə] sich beziehen auf
device [dɪˈvaɪs] Vorrichtung, Gerät
accessories [ækˈsesriz] Zubehör
projector [prəˈdʒektə] Projektionsgerät, Beamer
plotter [ˈplɒtə] Zeichengerät, Plotter
graphic digitizer [ˌgræfɪk ˈdɪdʒɪtaɪzə] Grafikdigitalisierer
light pen [ˈlaɪt ˌpen] Lichtgriffel
speaker [ˈspiːkə] Lautsprecher

A | Internal components

shape [ʃeɪp] Form
to make up [ˌmeɪk‿ˈʌp] ausmachen
chassis [ˈʃæsi] Gehäuse
power supply [ˈpaʊə səˌplaɪ] Stromversorgung
to transform [trænsˈfɔ:m] verwandeln, umwandeln
voltage [ˈvəʊltɪdʒ] elektrische Spannung
PCB (printed circuit board) [ˌpi:si:ˈbi: ˌprɪntɪd ˈsɜ:kɪt ˌbɔ:d] Leiterplatte
CPU [ˌsi:pi:ˈju: ˌsentrl ˈprəʊsesɪŋ ˌju:nɪt] Prozessor
request [rɪˈkwest] Nachfrage, Anfrage
mainboard [ˈmeɪnbɔ:d] Hauptplatine
to host [həʊst] beherbergen
expansion [ɪkˈspænʃn] Expansion, Erweiterung
access [ˈækses] Zugriff
hard disk drive [ˌhɑ:d ˈdɪsk ˌdraɪv] Festplattenlaufwerk
storage [ˈstɔ:rɪdʒ] Speicherung
operating system [ˈɒpreɪtɪŋ ˌsɪstəm] Betriebssystem
application [ˌæplɪˈkeɪʃn] Anwendung
optical disk drive [ˌɒptɪkl ˈdɪsk ˌdraɪv] optisches Laufwerk
to fit in [ˌfɪt‿ˈɪn] (hinein)passen
unless [ʌnˈles] wenn nicht, außer wenn
to enquire [ɪnˈkwaɪə] sich erkundigen, anfragen
to swap [swɒp] tauschen
enquiry [ɪnˈkwaɪəri] Anfrage
to submit [səbˈmɪt] vorlegen, einreichen, unterbreiten
corresponding [ˌkɒrɪˈspɒndɪŋ] entsprechend, dazugehörig
offer [ˈɒfə] Angebot

B | External components

peripheral devices [pəˌrɪfrl dɪˈvaɪsɪz] Peripheriegeräte

C | Assembling a computer

to assemble [əˈsembl] montieren, zusammenbauen

Module B Your company

regardless of [rɪˈgɑ:dləs‿əv] ungeachtet, unabhängig von
furniture [ˈfɜ:nɪtʃə] Möbel
likely [ˈlaɪkli] wahrscheinlich
supplier [səˈplaɪə] Lieferant
skill [skɪl] Fähigkeit, Fertigkeit
to express [ɪkˈspres] zum Ausdruck bringen
grease [gri:s] Fett
ratchet [ˈrætʃɪt] Knarre
tool [tu:l] Werkzeug

A | The company and its departments

department [dɪˈpɑ:tmənt] Abteilung
to distribute [dɪˈstrɪbju:t] vertreiben, verteilen
damaged [ˈdæmɪdʒd] beschädigt
employee [ɪmˈplɔɪi:] Beschäftigte(r), Angestellte(r)
accounts [əˈkaʊnts] Buchhaltung
raw materials [ˌrɔ: məˈtɪəriəlz] Rohstoffe
human resources [ˌhju:mən ˈri:zɔ:sɪz] Personalabteilung
to recruit [rɪˈkru:t] rekrutieren, anstellen
purchasing (department) [ˈpɜ:tʃəsɪŋ (dɪˌpɑ:tmənt)] Einkauf(-sabteilung)
to maintain [meɪnˈteɪn] warten, in Stand halten
R&D (Research and Development) [rɪˌsɜ:tʃ‿ən dɪˈveləpmənt] Forschungs- und Entwicklungsabteilung
to develop [dɪˈveləp] entwickeln
in charge of [ɪn ˈtʃɑ:dʒ‿əv] zuständig für

to cover [ˈkʌvə] abdecken, bedecken
headquarters [ˌhedˈkwɔ:təz] Hauptsitz
to found [faʊnd] gründen
family-owned [ˌfæmliˈəʊnd] in Familienbesitz
manufacturing plant [ˌmænjəˈfæktʃərɪŋ ˌplɑ:nt] Produktionsbetrieb
currently [ˈkʌrəntli] derzeit, zurzeit, momentan
braking system [ˈbreɪkɪŋ ˌsɪstəm] Bremsanlage
internship (AE) [ˈɪntɜ:rnʃɪp] Praktikum
device [dɪˈvaɪs] Gerät
cylinder head [ˈsɪlɪndə ˌhed] Zylinderkopf
to inspect [ɪnˈspekt] prüfen
operating system [ˈɒpreɪtɪŋ ˌsɪstəm] Betriebssystem
interface [ˈɪntəfeɪs] Schnittstelle, Interface

B | Tasks and responsibilities

task [tɑ:sk] Aufgabe
responsibility [rɪˌspɒnsəˈbɪləti] Verantwortung
to manufacture [ˌmænjəˈfæktʃə] herstellen
to occur [əˈkɜ:] vorkommen
apprenticeship [əˈprentɪsʃɪp] Ausbildung, Lehre

branch [brɑ:nʃ] Niederlassung
precision [prɪ'sɪʒn] Genauigkeit
essential [ɪ'senʃl] wesentlich, unbedingt erforderlich
to drill [drɪl] bohren
to shape [ʃeɪp] formen, fräsen
to polish ['pɒlɪʃ] abschleifen, polieren
to intervene [ˌɪntə'vi:n] einschreiten
to vibrate [vaɪ'breɪt] vibrieren
workpiece ['wɜ:kpi:s] Werkstück
to monitor ['mɒnɪtə] überwachen, kontrollieren, beobachten
to measure ['meʒə] messen
dimension [daɪ'menʃn] Maß, Abmessung
lubricated ['lu:brɪkeɪtɪd] geölt
lubricating oil ['lu:brɪkeɪtɪŋ‿ɔɪl] Schmieröl
generally ['dʒenrəli] normalerweise, im Allgemeinen
shift [ʃɪft] Schicht
to prefer [prɪ'fɜ:] bevorzugen
rarely ['reəli] selten
accuracy ['ækjərəsi] Genauigkeit
to include [ɪn'klu:d] einbeziehen, einschließen
to swap [swɒp] tauschen

C | Organisational structure

to employ [ɪm'plɔɪ] beschäftigen
to support [sə'pɔ:t] unterstützen
to split [splɪt] aufteilen
core area [ˌkɔ: 'eəriə] Kernbereich
to report to [rɪ'pɔ:t tu:] unterstehen
to belong to [bɪ'lɒŋ tu:] gehören zu
experienced [ɪk'spɪəriənst] erfahren
capable ['keɪpəbl] fähig
closely ['kləʊsli] eng

Module 3 Storing data

A | Storage devices

storage devices ['stɔ:rɪdʒ dɪˌvaɪsɪz] Speichergeräte, Datenspeicher
rewritable [ˌri:'raɪtəbl] überschreibbar
volatile ['vɒlətaɪl] flüchtig (Datenspeicher)
erasable [ɪ'reɪzəbl] löschbar
contents ['kɒntents] Inhalt
according to [ə'kɔ:dɪŋ tə] laut, gemäß
fragile ['frædʒaɪl] anfällig
to corrupt [kə'rʌpt] (Daten) beschädigen
flash memory ['flæʃ ˌmemri] Flash-Speicher
hard disk drive [ˌhɑ:d 'dɪsk ˌdraɪv] Festplatte(nlaufwerk)
floppy disk drive [ˌflɒpi 'dɪsk ˌdraɪv] Diskettenlaufwerk

B | Past and current developments in data storage

holographic [ˌhɒlə'græfɪk] holographisch
Giant Magneto Resistance (GMR) [ˌdʒaɪənt mæg'ni:təʊ rɪˌzɪstns, ˌdʒi:em'ɑ:] Riesenmagnetowiderstand
rumour ['ru:mə] Gerücht
to scan [skæn] absuchen
beam [bi:m] Strahl
unlikely [ʌn'laɪkli] unwahrscheinlich

C | The next storage revolution

brain [breɪn] Gehirn
molecule chain ['mɒlɪkju:l ˌtʃeɪn] Molekülkette
market ready [ˌmɑ:kɪt'redi] vermarktungsreif
to encode [ɪn'kəʊd] verschlüsseln, kodieren
laughable ['lɑ:fəbl] lächerlich

gist [dʒɪst] das Wesentliche
CERN [sɜ:n] Europäisches Nuklearforschungslabor
search engine ['sɜ:tʃ‿endʒɪn] Suchmaschine
relational database [rɪˌleɪʃnl 'deɪtəbeɪs] relationale Datenbank
foundations [faʊn'deɪʃnz] Grundlagen
mascot ['mæskɒt] Maskottchen
source code ['sɔ:s ˌkəʊd] Quellcode
alteration [ˌɔ:ltə'reɪʃn] Änderung
framework ['freɪmwɜ:k] Rahmenwerk, Rahmenbedingungen
toolbox ['tu:lbɒks] Werkzeugkiste
to enable [ɪ'neɪbl] in die Lage versetzen
cluster ['klʌstə] Anhäufung, Gruppe
to replace [rɪ'pleɪs] ersetzen
to handle ['hændl] handhaben, erledigen, bearbeiten
to gather ['gæðə] sammeln, zusammentragen
to crawl the Internet [krɔ:l] das Internet durchsuchen
to restructure [ˌri:'strʌktʃə] neu anordnen
to eliminate [ɪ'lɪmɪneɪt] beseitigen, entfernen, eliminieren
to boil down [ˌbɔɪl 'daʊn] *(hier:)* verdichten
implication [ˌɪmplɪ'keɪʃn] Auswirkung, Folge

Module C Telephoning

line [laɪn] *(hier:)* Branche
to fix [fɪks] reparieren
leak [li:k] undichte Stelle
to install [ɪn'stɔ:l] installieren, montieren, anschließen
complaint [kəm'pleɪnt] Beschwerde, Reklamation
order ['ɔ:də] Bestellung, Auftrag
necessary ['nesəsri] nötig, notwendig
delay [dɪ'leɪ] Verspätung, Verzögerung
breakdown ['breɪkdaʊn] Panne, Störung
solution [sə'lu:ʃn] Lösung
confused [kən'fju:zd] verwirrt
crash [kræʃ] Absturz

A | Making and receiving a phone call

meeting ['mi:tɪŋ] Sitzung, Besprechung
country code ['kʌntri ˌkəʊd] Ländervorwahl
area code ['eəriə ˌkəʊd] Vorwahl
extension number [ɪk'stenʃn ˌnʌmbə] Durchwahl
suitable ['su:təbl] geeignet, passend
polite [pə'laɪt] höflich
although [ɔ:l'ðəʊ] obwohl
to remain [rɪ'meɪn] bleiben
request [rɪ'kwest] Bitte
grateful ['greɪtfl] dankbar
whereas [weə'ræz] während
impolite [ˌɪmpə'laɪt] unhöflich

B | Giving information over the phone

valuable ['væljuəbl] *(hier:)* wichtig
figures ['fɪgəz] Nummern, Daten
clearly ['klɪəli] deutlich, klar

confused [kən'fju:zd] verwirrt
to divert [daɪ'vɜ:t] weiterleiten
extractor fan [ik'stræktəfæn] Dunstabzug
hob [hɒb] Kochfeld
diameter [daɪ'æmɪtə] Durchmesser
socket ['sɒkɪt] Steckdose

Module 4 BIOS and operating systems

BIOS ['baɪɒs] Basis-Eingabe-Ausgabe-System
operating system ['ɒpreɪtɪŋ ˌsɪstəm] Betriebssystem
firmware ['fɜ:mweə] Software in einem persistenten Speicherbaustein
access ['ækses] Zugang
motherboard ['mʌðəbɔ:d] Hauptplatine
setup ['setʌp] Programm zur Festlegung von Konfigurationsvariablen
arrow key ['ærəʊ ˌki:] Pfeiltaste
energy consumption ['enədʒi kənˌsʌmpʃn] Energieverbrauch
to select [sə'lekt] auswählen
fail-safe configuration [ˌfeɪlseɪf kənˌfɪg'reɪʃn] betriebssichere Konfiguration
entry ['entri] Eintrag
to protect [prə'tekt] schützen
unauthorised access [ʌnˌɔ:θraɪzd‿'ækses] unberechtigter Zugriff

A | BIOS or solving the chicken-or-the-egg dilemma

to solve [sɒlv] lösen
to resolve [rɪ'zɒlv] lösen
step [step] Schritt
to execute ['eksɪkju:t] ausführen
tailor-made [ˌteɪlə'meɪd] maßgeschneidert
central processing unit (CPU) [ˌsentrl 'prəʊsesɪŋ ˌju:nɪt] Hauptprozessor
instruction [ɪn'strʌkʃn] Anweisung
to keep track of [ˌki:p 'træk‿əv] verfolgen, kontrollieren
machine code [mə'ʃi:n ˌkəʊd] Programm-Code in einer Maschinensprache
setting ['setɪŋ] Einstellung
to constitute ['kɒnstɪtju:t] darstellen, bilden
to initialize [ɪ'nɪʃlaɪz] intialisieren
boot disk ['bu:t ˌdɪsk] Festplatte, CD/DVD oder USB Stick, von dem gebootet wird

B | Network booting

accessible [ək'sesəbl] für Zugriff verfügbar

C | Troubleshooting

accidentally [ˌæksɪ'dentli] unbeabsichtigt
to overwrite [ˌəʊvə'raɪt] überschreiben
configuration file [kənˌfɪg'reɪʃn ˌfaɪl] Konfigurationsdatei

D | Selecting an operating system

◎ **model installation** [ˌmɒdl͜ɪnstəˈleɪʃn] Beispielinstallation
to delete [dɪˈliːt] löschen
design application [dɪˌzaɪn͜æplɪˈkeɪʃn] Software zum Gestalten von z. B. Webseiten oder Druckerzeugnissen
boot menu list [ˌbuːt ˈmenjuː ˌlɪst] Liste von Betriebssystemen
to point out [ˌpɔɪnt͜ˈaʊt] hinweisen auf
default bootloader [dɪˌfɔːlt ˈbuːtˌləʊdə] Standard-Bootloader
cfg [ˌsiːefˈdʒiː] häufig verwendete Endung für Konfigurationsdateien
text editor [ˈtekst͜edɪtə] Textaufbereitungsprogramm
to append [əˈpend] anfügen

Module D Written communication

essential [ɪˈsenʃl] sehr wichtig
workshop [ˈwɜːkʃɒp] Werkstatt
efficiently [ɪˈfɪʃntli] effizient
necessary [ˈnesəsri] nötig, notwendig
enquiry [ɪnˈkwaɪəri] Anfrage
promptly [ˈprɒmtli] sofort
offer [ˈɒfə] Angebot
order [ˈɔːdə] Bestellung
to replace [rɪˈpleɪs] ersetzen
lesser [ˈlesə] geringer
advantage [ədˈvɑːntɪdʒ] Vorteil
disadvantage [ˌdɪsədˈvɑːntɪdʒ] Nachteil
confidential [ˌkɒnfɪˈdenʃl] vertraulich
time-consuming [ˈtaɪmkənˌsjuːmɪŋ] zeitraubend
reliable [rɪˈlaɪəbl] zuverlässig
misunderstanding [ˌmɪsʌndəˈstændɪŋ] Missverständnis

A | Enquiries

enquiry [ɪnˈkwaɪəri] Anfrage
car mechanic [ˈkɑː mɪˌkænɪk] Automechaniker(in)
appropriate [əˈprəʊpriət] angemessen, passend
salutation [ˌsæljəˈteɪʃn] (Brief:) Anrede
supplier [səˈplaɪə] Lieferant, Zulieferer
subject line [ˈsʌbdʒɪkt ˌlaɪn] (Brief:) Betreffzeile
bonnet (BE) [ˈbɒnɪt] Motorhaube
family-run [ˌfæmliˈrʌn] in Familienbesitz, familiengeführt
to expand [ɪkˈspænd] erweitern, vergrößern
catalogue [ˈkætəlɒg] Katalog
discount [ˈdɪskaʊnt] Rabatt, Preisnachlass
terms of payment [ˌtɜːmz͜əv ˈpeɪmənt] Zahlungsbedingungen
delivery times [dɪˈlɪvri ˌtaɪmz] Lieferzeiten
sample [ˈsæmpl] Muster
closing phrase [ˈkləʊzɪŋ ˌfreɪz] Schlussworte
complimentary close [ˌkɒmplɪmentri ˈkləʊz] Grußformel (am Briefende)
to recommend [ˌrekəˈmend] empfehlen
cost estimate [ˈkɒst͜estɪmət] Kostenvoranschlag
configure [kənˈfɪgə] konfigurieren
to appreciate [əˈpriːʃieɪt] etw. (wert-)schätzen
supply from stock [səˌplaɪ frəm ˈstɒk] ab Lager liefern

B | Offers

bank transfer [ˈbæŋk ˌtrænsfɜː] Banküberweisung
working day [ˌwɜːkɪŋ ˈdeɪ] Werktag
attachment [əˈtætʃmənt] Anhang
stock [stɒk] Bestand, Vorrat
to require [rɪˈkwaɪə] benötigen
ratchet [ˈrætʃɪt] Knarre, Ratsche
socket [ˈsɒkɪt] Stecknuss
(adjustable) wrench [əˌdʒʌstəbl ˈrenʃ] (verstellbarer) Schraubenschlüssel
screwdriver [ˈskruːˌdraɪvə] Schraubendreher
to dispatch [dɪˈspætʃ] versenden, verschicken
DIY (Do-it-yourself) [ˌdiːaɪˈwaɪ] Heimwerken

C | Orders

sum [sʌm] Betrag
consignment [kənˈsaɪnmənt] Lieferung, Sendung
torque wrench [ˈtɔːk ˌrenʃ] Drehmomentschlüssel

Module 5 Types of computer

stationary [ˈsteɪʃnri] feststehend
PDA [ˌpiːdiːˈeɪ] tragbarer elektronischer Organizer
device [dɪˈvaɪs] Gerät
advantage [ədˈvɑːntɪdʒ] Vorteil
disadvantage [ˌdɪsədˈvɑːntɪdʒ] Nachteil

keyboard ['ki:bɔ:d] Tastatur
memory ['memri] Speicher
external [ɪk'stɜ:nl] extern
portable ['pɔ:təbl] tragbar
lightweight ['laɪtweɪt] leicht(gewichtig)
suitable ['su:təbl] geeignet

A | Mainframes, minicomputers and microcomputers

mainframe ['meɪnfreɪm] Großrechner
to outline ['aʊtlaɪn] umreißen, skizzieren
input ['ɪnpʊt] Eingabe-
output ['aʊtpʊt] Ausgabe-
cabinet ['kæbɪnət] Schrank
component [kəm'pəʊnənt] (Bau)teil
integrated circuit [ˌɪntɪgreɪtɪd 'sɜ:kɪt] Schaltkreis
central processing unit [ˌsentrl 'prəʊsesɪŋ ˌju:nɪt] Prozessor, Zentraleinheit
transistor [træn'zɪstə] Transistor
to contain [kən'teɪn] enthalten
microprocessor [ˌmaɪkrə'prəʊsesə] Mikroprozessor
to process ['prəʊsəs] bearbeiten, verarbeiten
huge [hju:dʒ] riesig
case [keɪs] Fall
i.e. [ˌaɪ'i:] d.h., das heißt
weather forecasting ['weðə ˌfɔ:kɑ:stɪŋ] Wettervorhersage
to adapt [ə'dæpt] anpassen
to suit the needs of sth. [ˌsu:t ðə 'ni:dz‿əv ˌsʌmθɪŋ] die Bedürfnisse von etwas erfüllen
capacity [kə'pæsəti] Leistungsfähigkeit
e.g. [ˌi:'dʒi:] z.B., zum Beispiel
to vary ['veəri] sich unterscheiden
as regards [əz rɪ'gɑ:dz] bezüglich
distinction [dɪ'stɪŋkʃn] Unterscheidung
application [ˌæplɪ'keɪʃn] Anwendung
overlap ['əʊvəlæp] Überschneidung
to require [rɪ'kwaɪə] benötigen
moderate ['mɒdrət] mäßig, moderat
capability [ˌkeɪpə'bɪləti] Fähigkeit
range [reɪndʒ] Reichweite
multiple ['mʌltɪpl] mehrfach
to dedicate ['dedɪkeɪt] widmen
database ['deɪtəbeɪs] Datenbank
term [tɜ:m] Begriff

B | Microcomputers of today

branch [brɑ:nʃ] Niederlassung

to edit ['edɪt] bearbeiten
appropriate [ə'prəʊpriət] geeignet
word processing program ['wɜ:dˌprəʊsesɪŋ ˌprəʊgræm] Textverarbeitungsprogramm
to calculate ['kælkjəleɪt] berechnen
to manage ['mænɪdʒ] verwalten
library ['laɪbrəri] Bibliothek, Bücherei
spreadsheet ['spredʃi:t] Tabellenkalkulation
desk [desk] Schreibtisch
chassis ['ʃæsi] Gehäuse
storage ['stɔ:rɪdʒ] Speicherung
stationary ['steɪʃnri:] stationär
battery pack ['bætri ˌpæk] Akku
power supply ['paʊə səˌplaɪ] Stromversorgung
to recharge [ˌri:'tʃɑ:dʒ] wiederaufladen
LCD, liquid crystal display [ˌelsi:'di:, ˌlɪkwɪd 'krɪstl dɪ'spleɪ] Flüssigkristallanzeige
lid [lɪd] Deckel
optical disc drive [ˌɒptɪkl 'dɪsk ˌdraɪv] optisches Laufwerk
pointing device ['pɔɪntɪŋ dɪˌvaɪs] Zeigegerät
touchpad ['tʌtʃpæd] Tastfeld
cordless ['kɔ:dləs] schnurlos
via [vaɪə 'vi:ə] über
wireless ['waɪələs] kabellos
processing power ['prəʊsesɪŋ ˌpaʊə] Rechenleistung
to store [stɔ:] speichern
Handwriting Recognition (HR) ['hændraɪtɪŋ rekəgˌnɪʃn] Handschriftenerkennung
to afford [ə'fɔ:d] sich leisten

feature ['fi:tʃə] (Programm)Funktion
provider [prə'vaɪdə] Anbieter
app [æp] Anwendungsprogramm
palm [pɑ:m] Handfläche
stylus ['staɪləs] Stift, Griffel
icon ['aɪkɒn] Icon, Bildschirmsymbol
character ['kærɪktə] Buchstabe, Zeichen
virtual ['vɜ:tʃuəl] virtuell
recognition [ˌrekəg'nɪʃn] (Er)kennung
slot [slɒt] Einbaustelle, Schlitz
to devise [dɪ'vaɪz] vorsehen
diary ['daɪəri] Terminkalender, Tagebuch
to consider [kən'sɪdə] berücksichtigen, in Betracht ziehen
fee [fi:] Gebühr

contract ['kɒntrækt] Vertrag
whereas [weə'ræz] während, wohingegen
principal ['prɪnsɪpl] Haupt-
rotatable [rəʊ'teɪtəbl] drehbar
to support [sə'pɔ:t] unterstützen

C | Advising customers

battery ['bætri] Akku

Module E Applications

application [ˌæplɪ'keɪʃn] Bewerbung
opportunity [ˌɒpə'tju:nəti] Möglichkeit
to decide [dɪ'saɪd] sich entscheiden
branch [brɑ:nʃ] Niederlassung
advert ['ædvɜ:t] Anzeige
letter of application [ˌletər‿əv‿ˌæplɪ'keɪʃn] Bewerbungsschreiben
CV (curriculum vitae) [ˌsi:'vi:, kəˌrɪkjələm 'vi:taɪ] Lebenslauf
job interview ['dʒɒb‿ˌɪntəvju:] Vorstellungsgespräch
employment contract [ɪm'plɔɪmənt ˌkɒntrækt] Arbeitsvertrag
to invite [ɪn'vaɪt] einladen
skill [skɪl] Fähigkeit
industry ['ɪndəstri] *(hier:)* Branche
hard-working [ˌhɑ:d'wɜ:kɪŋ] fleißig

A | Job advertisements

recently ['ri:sntli] kürzlich
willing to learn [ˌwɪlɪŋ tə 'lɜ:n] lernbereit, lernwillig
responsible [rɪ'spɒnsəbl] verantwortlich
punctual ['pʌŋktʃuəl] pünktlich
pleasant ['pleznt] angenehm, sympathisch
working atmosphere [ˌwɜ:kɪŋ‿'ætməsfɪə] Arbeitsklima
valid ['vælɪd] gültig
troubleshooting ['trʌblˌʃu:tɪŋ] Fehlersuche
to maintain [meɪn'teɪn] bewahren
leading ['li:dɪŋ] führend
supplier [sə'plaɪə] Lieferant, Zulieferer
vacancy ['veɪknsi] freie Stelle
fault [fɒlt] Fehler
assembly [ə'sembli] Montage
summary ['sʌmri] Zusammenfassung

B | Letter of application

internship (AE) ['ɪntɜ:rnʃɪp] Praktikum
theoretical [θɪə'retɪkl] theoretisch
to gain [geɪn] *(hier:)* sammeln
reliable [rɪ'laɪəbl] zuverlässig
to consider [kən'sɪdə] betrachten
to require [rɪ'kwaɪə] benötigen

C | The CV

advice [əd'vaɪs] Rat
tip [tɪp] Tipp, Hinweis
to highlight ['haɪlaɪt] betonen
strength [streŋθ] Stärke
achievement [ə'tʃi:vmənt] Leistung
supervisor ['su:pəvaɪzə] Leiter(in), Kontrolleur(in)
truth [tru:θ] Wahrheit
embarrassing [ɪm'bærəsɪŋ] peinlich
to spell [spel] buchstabieren
grateful ['greɪtfl] dankbar

Module 6 Networks

synonym ['sɪnənɪm] Synonym, bedeutungsgleiches Wort
device [dɪ'vaɪs] Gerät
purpose ['pɜ:pəs] Zweck, Absicht
data storage ['deɪtə ˌstɔ:rɪdʒ] Datenspeicher
access ['ækses] Zugang
crimping tool ['krɪmpɪŋ ˌtu:l] Crimpzange
port [pɔ:t] Steckplatz für Netzwerkkabel

A | Introduction to networks and associated protocols

protocol ['prəʊtəkɒl] Protokoll
copper wire [ˌkɒpə 'waɪə] Kupferkabel
optic fiber [ˌɒptɪk 'faɪbə] Glasfaser
to rule [ru:l] regeln
to stack [stæk] stapeln
layer ['leɪə] Schicht
IP addressing [ˌaɪpi:‿ə'dresɪŋ] IP-Adressierung

B | Network topologies

node [nəʊd] Knotenpunkt
mesh [meʃ] Gitter

data delivery ['deɪtə dɪˌlɪvri] Datenauslieferung
central node [ˌsentrl 'nəʊd] zentraler Knotenpunkt
to go down [ˌgəʊ 'daʊn] ausfallen
cost effective [ˌkɒstɪ'fektɪv] kostengünstig
resilient [rɪ'zɪliənt] widerstandsfähig

C | Troubleshooting: Network access

helpdesk ['helpdesk] IT-Hotline

engineering department [ˌendʒɪ'nɪərɪŋ dɪˌpɑ:tmənt] Konstruktionsabteilung
to access ['ækses] zugreifen
email account [ˌi:meɪl‿ə'kaʊnt] E-Mail-Konto
operating system ['ɒpreɪtɪŋ ˌsɪstəm] Betriebssystem
secure connection [sɪˌkjʊə kə'nekʃn] sichere Verbindung
to call ahead [ˌkɔ:l‿ə'hed] im Voraus Bescheid geben
VPN client installer [ˌvi:pi:en 'klaɪənt‿ɪnˌstɔ:lə] Installationsprogramm für den VPN Client
setting ['setɪŋ] Einstellung
menu bar ['menju: ˌbɑ:] Menüleiste
mail server tab ['meɪl ˌsɜ:və ˌtæb] Mail-Server-Karteireiterkarte
IP address field [ˌaɪpi:‿ədres ˌfi:ld] IP-Adressfeld
incoming mail [ˌɪnkʌmɪŋ 'meɪl] eingehende Post
outgoing mail [ˌaʊtgəʊɪŋ 'meɪl] ausgehende Post

to plug in [ˌplʌg‿'ɪn] einstecken

D | Crimping your own cable

to strip [strɪp] entfernen
insulation [ˌɪnsjə'leɪʃn] Isolierung
insulation stripping pliers [ˌɪnsjəleɪʃn 'strɪpɪŋ ˌplaɪəz] Abisolierzange
to examine [ɪg'zæmɪn] prüfen
exposed [ɪk'spəʊzd] freigelegt
subsequently ['sʌbsɪkwəntli] anschließend
crosstalk ['krɒstɔ:k] Nebensignaleffekte
twisted pair [ˌtwɪstɪd 'peə] verdrilltes Paar
to untwist [ʌn'twɪst] aufdrehen
to align [ə'laɪn] anordnen
neatly ['ni:tli] ordentlich
plug [plʌg] Stecker
to insert [ɪn'sɜ:t] einfügen
firmly ['fɜ:mli] kräftig
evenly ['i:vnli] gleichmäßig
handle ['hændl] Griff

ratcheting sound ['rætʃɪtɪŋ ˌsaʊnd] knarrendes Geräusch
to release [rɪ'li:s] loslassen
circuit indicator ['sɜkɪt‿ɪndɪkeɪtə] Durchgangsprüfer

Module F Socialising

relationship [rɪ'leɪʃnʃɪp] Beziehung

A | Small talk

subsidiary [səb'sɪdɪəri] Tochtergesellschaft
trainee [ˌtreɪ'ni:] Auszubildende(r)
appropriate [ə'prəʊpriət] angemessen, passend

B | Small talk in business

to dismiss [dɪ'smɪs] nicht beachten
common ground [ˌkɒmən 'graʊnd] gemeinsame Basis
trivial ['trɪviəl] unwichtig
uneasiness [ʌn'i:zinəs] Unbehagen
tension ['tenʃn] Spannung
to avoid [ə'vɔɪd] vermeiden
awkward ['ɔ:kwəd] peinlich, unangenehm

C | Eating out

well-done [ˌwel'dʌn] (Steak) gut durchgebraten
pork [pɔ:k] Schweinefleisch
side order ['saɪd‿ɔ:də] Beilage
bill [bɪl] Rechnung
game [geɪm] *(hier:)* Wild
dessert [dɪ'zɜ:t] Nachtisch, Nachspeise
fork [fɔ:k] Gabel
main dish [ˌmeɪn 'dɪʃ] Hauptgericht
beef [bi:f] Rindfleisch
poultry ['pəʊltri] Geflügel
starter ['stɑ:tə] Vorspeise
tip [tɪp] Trinkgeld

Module 7 Telecommunications

distance ['dɪstns] Entfernung
time frame ['taɪm ˌfreɪm] Zeitfenster
delivery [dɪ'lɪvri] Zustellung
real time ['rɪəltaɪm] Echtzeit
cell phone ['sel ˌfəʊn] Mobiltelefon
range [reɪndʒ] Bereich, Reichweite

transmitter [trænz'mɪtə] Sendeeinrichtung
bandwidth ['bændwɪtθ] Bandbreite
high band network [ˌhaɪbænd 'netwɜ:k] Netzwerk mit hoher Bandbreite
approximately [ə'prɒksɪmətli] in etwa

A | Telecommunication in the past and the present

to encode [ɪn'kəʊd] codieren
to transmit [trænz'mɪt] übertragen
to decide on [dɪ'saɪd‿ɒn] sich entscheiden für
transport medium ['trænspɔ:t ˌmi:diəm] Übertragungsmedium
connection [kə'nekʃn] Verbindung
to convert [kən'vɜ:t] umwandeln
recipient [rɪ'sɪpiənt] Empfänger(in)
character ['kærəktə] Zeichen
conversion [kən'vɜ:ʃn] Verwandlung
process chain ['prəʊses ˌtʃeɪn] Ablaufkette
to reassemble [ˌri:ə'sembl] wieder zusammensetzen
dot [dɒt] Punkt
dash [dæʃ] Bindestrich
short on [ˌʃɔ:t‿'ɒn] kurzes An
long on [ˌlɒŋ‿'ɒn] langes An
age [eɪdʒ] Zeitalter
to vary ['veəri] variieren
dirty interface [ˌdɜ:ti‿'ɪntəfeɪs] fehleranfällige Schnittstelle
UMTS (universal mobile telecommunications system) [ˌju:emti:'es, ˌju:nɪvɜ:sl ˌməʊbaɪl ˌtelɪkəˌmju:nɪ'keɪʃnz ˌsɪstəm] Mobilfunkstandard
LTE (long term evolution) [ˌelti:'i:, ˌlɒŋtɜ:m‿ˌi:və'lu:ʃn] Mobilfunkstandard mit hoher Bandbreite
device [dɪ'vaɪs] Gerät
to interface ['ɪntəfeɪs] sich verbinden
unreliable [ˌʌnrɪ'laɪəbl] unzuverlässig
underground ['ʌndəgraʊnd] unterirdisch
fibre optic wire [ˌfaɪbər‿ɒptɪk 'waɪə] Glasfaserkabel
to provide [prə'vaɪd] zur Verfügung stellen
long-distance line [ˌlɒŋdɪstns 'laɪn] Langstreckenverbindung
broadband ['brɔ:dbænd] Breitband
to connect [kə'nekt] (sich) verbinden
digital subscriber line (DSL) [ˌdɪdʒɪtl səb'skraɪbə ˌlaɪn, ˌdi:es'el] eine Art von Breitband-Internetverbindung

B | Telecommunications networks: future problems

node [nəʊd] Verbindungsknoten
link [lɪŋk] Verbindung
terminal ['tɜ:mɪnl] Endpunkt einer Verbindung

outdated [ˌaʊt'deɪtɪd] veraltet
HSDPA (high-speed downlink packet access) [ˌeɪtʃesdi:pi:'eɪ, ˌhaɪspi:d ˌdaʊnlɪŋk 'pækɪdʒ‿ækses] Erweiterung des UMTS-Standards
Tier 1 provider [ˌtɪə ˌwʌn prə'vaɪdə] Stufe 1 (Internet) Anbieter
access node ['ækses ˌnəʊd] Zugangsknotenpunkt
to colour ['kʌlə] einfärben, markieren
That's not a big deal! [ðæts ˌnɒt‿ə ˌbɪg 'di:l] Das ist keine große Sache!
MAN (metropolitan area network) [mæn, em‿eɪ en, ˌmetrə'pɒlitən 'eəriə 'net,wɜ:k] regionales Mobilfunknetz, z. B. für eine größere Stadt
transport node ['trænspɔ:t ˌnəʊd] Transportknotenpunkt
core network [ˌkɔ: 'netwɜ:k] Verbindungsnetzwerk, das mehrere MAN miteinander verbindet
service node ['sɜ:vɪs ˌnəʊd] Serviceknotenpunkt, der Daten von einem Netzwerkformat in ein anderes übersetzt

C | Finding the right telecommunications provider

questionnaire [ˌkwestʃə'neə] Fragebogen, Umfrage
out of office [ˌaʊt‿əv‿'ɒfɪs] außer Haus
rural ['rʊərl] ländlich
reception [rɪ'sepʃn] Empfang
to shift [ʃɪft] sich verlagern
data traffic ['deɪtə ˌtræfɪk] Datenverkehr
to require [rɪ'kwaɪə] benötigen
supported [səˌpɔ:tɪd] unterstützt
network coverage [ˌnetwɜ:k 'kʌvrɪdʒ] Netzabdeckung

Module G Presentations

required [rɪ'kwaɪəd] erforderlich, verlangt, erwünscht
service ['sɜ:vɪs] Dienstleistung
positional sketch [pəˌzɪʃnl 'sketʃ] Technologieschema
to develop [dɪ'veləp] entwickeln
to improve [ɪm'pru:v] besser werden, sich verbessern
meeting ['mi:tɪŋ] Sitzung, Besprechung
graph [grɑ:f] Diagramm
chart [tʃɑ:t] Schaubild, Diagramm
preparation [ˌprepr'eɪʃn] Vorbereitung
to explain [ɪk'spleɪn] erklären
sales pitch ['seɪlz ˌpɪtʃ] Verkaufspräsentation
reason ['ri:zn] Grund

A | Preparing a presentation

audience ['ɔ:diəns] Zuhörer (Pl.), Publikum
body language ['bɒdi ˌlæŋgwɪdʒ] Körpersprache
handout ['hændaʊt] Informationsblatt
to prepare [prɪ'peə] vorbereiten
visual aids [ˌvɪʒuəl‿'eɪdz] Anschauungsmaterial, visuelle Hilfen
to describe [dɪ'skraɪb] beschreiben
summary ['sʌmri] Zusammenfassung
overview ['əʊvəvju:] Überblick
to reinforce [ˌri:ɪn'fɔ:s] verstärken, betonen
guidelines ['gaɪdlaɪnz] Leitlinien

B | Describing materials and products

sturdy ['stɜ:di] robust
shiny ['ʃaɪni] glänzend
robust [rə'bʌst] stabil
state-of-the-art [ˌsteɪt‿əv ðiˈ‿ɑ:t] auf dem neuesten Stand (der Technik)
user-friendly [ˌju:zə'frendli] benutzerfreundlich
reliable [rɪ'laɪəbl] zuverlässig
hand-crafted [ˌhæn'krɑ:ftɪd] handgefertigt

C | Delivering a presentation

carpenter ['kɑ:pɪntə] Tischler(in), Zimmerer, Zimmerin
furniture ['fɜ:nɪtʃə] Möbel
trade show ['treɪd ˌʃəʊ] Messe

lounger ['laʊndʒə] Liegesessel
softwood ['sɒftˌwʊd] Weichholz
timber ['tɪmbə] Holz, Bauholz
joiner ['dʒɔɪnə] Tischler(in), Schreiner(in)
convenience [kənˌvi:niəns] Zweckmäßigkeit, Bequemlichkeit
varnish ['vɑ:nɪʃ] Lack
durable ['djʊərəbl] haltbar
polyurethane coating [ˌpɒlɪjʊərəθeɪn 'kəʊtɪŋ] Polyurethanbeschichtung

Module 8 The Internet

A | FAQs on Internet milestones

node [nəʊd] Knotenpunkt
stable ['steɪbl] stabil
to enable [ɪ'neɪbl] ermöglichen
application layer protocol [æplɪˌkeɪʃn ˌleɪə 'prəʊtəkɒl] Protokoll auf Anwendungsebene
numerical [nju:'merɪkl] numerisch
to convert [kən'vɜ:t] verwandeln, umwandeln
to transmit [trænz'mɪt] übermitteln
to distribute [dɪ'strɪbju:t] vertreiben, verteilen
subscriber [səb'skraɪbə] Abonnent(in), Kunde, Kundin
access ['ækses] Zugang
packet switching ['pækɪt ˌswɪtʃɪŋ] Paketaustausch
precursor [ˌpri:'kɜ:sə] Vorläufer

B | The future of the Internet and the World Wide Web

maintenance ['meɪntnəns] Instandhaltung
software suite ['sɒftweə ˌswi:t] Anwendungssystem
custom-designed [ˌkʌstəmdɪ'zaɪnd] anwendungsspezifisch
to host [həʊst] beherbergen
to administer [əd'mɪnɪstə] verwalten
to streamline ['stri:mlaɪn] rationalisieren, vereinfachen
heterogeneous [ˌhetrə'dʒi:niəs] uneinheitlich
encryption standard [ɪn'krɪpʃn ˌstændəd] Verschlüsselungsstandard
authentication [ɔ:ˌθentɪ'keɪʃn] Authentifizierung

reprocessing [ˌriːˈprəʊsesɪŋ] Wiederaufbereitung
collaboration [kəˌlæbˈreɪʃn] Zusammenarbeit
feature [ˈfiːtʃə] Merkmal, Bestandteil

C | Connecting to the Internet

access point [ˈækses ˌpɔɪnt] Anschlussknoten, Zugangspunkt
to expand [ɪkˈspænd] expandieren, erweitern, vergrößern
to intercept [ˌɪntəˈsept] abfangen
to access [ˈækses] zugreifen
cookie [ˈkʊki] Keks, Cookie
tag [tæg] Etikett, Anhängeschildchen, Identifizierungskennzeichen
gateway [ˈgeɪtweɪ] Eingangstor, Leitcomputer
bookmark [ˈbʊkmɑːk] Lesezeichen, Bookmark

Module H Dealing with customers

to deal with [ˈdiːl wɪð] umgehen mit, sich befassen mit
customer [ˈkʌstəmə] Kunde, Kundin
success [səkˈses] Erfolg
appointment [əˈpɔɪntmənt] Termin
enquiry [ɪnˈkwaɪəri] Anfrage
complaint [kəmˈpleɪnt] Beschwerde
essential [ɪˈsenʃl] sehr wichtig
builder [ˈbɪldə] Bauunternehmer(in)
building site [ˈbɪldɪŋ ˌsaɪt] Baustelle
to explain [ɪkˈspleɪn] erklären

A | Complaints

solution [səˈluːʃn] Lösung
delay [dɪˈleɪ] Verzögerung, Verspätung
price reduction [ˈpraɪs rɪˌdʌkʃn] Preisnachlass
faulty [ˈfɒlti] fehlerhaft, defekt, mangelhaft
damaged [ˈdæmɪdʒd] beschädigt
unsatisfactory [ʌnˌsætɪsˈfæktri] unbefriedigend, ungenügend, unzureichend
to replace [rɪˈpleɪs] ersetzen
air freight [ˈeə ˌfreɪt] Luftfracht
surplus [ˈsɜːpləs] überschüssig
credit note [ˈkredɪt ˌnəʊt] Gutschrift
specific [spəˈsɪfɪk] bestimmt, spezifisch

◎
access [ˈækses] Zugang
to log on [ˌlɒg‿ˈɒn] sich anmelden, sich einwählen
migration [maɪˈgreɪʃn] *(hier:)* Umstellung
to redo [ˌriːˈduː] noch einmal machen
to look into sth. [ˌlʊk‿ˈɪntə] einer Sache nachgehen

technician [tekˈnɪʃn] Techniker(in)
plumbing and heating [ˌplʌmɪŋ‿ənd ˈhiːtɪŋ] Heizung und Sanitär

B | Customer service

upset [ʌpˈset] verärgert
to avoid [əˈvɔɪd] vermeiden
argument [ˈɑːgjəmənt] Streit, Auseinandersetzung
to calm sb. [kɑːm] jmdn. beruhigen
to reassure [ˌriːəˈʃʊə] beruhigen
patient [ˈpeɪʃnt] geduldig
to solve [sɒlv] lösen
frame of mind [ˌfreɪm‿əv ˈmaɪnd] geistige Verfassung
furious [ˈfjʊəriəs] wütend
to affect [əˈfekt] Einfluss nehmen auf
mood [muːd] Laune
to blame sb./sth. for sth. [bleɪm] jmdm./etw. die Schuld an etw. geben, jmdn. verantwortlich machen
excuse [ɪkˈskjuːs] Ausrede

Module 9 Writing software

to model software [ˌmɒdl ˈsɒftweə] Software entwerfen
to dimension [daɪˈmenʃn] vermaßen
data centre infrastructure [ˌdeɪtə ˌsentər‿ˈɪnfrəˌstrʌktʃə] Rechenzentrumsinfrastruktur
lead tester [ˌliːd ˈtestə] Hauptverantwortliche(r) für das Testen einer Software, Leiter(in) eines Tests
to ensure [ɪnˈʃɔː] sicherstellen
software architect [ˌsɒftweər‿ˈɑːkɪtekt] Software-Architekt(in)
deployment specialist [dɪˈplɔɪmənt ˌspeʃlɪst] Experte, Expertin für den Einsatz von Software
to implement [ˈɪmplɪment] umsetzen
functionality [ˌfʌŋkʃnˈælɪti] Funktionalität
bug [bʌg] Fehler in einem Software-Programm

A | Writing code: the IDE

IDE (integrated development environment) [ˌaɪdiː'iː, ˌɪntɪɡreɪtɪd dɪ'veləpmənt‿ɪnˌvaɪrnmənt] Entwicklungsumgebung
source code ['sɔːs ˌkəʊd] Quellcode
spelling mistake ['spelɪŋ mɪˌsteɪk] Rechtschreibfehler
to debug [ˌdiː'bʌɡ] Fehler beseitigen
compilation [ˌkɒmpɪ'leɪʃn] Kompilierung
execution [ˌeksɪ'kjuːʃn] Ausführung
free of charge [ˌfriː‿əv 'tʃɑːdʒ] kostenfrei
word processing program ['wɜːd ˌprəʊsesɪŋ ˌprəʊɡræm] Textverarbeitungsprogramm
open source [ˌəʊpn 'sɔːs] Open Source
to detect [dɪ'tekt] erkennen
compiler [kəm'paɪlə] Compiler
debug mode ['diːbʌɡ ˌməʊd] Debug-Modus
to pause [pɔːz] anhalten
hence [hens] folglich
proprietary [prə'praɪətri] proprietär

B | Debugging

to cause [kɔːz] verursachen, auslösen
multiplayer module ['mʌltɪˌpleɪə ˌmɒdjuːl] Mehrspieler-Modul
to release [rɪ'liːs] veröffentlichen

Be my guest. [ˌbi maɪ 'ɡest] Bitte, nur zu.
hotfix ['hɒtfɪks] Hotfix
multiplayer matchmaking [ˌmʌltɪpleɪə 'mætʃˌmeɪkɪŋ] Mehrspieler-Spielvermittlung
to make available [ˌmeɪk‿ə'veɪləbl] verfügbar machen
issue ['ɪʃuː] Problem
to reschedule [ˌriː'ʃedjuːl] verschieben
compile report [kəm'paɪl rɪˌpɔːt] Kompilierungsbericht
to run into an exception [ˌrʌn‿ɪntʊ‿ən‿ɪk'sepʃn] in einen nicht erwarteten Zustand geraten
to arise [ə'raɪz] auftreten
beta testing phase [ˌbiːtə 'testɪŋ ˌfeɪz] Betatest-Phase
bug report ['bʌɡ rɪˌpɔːt] Fehlerbericht
to take a nap [ˌteɪk‿ə 'næp] ein Nickerchen machen
router ['ruːtə] Gerät, das es ermöglicht, gemeinsam einen Internetanschluss zu nutzen

firmware ['fɜːmweə] in Hardware-Geräte eingebettetes Betriebssystem
patch [pætʃ] Aktualisierung, die einen oder mehrere Fehler behebt
to ship [ʃɪp] ausliefern
to determine [dɪ'tɜːmɪn] ermitteln
session ['seʃn] Sitzung
to tune [tjuːn] fein abstimmen
to reset [ˌriː'set] zurücksetzen
timeout value ['taɪmaʊt ˌvæljuː] Zeitüberschreitungswert

supervisor ['suːpəvaɪzə] Dienstvorgesetzte(r)
ranking management module ['ræŋkɪŋ ˌmænɪdʒmənt ˌmɒdjuːl] Punkteverwaltungs-Modul

C | Comments and documentation

to insert [ɪn'sɜːt] einfügen

Module 10 Tools and applications

media development [ˌmiːdɪə dɪ'veləpmənt] Mediengestaltung
content access software [ˌkɒntent‿'ækses ˌsɒftweə] Zugangssoftware
information worker software [ˌɪnfə'meɪʃn ˌwɜːkə ˌsɒftweə] Datenverarbeitungssoftware
enterprise ['entəpraɪz] Unternehmen
entertainment software [ˌentə'teɪnmənt ˌsɒftweə] Unterhaltungssoftware

A | Web-based application software

word processor ['wɜːd ˌprəʊsesə] Textverarbeitungsprogramm
spreadsheet ['spredʃiːt] Tabellenkalkulation
revision history [rɪ'vɪʒn 'hɪstri] Überarbeitungshistorie
to grant copyright [ɡrɑːnt 'kɒpiˌraɪt] Urheberrecht gewähren
to undo [ʌn'duː] rückgängig machen
to redo [ˌriː'duː] etw. noch einmal machen
toolbar ['tuːlbɑː] Symbolleiste

B | Computer health maintenance

system registry [ˌsɪstəm ˈredʒɪstri] Systemregistrierung
disk defragmenter [ˈdɪsk ˌdi:frægmentə] Defragmentierungsprogramm
temporary files [ˌtemprəri ˈfaɪlz] temporäre Dateien
extensions [ɪkˈstenʃnz] Dateierweiterungen

C | Data backup methods and data recovery

self-contained [ˌselfkənˈteɪnd] unabhängig
restoration [ˌrestˈreɪʃn] Wiederherstellung
storage space [ˈstɔ:rɪdʒ ˌspeɪs] Speicherplatz
reference point [ˈrefrns ˌpɔɪnt] Bezugspunkt
to track [træk] verfolgen

Module 11 Enterprise software

financial management [faɪˌnænʃl ˈmænɪdʒmənt] Buchhaltung
warehouse [ˈweəhaʊs] Warenlager
manufacturing [ˌmænjəˈfæktʃrɪŋ] Fertigung
human resources [ˌhju:mən ˈri:sɔ:sɪz] Personalabteilung
expense account [ɪkˈspens‿əˌkaʊnt] Spesenkonto
to divide into [dɪˈvaɪd‿ɪntə] aufteilen in
to class [klɑ:s] klassifizieren
consumer [kənˈsju:mə] Konsument(in)
alike [əˈlaɪk] sowohl … als auch …
to target [ˈtɑ:gɪt] anpeilen, zielen auf
use case [ˈju:s ˌkeɪs] Anwendungsfall
operating system [ˈɒpreɪtɪŋ ˌsɪstəm] Betriebssystem
broad ranged [ˌbrɔ:d ˈreɪndʒd] breit angelegt
enterprise resource planning [ˌentəpraɪz rɪˈzɔ:s ˌplænɪŋ] Warenwirtschaft
payroll system [ˈpeɪrəʊl ˌsɪstəm] Lohnabrechnungssystem
to speed up [ˌspi:d‿ˈʌp] beschleunigen
currently [ˈkʌrntli] zurzeit, derzeit
raw materials [ˌrɔ: məˈtɪəriəlz] Rohstoffe
in stock [ɪn ˈstɒk] vorrätig
setting [ˈsetɪŋ] Einstellung

A | Enterprise resource planning

just in time [ˌdʒʌst‿ɪn ˈtaɪm] just-in-time
manufacturer [ˌmænjəˈfæktʃrə] Hersteller, Produzent
to rely on [rɪˈlaɪ‿ɒn] sich verlassen auf
heavily [ˈhevɪli] in hohem Maße
feature [ˈfi:tʃə] Eigenschaft, Merkmal
purpose [ˈpɜ:pəs] Zweck
to tailor [ˈteɪlə] anpassen
to map a process to a module [ˌmæp‿ə ˌprəʊses tu‿ə ˈmɒdju:l] einen (Geschäfts)prozess in einem Modul abbilden
invoice [ˈɪnvɔɪs] Rechnung
accounting [əˈkaʊntɪŋ] Rechnungswesen
sale [seɪl] Verkauf
shipment [ˈʃɪpmənt] Versand, Lieferung
accounting [əˈkaʊntɪŋ] Buchhaltung
customer relations [ˌkʌstəmə rɪˈleɪʃnz] Kundendienst
customer relationship management [ˌkʌstəmə rɪˈleɪʃnʃɪp ˌmænɪdʒmənt] Kundenbeziehungsmanagement
to keep up to date [ˌki:p‿ʌp tə ˈdeɪt] auf dem neuesten Stand halten
to keep track of [ˌki:p ˈtræk‿əv] im Auge behalten
tax declaration [ˈtæks dekləˌreɪʃn] Steuererklärung
commonly [ˈkɒmənli] üblicherweise
supplier [səˈplaɪə] Lieferant
tax advisor [ˈtæks‿ədˌvaɪzə] Steuerberater(in)
to be around [bi‿əˈraʊnd] vorhanden sein, (es) geben
service sector [ˈsɜ:vɪs ˌsektə] Dienstleistungssektor
process [ˈprəʊsəs] Verfahren, Vorgang, Ablauf
instance [ˈɪnstns] Beispiel

B | Business intelligence

to generate [ˈdʒenreɪt] verursachen
efficiency [ɪˈfɪʃnsi] Leistungsfähigkeit
relationship [rɪˈleɪʃnʃɪp] Beziehung
to relate to [rɪˈleɪt‿tə] sich beziehen auf
to coin [kɔɪn] ins Leben rufen
hence [hens] daher
decision support system [dɪˌsɪʒn səˈpɔ:t ˌsɪstəm] Entscheidungsfindungssystem
computer scientist [kəmˈpju:tə ˌsaɪəntɪst] Informatiker(in)
widespread [ˈwaɪdspred] weitverbreitet

sales representative ['seɪlz reprɪˌzentətɪv] Außendienst-mitarbeiter(in)
to file a report [ˌfaɪl‿ə rɪ'pɔ:t] einen Bericht abgeben
defective [dɪ'fektɪv] fehlerhaft, defekt
manufacturing process [ˌmænjə'fæktʃrɪŋ ˌprəʊses] Herstellungsverfahren
to interact [ˌɪntə'ækt] interagieren, zusammenwirken
to take a day off [ˌteɪk‿ə ˌdeɪ‿'ɒf] sich einen Tag frei nehmen
to update [ʌp'deɪt] aktualisieren
in response to [ɪn rɪ'spɒns tə] als Antwort auf
to come in [ˌkʌm‿'ɪn] seinen Einsatz finden
to request [rɪ'kwest] wünschen, bitten um
inconvenient [ˌɪnkən'vi:niənt] ungünstig

◎
to forgive [fə'gɪv] verzeihen
performant [pə'fɔ:mənt] leistungsfähig
previous ['pri:viəs] vorherig, früher
manually ['mænjuəli] von Hand, manuell
to clutter ['klʌtə] in einem Durcheinander sein
to remind [rɪ'maɪnd] erinnern
available [ə'veɪləbl] verfügbar, erhältlich
menu bar ['menju: ˌbɑ:] Menüleiste
to deserve [dɪ'zɜ:v] verdienen
entry ['entri] Eintrag
to select [sə'lekt] auswählen
to bear with ['beə wɪð] Geduld haben
by [baɪ] *(hier:)* geordnet nach
revenue ['revnju:] Umsatz
at your finger tips [ət jɔ: 'fɪŋgə ˌtɪps] zur Hand
once in a while [ˌwʌns‿ɪn‿ə 'waɪl] ab und zu, gelegentlich
impressed [ɪm'prest] beeindruckt
advanced [əd'vɑ:nst] fortgeschritten
to set oneself apart from [ˌset‿ə'pɑ:t frm] sich abheben von
to interfere [ˌɪntə'fɪə] stören, beeinträchtigen
gladly ['glædli] gerne

to configure [kən'fɪgə] konfigurieren
interface ['ɪntəfeɪs] Schnittstelle, Interface

C | Customizing enterprise software

to customize ['kʌstəmaɪz] (an Kundenwünsche) anpassen
font size ['fɒnt ˌsaɪz] Schriftgröße
checkbox ['tʃekbɒks] Checkbox

to recommend [ˌrekə'mend] empfehlen
regarding [rɪ'gɑ:dɪŋ] bezüglich
best regards [ˌbest rɪ'gɑ:dz] beste Grüße

Module 12 Computers in danger

public transport [ˌpʌblɪk 'trænspɔ:t] öffentliche Verkehrsmittel
power grid [pauə'grɪd] Stromversorgungsnetz
emergency services [i'mɜ:dʒensi 'sɜ:vɪsɪz] Notfalldienste

A | Types of malware

distributor [dɪ'strɪbjətə] Verteiler
victim ['vɪktɪm] Opfer
to modify ['mɒdɪfaɪ] verändern, modifizieren
to self-replicate [self 'replɪkeɪt] selbstreplizieren
to infect [in'fekt] infizieren
to redirect [ˌri:daɪ'rekt, ˌri:dɪ'rekt] umleiten
multiple request ['mʌltɪpl ri'kwest] mehrfache Anfragen
fake [feɪk] gefälscht
drive-by [draiv baɪ] beiläufig
to hijack ['haɪdʒæk] entführen, klauen
to spy [spaɪ] jmdm. nachspionieren, jmdn. abhören
buffer overflow [bʌfə'eʊvəfləʊ] Pufferüberlauf
macro ['mækreʊ] kleiner Programmcode

B | Remedies for computers in danger

◎
resistant [rɪ'zɪstənt] widerstandsfähig, resistent
on board [ɒn bɔ:d] integriert
to configure [kən'fɪgə] aufbauen, gestalten, konfigurieren

phishing ['fɪʃɪŋ] Identitätsdiebstahl
recovery [rɪ'kʌvərɪ] Erholung, Genesung, Wiederherstellung
restrictive [rɪ'strɪktɪv] eingeschränkt, restriktiv

C | Setting up a firewall

access ['ækses] Zugang
to shield [ʃi:ld] abschirmen, schützen
to supervise ['su:pəvaɪz] beaufsichtigen, überwachen
to import [ɪm'pɔ:t] importieren
to migrate [maɪ'greɪt] migrieren

Module 13 Customer support

A | Saying the right things on the phone

close-ended [ˌkləʊz'endɪd] geschlossen
follow-up [ˌfɒləʊ'ʌp] Folge-
to determine [dɪ'tɜ:mɪn] bestimmen, festlegen
sensitive ['sensətɪv] einfühlsam, sensibel

to enhance [ɪn'hɑ:ns] erhöhen, verbessern
rapport [ræ'pɔ:] Verhältnis
talkative ['tɔ:kətɪv] gesprächig
rude [ru:d] unhöflich, unverschämt
abusive [ə'bju:sɪv] beleidigend
knowledgeable ['nɒlɪdʒəbl] kenntnisreich
level-two technician [ˌlevlˌtu: tek'nɪʃn] Sachverständige(r) auf höherer Ebene
condescending [ˌkɒndɪ'sendɪŋ] herablassend
in plain terms [ɪn ˌpleɪn 'tɜ:mz] freiweg, unverblümt
industry jargon [ˌɪndəstri 'dʒɑ:gən] Fachjargon, Fachsprache

B | Troubleshooting and troubleshooting software

troubleshooting ['trʌblˌʃu:tɪŋ] Fehlersuche und Fehlerbehebung
newsgroup ['nju:zgru:p] Nachrichtenforum
remote maintenance [rɪˌməʊt 'meɪntnəns] Fernwartung
encrypted [ɪn'krɪptɪd] verschlüsselt
to migrate [maɪ'greɪt] migrieren

Alphabetical word list

A

abusive beleidigend 89
to access zugreifen 50, 67
access Zugang 32, 48
accessible für Zugriff verfügbar 34
access node Zugangsknotenpunkt 58
accessories Zubehör 16
access point Anschlussknoten, Zugangspunkt 67
accidentally unbeabsichtigt 34
according to laut, gemäß 25
accounting Buchhaltung 10, 81
accounts Buchhaltung 21
accuracy Genauigkeit 23
achievement Leistung 47
actually eigentlich, tatsächlich 10
to adapt anpassen 41
to administer verwalten 66
advanced fortgeschritten 82
advantage Vorteil 40
advert Anzeige 44
advice Rat 47
to advise beraten 9
to affect Einfluss nehmen auf 71
to afford sich leisten 42
age Zeitalter 57
air freight Luftfracht 69
to align anordnen 51
alike sowohl …, als auch … 80
alteration Änderung 27
although obwohl 30
analytical analytisch 9
app Anwendungsprogramm 42
to append anfügen 34
application Bewerbung 44
application layer protocol Protokoll auf Anwendungsebene 65
to apply anwenden 9
appointment Termin 68
to appreciate etw. (wert-)schätzen 37
apprenticeship Ausbildung, Lehre 10, 22
appropriate angenehm, passend, geeignet 12, 42
approximately in etwa 56
area code Vorwahl 29
argument Streit, Auseinandersetzung 71
to arise auftreten 74
arrow key Pfeiltaste 32
as regards bezüglich 41
to assemble montieren, zusammenbauen 19
assembly Montage 45
to assess bewerten, einschätzen, abschätzen 10
attachment Anhang 38
at your finger tips zur Hand 82
audience Zuhörer (Pl.), Publikum 61
authentication Authentifizierung 66
available verfügbar, erhältlich 82
to avoid vermeiden 71
awkward peinlich, unangenehm 54

B

bandwidth Bandbreite 56
bank transfer Banküberweisung 38
battery Akku
battery pack Akku 42
beam Strahl 26
to be around vorhanden sein, (es) geben 81
to bear with Geduld haben 82
beef Rindfleisch 55
to belong to gehören zu 23
Be my guest. Bitte, nur zu. 74
benefit Leistung, Nutzen 9
best regards beste Grüße 83
beta testing phase Beta Test Phase 74
bill Rechnung 55
BIOS Basis-Eingabe-Ausgabe-System 32
to blame sb. / sth. for sth. jmdm. / etw. die Schuld an etw. geben, jmdn. verantwortlich machen 71
body language Körpersprache 61
to boil down verdichten 27
bonnet (BE) Motorhaube 37
bookmark Lesezeichen; Bookmark 67
boot disk Festplatte, CD/DVD oder USB Stick, von dem gebootet wird 33
boot menu list Liste von Betriebssystemen 34
brain Gehirn 27
braking system Bremsanlage 21
branch Niederlassung 44
breakdown Panne, Störung 28
broad breit angelegt 9
broadband Breitband 57
broad ranged breit angelegt 80
buffer overflow Pufferüberlauf 85
bug Fehler in einem Software-Programm 72
bug report Fehlerbericht 74
builder Bauunternehmer(in) 68
building site Baustelle 68
by *(hier:)* geordnet nach 82

C

cabinet Schrank 41
to calculate berechnen 42
to call ahead im Voraus Bescheid geben 50
to calm sb. jmdn. beruhigen 71
capability Fähigkeit 41
capable fähig 23
capacity Leistungsfähigkeit 41
career Beruf, Laufbahn, Karriere 9
car mechanic Automechaniker(in) 37
carpenter Tischler(in), Zimmerer, Zimmerin 63
case Fall 41
cash register Kasse 15
catalogue Katalog 37
to cause verursachen, auslösen 74
cell phone Mobiltelefon 56
central node zentraler Knotenpunkt 50
central processing unit (CPU) Hauptprozessor, Prozessor, Zentraleinheit 33, 41

D

H

I

J

K

L

M

machine code Programm-Code in einer Maschinensprache 33
macro kleiner Programmcode 85
mail server tab Mail-Server Karteireiterkarte 50
mainboard Hauptplatine 17
main dish Hauptgericht 55
mainframe Großrechner 41
to maintain bewahren 45
maintenance Wartung 9
major Haupt-, bedeutend 10
to make available verfügbar machen 74
to make up (made, made) ausmachen 17
MAN (metropolitan area network) regionales Mobilfunknetz, z.B. für eine größere Stadt 58
to manage verwalten 42
to manufacture herstellen 22
manufacturer Hersteller, Produzent 81
manufacturing Fertigung 80
manufacturing plant Produktionsbetrieb 21
manufacturing process Herstellungsverfahren 82
to map a process to a module einen (Geschäfts)prozess in einem Modul abbilden 81
market ready vermarktungsreif 27
mascot Maskottchen 27
to match zuordnen 10
to measure messen 22
media development Mediengestaltung 76
meeting Sitzung, Besprechung 60
memory Speicher 40
menu bar Menuleiste 82
mesh Gitter 50
microprocessor Mikroprozessor 41
to migrate migrieren 87
migration *(hier:)* Umstellung 69
minutes Protokoll 15
misunderstanding Missverständnis 36
model installation Beispielinstallation 34
to model software Software entwerfen 72
moderate mäßig, moderat 41
to modify verändern, modifizieren 85
molecule chain Molekülkette 27
to monitor überwachen, kontrollieren, beobachten 22
mood Laune 71
motherboard Hauptplatine 32
multiplayer matchmaking Mehrspieler Spielvermittlung 74
multiplayer module Mehrspieler Modul 74
multiple mehrfach 41
multiple request mehrfache Anfragen 85

N

neatly ordentlich 51
necessary nötig, notwendig 36
network coverage Netzabdeckung 59
newsgroup Nachrichtenforum 90
node Knotenpunkt 65
numerical numerisch 65

O

to occur vorkommen 22
offer Angebot 36
on board integriert 86
once in a while ab und zu, gelegentlich 82
on the other hand andererseits 15
open source Open Source 73
operating system Betriebssystem 80
opportunity Möglichkeit 44
optical disc drive optisches Laufwerk 17, 42
optic fiber Glasfaser 49
option Alternative, Möglichkeit 9
order Bestellung 36
organigram Organigramm 10
organisation chart (org chart) Organigramm, Organisationsschema 10
outdated veraltet 58
outgoing mail abgehende Mail 50
to outline umreißen, skizzieren 41
out of office außer Haus 59
output Ausgabe- 41
overall gesamt 9
overlap Überschneidung 41
overview Überblick 61
to overwrite überschreiben 34

P

packet switching Paketaustausch 65
palm Handfläche 42
patch Aktualisierung, die einen oder mehrere Fehler behebt 74
patient geduldig 71
to pause anhalten 73
payroll system Lohnabrechnungssystem 80
PCB (printed circuit board) Leiterplatte 17
PDA tragbarer elektronischer Organizer 40
performance Ergebnis, Erfolg 9
performant leistungsfähig 82
peripheral devices Peripheriegeräte 18
phishing Identitätsdiebstahl 86
pleasant angenehm 15
pleasantry höfliche Floskel 15
plotter Zeichengerät, Plotter 16
plug Stecker 51
to plug in einstecken 50
plumbing and heating Heizung und Sanitär 70
pointing device Zeigegerät 42
to point out hinweisen auf 34
to polish abschleifen, polieren 22
polite höflich 15
politeness Höflichkeit 15
polyurethane coating Polyurethanbeschichtung 63
pork Schweinefleisch 55
port Steckplatz für Netzwerkkabel 48
portable tragbar 40
positional sketch Technologieschema 60
poultry Geflügel 55
power grid Stromversorgungsnetz 84
power supply Stromversorgung 42
precision Genauigkeit 22
precursor Vorläufer 65
to prefer bevorzugen 22
premises Firmengelände 10
preparation Vorbereitung 60

Q

R

S

to shape formen, fräsen 22
sheet Blatt 10
to shield abschirmen, schützen
shift Schicht 22
to shift sich verlagern 59
shiny glänzend 62
to ship ausliefern 74
shipment Versand, Lieferung 81
short on kurzes An 57
side order Beilage 55
to sign unterschreiben 44
skill Fähigkeit 44
slot Einbaustelle, Schlitz 42
socket Steckdose, Stecknuss 31, 38
software architect Software-Architekt(in) 72
software suite Anwendungssystem 66
softwood Weichholz 63
solution Lösung 28
to solve lösen 33
source code Quellcode 73
speaker Lautsprecher 16
specific bestimmt, spezifisch 69
to speed up beschleunigen 80
to spell buchstabieren 47
spelling mistake Rechtschreibfehler 73
to split aufteilen 23
spreadsheet Tabellenkalkulation 42, 77
to spy jmdm. nach spionieren, jmdn. abhören 85
stable stabil 65
to stack stapeln 49
starter Vorspeise 55
state-of-the-art auf dem neuesten Stand (der Technik) 62
stationary feststehend, stationär 40, 42
stay Aufenthalt 10
step Schritt 33
stock Bestand, Vorrat 38
stockkeeping Lagerhaltung 10
storage Speicherung 42
storage devices Speichergeräte, Datenspeicher 25
storage space Speicherplatz 79
to store speichern 42
stranger Unbekannte(r) 15
to streamline rationalisieren, vereinfachen 66
strength Stärke 47
to strip entfernen 51
sturdy robust 62
stylus Stift, Griffel 42
subject line *(Brief:)* Betreffzeile 37
to submit vorlegen, einreichen, unterbreiten 17
subscriber Abonnent(in), Kunde, Kundin 65
subsequently anschließend 51
subsidiary Tochtergesellschaft 53
success Erfolg 68
suggestion Vorschlag 9
suitable geeignet 40
to suit the needs of sth. die Bedürfnisse von etwas erfüllen 41
sum Betrag 39
summary Zusammenfassung 61
to supervise beaufsichtigen, überwachen 87
supervisor Dienstvorgesetzte(r) 74
supplier Lieferant 20
supply from stock ab Lager liefern 37
to support unterstützen 42
supported unterstützt 59
surplus überschüssig 69
to swap tauschen 17
synonym Synonym, bedeutungsgleiches Wort 48
system registry Systemregistrierung 78
systems analyst Systemberater(in) 9

T

tag Etikett, Anhängeschildchen, Identifizierungskennzeichen 67
to tailor anpassen 81
tailor-made maßgeschneidert 33
to take a day off sich einen Tag frei nehmen 82
to take a nap ein Nickerchen machen 74
talkative gesprächig 89
to target anpeilen, zielen auf 80
task Aufgabe 22
tax advisor Steuerberater(in) 81
tax declaration Steuererklärung 81
technician Techniker(in) 69
temporary files temporäre Dateien 78
tension Spannung 54
term Begriff 41
terminal Endpunkt einer Verbindung 58
terms of payment Zahlungsbedingungen 37
text editor Textaufbereitungsprogramm 34
That's not a big deal! Das ist keine große Sache! 58
theoretical theoretisch 46
thorough gründlich 9
Tier 1 provider Stufe 1 (Internet) Anbieter 58
timber Holz, Bauholz 63
time-consuming zeitraubend 36
time frame Zeitfenster 56
timeout value Zeitüberschreitungswert 74
tip Trinkgeld 55
tool Werkzeug 20
toolbar Symbolleiste 77
toolbox Werkzeugkiste 27
torque wrench Drehmomentschlüssel 39
touchpad Tastfeld 42
to track verfolgen 79
trade fair Messe 13
trade show Messe 63
trainee Auszubildende(r) 53
to transform verwandeln, umwandeln 17
transistor Transistor 41
to transmit übermitteln 65
transmitter Sendeeinrichtung 56
transport medium Übertragungsmedium 57
transport node Transportknotenpunkt 58
trivial unwichtig 54
to troubleshoot Fehler beheben 9
troubleshooting Fehlersuche 45
truth Wahrheit 47
to tune fein abstimmen 74
tutor Klassenlehrer(in), Betreuer(in) 10
twisted pair verdrilltes Paar 51

U

V

W

Bildquellenverzeichnis

4 Thinkstock (Comstock), München; **4** iStockphoto (Petar Chernaev), Calgary, Alberta; **5** iStockphoto (Chris Schmidt), Calgary, Alberta; **8** Thinkstock (iStockphoto), München; **8** Fotolia.com (Eimantas Buzas), New York; **8** iStockphoto (Clerkenwell_Images), Calgary, Alberta; **8** Thinkstock (Comstock), München; **10** shutterstock (Michal Kowalski), New York, NY; **11** dreamstime.com (Kmiragaya), Brentwood, TN; **12** iStockphoto (daniel rodriguez), Calgary, Alberta; **12** Thinkstock (Stockbyte), München; **12** iStockphoto (David Jones), Calgary, Alberta; **12** iStockphoto (Helder Almeida), Calgary, Alberta; **14** iStockphoto (Dean Mitchell), Calgary, Alberta; **15** iStockphoto (4x6), Calgary, Alberta; **16** shutterstock (Vitaly Korovin), New York, NY; **16** shutterstock (Your lucky photo), New York, NY; **16** shutterstock (Lipowski Milan), New York, NY; **16** shutterstock (Zadorozhnyi Viktor), New York, NY; **18** iStockphoto (Dino Ablakovic), Calgary, Alberta; **19** Thinkstock (iStockphoto), München; **20** shutterstock (Dmitry Kalinovsky), New York, NY; **20** Thinkstock (BananaStock), München; **20** iStockphoto (sturti), Calgary, Alberta; **20** Thinkstock (iStockphoto), München; **22** shutterstock (Dmitry Kalinovsky), New York, NY; **23** iStockphoto (mediaphotos), Calgary, Alberta; **24** iStockphoto (-Oxford-), Calgary, Alberta; **24** MEV Verlag GmbH, Augsburg; **24** iStockphoto (Kevin Landwer-Johan), Calgary, Alberta; **24** shutterstock (scyther5), New York, NY; **25** Thinkstock (Photos.com/Jupiterimages), München; **27** shutterstock (YasnaTen), New York, NY; **28** iStockphoto (diego cervo), Calgary, Alberta; **28** iStockphoto (nolimitpictures), Calgary, Alberta; **28** Thinkstock (Wavebreak Media), München; **28** PantherMedia GmbH (Benis Arapovic), München; **30** iStockphoto (PeskyMonkey), Calgary, Alberta; **33** shutterstock (CyberVam), New York, NY; **34** shutterstock (Charles Knox Photo Inc.), New York, NY; **34** Thinkstock (iStockphoto), München; **36** iStockphoto (David Jones), Calgary, Alberta; **36** iStockphoto (Warwick Lister-Kaye), Calgary, Alberta; **36** shutterstock (Stephen Coburn), New York, NY; **36** shutterstock (rangizzz), New York, NY; **40** shutterstock (Venus Angel), New York, NY; **40** iStockphoto (Petar Chernaev), Calgary, Alberta; **40** Thinkstock (Stockbyte), München; **40** shutterstock (EDHAR), New York, NY; **41** dreamstime.com (Sandra Howard), Brentwood, TN; **43** shutterstock (AISPIX by Image Source), New York, NY; **43** iStockphoto (Tova Teitelbaum), Calgary, Alberta; **43** Thinkstock (iStockphoto), München; **44** shutterstock (Minerva Studio), New York, NY; **44** iStockphoto (Brian Jackson), Calgary, Alberta; **44** shutterstock (StockLite), New York, NY; **44** iStockphoto (Willie B. Thomas), Calgary, Alberta; **46** shutterstock (Goodluz), New York, NY; **48** dreamstime.com (Youssouf Cader), Brentwood, TN; **48** dreamstime.com (Vasily Topko), Brentwood, TN; **48** dreamstime.com (Benis Arapovic), Brentwood, TN; **48** Thinkstock (iStockphoto), München; **51** dreamstime.com (Danieloizo), Brentwood, TN; **52** iStockphoto (Clerkenwell_Images), Calgary, Alberta; **52** Thinkstock (Purestock), München; **52** iStockphoto (Chris Schmidt), Calgary, Alberta; **52** iStockphoto (fatihhoca), Calgary, Alberta; **53** Thinkstock (BananaStock), München; **54** Thinkstock (Stockbyte), München; **55** iStockphoto (kristian sekulic), Calgary, Alberta; **56** dreamstime.com (Hupeng), Brentwood, TN; **56** dreamstime.com (Aviahuismanphotography), Brentwood, TN; **56** dreamstime.com (Eimantas Buzas), Brentwood, TN; **56** dreamstime.com (Sebastian Czapnik), Brentwood, TN; **60** iStockphoto (Clerkenwell_Images), Calgary, Alberta; **60** shutterstock (wavebreakmedia ltd), New York, NY; **60** Thinkstock (Purestock), München; **60** iStockphoto (Oleg Prikhodko), Calgary, Alberta; **61** iStockphoto (bluecinema), Calgary, Alberta; **63** iStockphoto (Joshua Hodge Photography), Calgary, Alberta; **64** iStockphoto (JazzIRT), Calgary, Alberta; **64** iStockphoto (Yunus Arakon), Calgary, Alberta; **64** shutterstock (vichie81), New York, NY; **64** BigStockPhoto.com (stocksnapp), Davis, CA; **68** iStockphoto (YanLev), Calgary, Alberta; **68** iStockphoto (Steve Debenport), Calgary, Alberta; **68** iStockphoto (Sean Locke), Calgary, Alberta; **68** iStockphoto (Louis-Paul St-Onge), Calgary, Alberta; **69** iStockphoto (Sean Locke), Calgary, Alberta; **72** dreamstime.com (Margol), Brentwood, TN; **72** shutterstock (Yuri Arcurs), New York, NY; **72** dreamstime.com (Jonathan Ross), Brentwood, TN; **72** iStockphoto (Baran Özdemir), Calgary, Alberta; **73** dreamstime.com (Karol Brandys), Brentwood, TN; **76** BigStockPhoto.com (badboo), Davis, CA; **76** BigStockPhoto.com (igor stevanovic), Davis, CA; **76** iStockphoto (Micah Young), Calgary, Alberta; **76** Thinkstock (iStockphoto), München; **78** iStockphoto (Don Bayley), Calgary, Alberta; **79** shutterstock (PRILL), New York, NY; **81** iStockphoto (Helder Almeida), Calgary, Alberta; **84** iStockphoto (4FR), Calgary, Alberta; **84** iStockphoto (Vetta Collection/H-Gall), Calgary, Alberta; **84** iStockphoto (Rafal Olechowski), Calgary, Alberta; **84** Thinkstock (Wavebreak Media), München; **86** iStockphoto (Rob Broek), Calgary, Alberta; **87** dreamstime.com (Hans Joachim Roy), Brentwood, TN; **88** Corbis (Blend Images/Terry Vine), Düsseldorf; **89** iStockphoto (vm), Calgary, Alberta; **90** shutterstock (Kaspri), New York, NY; **91** iStockphoto (Abel Mitja Varela), Calgary, Alberta; **92** LinguaTV GmbH, Berlin; **93** LinguaTV GmbH, Berlin; **94** ZDF Enterprises GmbH, Mainz; **95** ZDF Enterprises GmbH, Mainz; **96** ZDF, Mainz; **96** ZDF Enterprises GmbH, Mainz; **97** Video(s) supplied by BBC Motion Gallery, London; **146** Klett-Archiv, Stuttgart; **COVER** Getty Images RF (Blend Images/Shalom Ormsby), München; **COVER** Getty Images RF (Flickr/Csaba Bajko photography. Szentendre/Hungary), München

Sollte es in einem Einzelfall nicht gelungen sein, den korrekten Rechteinhaber ausfindig zu machen, so werden berechtigte Ansprüche selbstverständlich im Rahmen der üblichen Regelungen abgegolten.